Arts and Crafts Architecture

Arts and Crafts Architecture:

The Search for Earthly Paradise

Peter Davey

The Architectural Press: London

With love to my parents who brought me up in two Arts and Crafts houses (though none of us knew it at the time).

Frontispiece: Edgar Wood. Lindley Tower, near Huddersfield (1900–02)

First published in 1980 by the Architectural Press Ltd: London

ISBN: 0 85139 049 8

Filmset and printed in Great Britain
by W & J Mackay Limited, Chatham

Photographic Credits
Aerofilms Ltd. 198, 199; Architectural Press (Bill Toomey) 1, 6, 12, 16, 17, 18, 21, 23, 28, 29, 33, 35, 44, 46, 47, 58, 59–62, 63, 64, 70, 78, 90–94, 95, 97, 98, 101, 103, 105, 109, 111, 113, 114, 115, 116, 118, 121, 130, 134, 136, 140, 147, 151, 163, 165, 166, 167, 176, 177, 187, 188, 189, 190, 193, 195, 196, 201, 207, 208–211, 217–219, 228, 229, 232, 234, 235, 236, 237; Martin Charles 137; Country Life 179, 180, 181, 182, 183, 184; Gillian Darley 197; Michael Devereux 186; Louis Dezart 185; Finnish Architectural Museum 221; André Goulancourt 99, 112, 123, 178; Hamlyn Group (Keith Gibson) 106, 107, 152–154; Charles Knevitt 220; Knight, Frank & Rutley 24; Sam Lambert 156; Mrs Levson 122; Duncan McNeill 74; 80; Mervyn Miller 202; William Morris Museum 36; Graham Morrison 216; Eckhart Muthesius 226, 227; National Trust 22; RIBA (British Architectural Library) 2, 71, 73, 77, 81, 86, 88, 102, 108, 160, 162; Martin Richardson 212; Collection Alastair Service 27, 31, 37, 50, 51, 57, 66, 67, 119, 127, 133, 138, 139, 174; Swedish Tourist Office 222, 223; Victoria & Albert Museum p. 29, 157, 158, 161; Walker Art Gallery 34. All other photographs by the author.

Contents

Preface

I started to write this book because I needed it myself. There was no history of Arts and Crafts thinking as a whole with the exception of Gillian Naylor's pioneering work which scarcely touches on architecture. General histories of the period described the Arts and Crafts movement as no more than an aberrant offshore version of Art Nouveau or as the British John the Baptist for the messianic Modern Movement. Yet as that movement waned, the ideas of Morris, the buildings of people like Voysey, Prior and Lutyens began to seem more and more relevant to a contemporary architecture fumbling to rediscover compassion and individualism.

What were all those half forgotten architects doing and thinking about nearly a century ago? Why are their buildings so attractive? Why, suddenly and briefly, did British architecture become the cynosure of the western world?

This book tries to explain, and, like all efforts to encapsulate real life, it has a heavy bias. People are so complicated, so illogical and contradictory that any attempt to describe a period fully would fill the world with paper. There are always alternative explanations—especially of something so ill defined as the Arts and Crafts movement, which never produced a manifesto to which all subscribed, nor a very recognizable style, nor a clear ideology.

I have tried to take a microscope section through the truth to show how, in architecture, the ideals of Pugin* and Ruskin and Morris grew from the Gothic revival, interacted and, in the end, lost cohesion and fell apart to help generate quite other architectures which would have revolted the founding spirits of

Arts and Crafts. I hope that within its limits the story is truthful.

The account is as restricted in its coverage as in emphasis. Some architects and thinkers have been given star billing because I think they most clearly illuminate the period. Others like Sedding, Weir, Cave, Troup, Ricardo and many more would, in a book five times this size, have merited treatment as long as I have given Lethaby, Voysey and Ashbee. I am sorry so many good architects can have no more than walk-on parts.

Of the many people who have helped in writing, Gavin Stamp must be mentioned first; he read all the English chapters, and without his many stimulating and restraining comments the book would be more heavily biased than it is. Long discussions with Alastair Service have been almost equally formative. Lionel Lambourne, whose book *Utopian Craftsmen* was running roughly parallel with this one, has always been helpful.

On individuals, Alan Crawford's comments on my Ashbee chapter have been invaluable, so have Lynne Walker's on Prior. Godfrey Rubens has given me information on Lethaby; Richard Crofton kindly allowed me access to his original research on Parker and Unwin. Michael Devereaux painstakingly obtained material from the Isle of Man on Baillie Scott. Eckhart Muthesius generously gave me information on his father and allowed me to use his original photographs. Just before this book went to press, Mervyn Miller made many helpful comments on the Parker and Unwin chapter; I am sorry not to have been able to respond to them all.

My colleagues, Dan Cruickshank and Colin Amery have put up with an obsession which must on occasion have seemed like monomania, and have given many comments which helped keep some semblance of perspective.

---

* Any history must begin arbitrarily, but my choice of Pugin to kick off with had some contemporary sanction. John Dando Sedding remarked in 1888 that "we should have had no Morris, no Street, no Burges, no Shaw, no Webb, no Bodley, no Rossetti, no Burne-Jones, no Crane, but for Pugin."

Very many owners and managers of Arts and Crafts buildings have kindly allowed me access for photography and given information—particularly Mr. and Mrs. Gimson of Stoneywell Cottage. The West Yorkshire police were most understanding when they picked me up as a possible terrorist, apparently preparing to blow up High Court judges in Leeds.

The librarians of the London Library, the Victoria and Albert Museum and the Royal Institute of British Architects have been unfailingly helpful, particularly on Saturdays when no librarian likes to work. In particular Ruth Kamen of the RIBA has stretched many points to help a part-time historian; she made me do a bibliography and gave many helpful comments on it.

I owe thanks to my employers, the Architectural Press, for giving me access to original research into the origins of the firm and for giving me time off from the magazines to finish the book. On the publishing side of the firm, editors, particularly Margaret Crowther, have patiently held my hand; Godfrey Golzen has been an unfailing support in times of crisis and has helped shape the book.

Above all, I must thank my wife. Without her unfailing help as driver, navigator, typist, critic and constant support, I could scarcely have started, and certainly would never have finished.

William Reynolds-Stephens. Screen, in Charles Harrison Townsend's church of St. Mary the Virgin, Great Warley, Essex (1902–04) (p. 111)

1 Once Upon a Time

Folk say, a wizard to a northern king
At Christmas-tide such wondrous things did show,
That through one window men beheld the spring,
And through another saw the summer glow,
And through a third the fruited vines a-row,
While still, unheard, but in its wonted way
Piped the drear wind of that December day.

So with this Earthly Paradise it is,
If ye will read aright, and pardon me,
Who strive to build a shadowy isle of bliss
Midmost the beating of the steely sea.

From *The Earthly Paradise*, William Morris 1868–70

On a fine summer's morning in Hammersmith, a man awoke to find himself in the middle of a miracle. He had gone to bed on a winter night in 1890, but as he gathered his senses in the hot early sunshine, he gradually realized that not only had the season changed but the whole of society and its buildings had been wonderfully altered.

The hero of William Morris's *News from Nowhere* had, by a trick of time, entered the post-Revolutionary world. It was a world in which money did not exist, in which everyone freely laboured at the dreary tasks, allowing all to devote time to creating beautiful and useful artefacts which they gave to each other whenever they were asked.

A pellucid Thames flowed softly through a London freed of smoke and congestion, where gardens and orchards ran down to the river banks half hiding "very pretty houses, low and not large, standing back a little way from the river; they were mostly built of red brick and roofed with tiles, and looked, above all, comfortable, and as if they were, so to say, alive and sympathetic with the life of the dwellers in them."[1]

Rising above these little houses were the public buildings, and Morris's hero finds himself lodging in one—the Guest House of Hammersmith. "It was a longish building with its gable ends turned away from the road, and long traceried windows coming rather low down set in the wall that faced us. It was very handsomely built of red brick with a lead roof; and high up about the windows there ran a frieze of figure subjects in baked clay, very well executed, and designed with a force and directness which I had never noticed in modern work before."[2]

Morris set his story more than a hundred years ahead of 1890, when it was first published in the *Commonweal*, the journal of the Socialist League. But, though the English Revolution has even now not occurred, when *News* was published, English architects and craftsmen were building a world that much resembled that seen by Morris's time traveller. These people centred around the Arts and Crafts Exhibition Society, founded in 1888 with the aim of initiating a new, original and vigorous approach to design. The approach was strongly rooted in the ideals of Morris as shown in the work of his firm and in his writings.

Arts and Craftsfolk were a highly individualistic lot but all shared Morris's affection for simplicity, truth-to-materials and the unity of handicraft and design. And they shared his affection for the Gothic—not the scholastic and religious Gothic of the High Victorians but for a Gothic spirit. It was a Gothic free of Rule, derived more from the unselfconscious cottages, almshouses and barns of ordinary medieval people than from palaces, town halls and churches. In an 1889 lecture on Gothic architecture Morris spelt out the Arts and Crafts ideal: "Now a Gothic building has walls that it is not ashamed of;

and in those walls you may cut windows wherever you please; and, if you please may decorate them to show that you are not ashamed of them; your windows, which you must have, become one of the great beauties of your house and you have no longer to make a lesson in logic in order not to sit in pitchy darkness in your own house, as in the sham sham-Roman style; your window, I say, is no longer a concession to human weakness, an ugly necessity (generally ugly enough in all conscience) but a glory of the art of Building. As for the roof in the sham style: unless the building is infected with Gothic common sense, you must pretend that you are living in a hot country which needs nothing but an awning, and that it never rains or snows in these islands."[3]

Hand in hand with these rather austere principles, a thoroughly Victorian affection for comfort and gentle ease ran throughout the Arts and Crafts movement. And there was a strong feeling for nationality—English and sometimes Scottish—as befitted a nation which had ruled the waves unhindered for the most part of a century.

The Arts and Crafts movement was of and for the Victorian upper middle class. The inhabitants of William Morris's visionary world have all the nice characteristics of Victorian gentlefolk, they are hobbits without furry feet: kind, generous, polite, energetic, moral, nationalistic (in the best sense), intellectual, practical, comfort loving and fond of "beauty". They are purged of the reverse of the Victorian coin: hypocrisy, philistinism, selfishness, puritanism, arrogant chauvinism, indifference to others and terrible class consciousness.

The upper middle classes were the only people who could enjoy individual freedom in Victorian England; they were free of the grinding poverty of the lower orders, the inverted snobbery of the lower middle classes and the increasingly rigid formality of the aristocracy. Because Britain was the richest and most powerful nation, they were probably the most free people in the world. It was for them that Arts and Crafts architects worked, evolving a new easy style which was most often seen in the small country houses of a free, proud, individualistic breed who, in three decades from 1880 to 1910, were the patrons of some of the finest and most original architecture and artefacts ever produced in Britain.

The achievements of Arts and Crafts architecture were widely recognized by continental contemporaries and by no-one more clearly than Hermann Muthesius, an architect attached to the German embassy in London between 1896 and 1903, who produced his monumental *Das englische Haus*, the definitive analysis of the domestic scene at the turn of the century, in 1904 and 1905.

Muthesius was clear that the mainspring of the British success was modest individuality. "The Englishman builds his house for himself alone. He feels no urge to impress, has no thought of festive occasions or banquets and the idea of shining in the eyes of the world through lavishness in and of his house simply does not occur to him. Indeed, he even avoids attracting attention to his house by means of striking design or architectonic extravagance, just as he would be loth to appear personally eccentric by wearing a fantastic suit. In particular, the architectonic ostentation, the creation of 'architecture' and 'style' to which we in Germany are still so prone, is no longer to be found in England. It is most instructive to note . . . that a movement opposing the imitation of styles and seeking closer ties with simple rural buildings, which began over forty years ago, has had the most gratifying results."[4]

1 Morris, William *News from Nowhere*, reprinted in *William Morris*, Nonesuch Press 1974, p. 9
2 *Ibid*, p. 13
3 Morris, William *Gothic Architecture*, reprinted in *William Morris*, Nonesuch Press 1974, p. 491
4 Muthesius, Hermann *The English House*, Crosby Lockwood Staples, London 1979, p. 10. This is the first English translation (by Janet Seligman).

2 Gathering Grounds

Forty years before Morris brought News from Nowhere, the Queen and Prince Albert had opened the Great Exhibition. Sixty thousand people a day flocked to a Crystal Palace crammed with locomotives, printing presses, electric telegraphs, Indian umbrellas, astronomical clocks, the Koh-i-noor, light house lanterns, Turkish carpets and rows of the most sentimental sculpture the world has ever seen.

In the middle of the vast and chaotic collection of up-to-date inventions (condemned by *The Times* as exhibiting "Universal infidelity in principles of design"[1]) was one court devoted with firm principle entirely to the thirteenth and fourteenth centuries: there were embroidered copes, jewelled chains, stained glass widows, painted tiles, pews, silver and metal gilt vessels, great carved font covers, ironwork

1 *The Medieval Court at the 1851 Great Exhibition*

screens and lamps, even, as the *Illustrated Exhibitor* commented, "a pianoforte attempted in the Revived style".

"The Medieval Court", announced the *Exhibitor*, "in the strikingly-harmonious combination of its stained glass, hardware, woodcarving, hangings, encaustic tiles—all successful repetitions of Gothic models—will at least have the merit of suggesting to many, who would not otherwise have heard of such facts, the fullness of beauty and character, and the homogenousness, of medieval design, however applied, to domestic as to ecclesiastic purposes . . . It is almost needless to say . . . that to the Messrs Pugin are due the entire design."[2] *Messrs* Pugin was an exaggeration since Augustus Welby Northmore Pugin (1812–1852) had designed virtually everything in the court. He now had little more than a year to live before he died at forty of overwork. He married three times, fathered eight children and designed more than a hundred buildings (mostly churches) as well as great quantities of church ornament, plate, furniture and vestments. He drew virtually every line himself and "asked why he didn't give the mere mechanical part of his working drawings to a clerk to do, he reposted, 'Clerk, my dear sir, clerk, I never employ one; I should kill him in a week.'"[3]

The taste for Gothic was very well established by the second quarter of the nineteenth century. Starting as an aristocratic fashion for picturesque Gothick country houses in the eighteenth century, by the time Pugin started to practise, Gothic was the accepted proper style for churches and widely used for other kinds of buildings. Pugin was himself deeply involved in the later years of Gothick. His father, A. C. Pugin, an aristocratic French emigré, had built up a flourishing practice from the 1790s onwards as a Gothic ghost who provided "correct" detailing for picturesquely medieval country houses of architects like Nash. The younger Pugin was thought even more knowledgable than his father and, at fifteen, he was delegated to design the Gothic furniture for Sir Jeffrey Wyatville's reconstructions of Windsor Castle. (He later called these designs "enormities" and remarked that "a man who remains any length of time in a modern Gothic room, and escapes without being wounded by some of its minutiae, may consider himself extremely fortunate."[4])

In his late teens, Pugin set up a business which provided "all the ornamental portions of buildings which could by possibility be executed apart from the structure and be fixed afterwards".[5] The firm was

2 *Pugin's satirical modern Gothic room from which a man who escapes "without being wounded by some of its minutiae may consider himself extremely fortunate"*

needed because after the long reign of classical architecture, there were very few craftsmen who could do Gothic work with correct feeling. It seems to have thrived for a short while but failed because he was no businessman.

He contrived an intimate connection with craftsmen throughout his career. With his friends the manufacturers Hardman and Herbert Minton, Pugin revitalized the crafts of ironwork, stained glass and ceramics; he was a partner* in Hardman's firm, doing most of the design work himself. Yet there was a contradiction; in the fourteenth century, a church was (in Pugin's theory) produced by craftsmen working together, sometimes for several generations. They worked to a general design but within it each mason,

---

* Several Victorian Gothic architects had to set up similar close links with manufacturers and craftsmen. For instance Sir George Gilbert Scott (1811–1878) worked closely with the Skidmore Art Manufacturers Company, metal craftsmen, and Clayton & Bell, stained glass manufacturers. His Albert Memorial (1863–1872) was in a sense a very early example of Arts and Crafts fusion of architecture, sculpture and craft work. (I am indebted to Gavin Stamp for this observation.) Integration of the arts was characteristic of the later Gothic revival, brought to a luxuriant (and witty) high pitch by William Burges (1827–1881).

carpenter and smith produced his own details. Pugin's paradox was that because of the lack of good "out workmen" he had to design down to the last nail to try to recreate the effect of a group of craftsmen working together. Pugin himself seems to have been unworried by the contradiction, but his paradox haunted succeeding generations of architects.

The great turning point in Pugin's life was his conversion to Catholicism in 1834. Its immediate result was *Contrasts*, in which Pugin preached the cause of Gothic as the only true Christian architecture by comparing a warm, Gothic pre-reformation England with the buildings and institutions of his own day shown at their meanest, most cold hearted and classical. "Catholic England", he believed, "was Merry England, at least for the humblest classes."[6] If Gothic was to be the style of a truly Christian architecture, what was the real nature of Gothic?

Pugin provided the answer on the first page of his next book, *The True Principles of Pointed or Christian Architecture*. "The two great rules for design are these: *1st, that there should be no features about a building which are not necessary for convenience, construction or propriety; 2nd, that all ornament should consist of the essential construction of the building.* The neglect of these two rules is the cause of all the bad architecture of the present time."[7] These two principles were to influence the whole of the Arts and Crafts movement.

Pugin expounded: "Architectural features are continually tacked on buildings with which they have no connexion, merely for the sake of what is termed effect; and ornaments are *actually constructed*, instead of forming the decoration of *construction*, to which in good taste they should always be subservient."[8] He went on, with surprising effect, to show how the individual elements of Gothic church architecture all had some functional purpose. And he emphasized that "the architects of the middle ages were the first who *turned the natural properties of the various materials to their full account*, and made *their mechanism a vehicle for their art*."[9]

In the early years of Victoria's reign, "How many objects of ordinary use are rendered monstrous and ridiculous simply because the artist, instead of seeking the *most convenient form*, and *then decorating it*, has embodied some extravagance *to conceal the real purpose for which the article has been made!* If a clock is required, it is not unusual to cast a Roman warrior in a flying chariot, round one of the wheels of which, on close inspection, the hours may be descried; or the whole front of a cathedral church reduced to a few inches in height, with the clock face occupying the position of a magnificent rose window."[10]

A building and everything in it should be honest reflections of materials as well as of functions: "all plaster, cast iron, and composition ornaments, painted like stone or oak, are mere impositions, and, although very suitable for a tea garden, are utterly unworthy of a sacred edifice."[11]

It was not merely his approach to decorative details, but also Pugin's principles of domestic planning which foreshadowed the approach of the Arts and Crafts movement. "An architect should exhibit his skill by turning the difficulties which occur in raising an elevation from *a convenient plan* into so many *picturesque beauties*; and this constitutes the great difference between the principles of classic and pointed domestic architecture. In the former *he would be compelled to devise expedients to conceal these irregularities*; in the latter he has *only to beautify them*."[12]

Pugin's practical and picturesque approach to planning and elevating is perfectly shown in his own cliff-top house at Ramsgate, the Grange, built in 1844. It is of plain buff local brick with stone dressings. The principal elevation overlooks the sea and is dominated by the tower from which Pugin, an ardent sailor always dressed in shabby nautical rig, who once exclaimed, "there is nothing worth living for but Christian Architecture and a boat"[13] used to watch in charity for ships in distress. The tower is balanced by a double-height bay window at the other end of the elevation. This, in proper Gothic style, fronts the most important rooms—the drawing room and the study above. The rest is very quiet; all with square-headed windows, apart from the simple pointed lights of his private chantry which sticks out towards the church of St. Augustine next door.

The exterior of St. Augustine's, built at Pugin's own expense, reveals another doctrine—fidelity to place—adopted by the Arts and Crafts movement. Like the Grange, the facade of the church is very simple. It is made of local Kentish black knapped flints banded in brown Whitby stone which was traditionally brought down the coast by sea. Perhaps because of his origins, Pugin had become an ardent English patriot: "What does an Italian house do in England?", he railed against the prevailing fashion for Italianate villas. "Is there any similarity between our climate and that of Italy? Not in the least . . . Another objection to Italian architecture is this—we

3 *A. W. M. Pugin's house at Ramsgate, Kent, The Grange (1843–4)*

are not Italians, we are Englishmen." He raged against the international style of his day: "a bastard Greek, a nondescript modern style has ravaged many of the most interesting cities of Europe."[14]

As St. Augustine's shows, Pugin wanted not only to escape from internationalism; he wanted to revive local as well as national architecture. "I would also have travelling students but I would circumscribe their limits. Durham, the destination of some—Lincolnshire's steepled fens for others . . . each county should be indeed a school—for each *is* a school."[15]

On Pugin's death, a memorial fund for travelling scholarships was set up on his model. It raised more than a thousand pounds, which was given to the Royal Institute of British Architects to provide the Pugin scholarship.* Most of the leading architects

---

* The RIBA has scandalously betrayed its trust and amalgamated the fund with others. Several Arts and Crafts architects benefited from the Pugin fund, including Lethaby and Stokes.

4 *Pugin. St. Augustine's, Ramsgate (1845–52)*

and critics of the day subscribed to the fund; even the young Norman Shaw put in his half guinea.[16]

One conspicuous absentee from the subscribers list was John Ruskin (1819–1900), by then the most widely acclaimed architectural critic and the archpriest of Gothic.

Despite a common dedication to Gothic, Ruskin was extremely hostile to Pugin, perhaps because he was thought by many to be a Puginite.

Ruskin vehemently denied any debt to Pugin and made the unlikely claim that "I glanced at Pugin's *Contrasts* once in the Oxford architectural reading room during an idle forenoon. His 'Remarks on Articles in the *Rambler*' were brought under my notice by some of the reviews. I never read a word of any other of his works, not feeling, from the style of his architecture, the smallest interest in his opinions."[17]

He thundered against Pugin in an appendix to *The Stones of Venice:** "He is not a great architect but one of the smallest possible or conceivable architects."[18] He savaged Pugin for "being lured into the Romanist Church by the glitter of it . . . blown into a change of religion by the whine of an organ pipe; switched into a new creed by the gold threads of priests' petticoats; jangled into a change of conscience by the chimes of a belfry."[19]

Ruskin was out to prove that Gothic, though it had originally been built by Catholics, was the true style for Protestants in England. He performed this feat of intellectual sleight of hand in the great chapter in *The Stones of Venice* on "The Nature of Gothic" which, through Morris, was to have a formative effect on the Arts and Crafts movement.† Ruskin emphasized that Gothic was the architecture of northern Europe and that, unlike classical architecture built by slaves, it was the product of free craftsmen: in effect proto Protestants.

According to Ruskin, classical architecture was the architecture of slavery, aiming at perfection of execution according to a series of clearly defined rules; in the end, any workman could produce it if he were beaten hard enough. But a truly Christian and humane architecture, Ruskin believed, *must* be imperfect—what he called "Savage". "You can teach a man to draw a straight line, and to cut one; to strike a curved line, and to carve it; and to copy and carve

any number of given lines and forms, with admirable speed and perfect precision; and you will find his work perfect of its kind: but if you ask him to think about any of those forms, to consider if he cannot find any better in his own head, he stops; his execution becomes hesitating; he thinks, and ten to one he makes a mistake in the first touch he gives to his work as a thinking being. But you have made a man of him for all that. He was only a machine before, an animated tool."[20]

This argument had profound consequences. Pugin was prepared to grant machinery a limited role provided it was not used to imitate handwork—machines were widely used in the Hardman workshops for instance, and he urged that "We do not want to arrest the course of inventions, but to confine these inventions to their legitimate uses, and to prevent their substitution for nobler arts."[21]

Ruskin was far more radical. In *The Lamp of Truth* he had already proclaimed that "all cast and machine work is bad, as work . . . it is dishonest".[22] In *The Stones* he was more explicit: "the great cry that rises from all our manufacturing cities, louder than their furnace blast, is . . . that we manufacture everything there except men . . . to brighten, to strengthen, to refine or to form a single living spirit, never enters into our estimate of advantages".[23] The only remedy could be "a determined sacrifice of such convenience, or beauty, or cheapness as is to be got only by the degradation of the workman; and by equally determined demand for the products and results of healthy and ennobling labour". He laid down three rules for encouraging such products. "1: Never encourage the manufacture of any article not absolutely necessary in the production of which *Invention* has no share. 2: Never demand an exact finish for its own sake, but only for some practical or noble end. 3: Never encourage imitation or copying of any kind except for the sake of preserving record of great works."[24] These were the rules of Ruskinian "savageness" that for the next fifty years were applied by Arts and Crafts designers to everything they created from cathedrals to teapots.

Related to savageness was Gothic "naturalism". The Gothic craftsman, Ruskin believed, not only expressed his own imperfections in his art but, by close observation of nature, the imperfections of his subjects too. Unlike the Greek sculptor who "could neither bear to confess his own feebleness nor to tell the faults of the forms that he portrayed"[25] the Gothic craftsman did not idealize, and struggled to render

---

* Ruskin later regretted his outburst, and the appendix was dropped from editions of *Stones* published after Pugin's death.

† And a much wider public. It was published as a penny pamphlet for working men and was widely sold.

5 *William Butterfield. Coalpit Heath Vicarage, Avon (1844–5)*

the characteristics of foliage "with as much accuracy as was compatible with the laws of his design and the nature of his materials".

Parallel to savageness in Ruskin's analysis of Gothic was "changefulness". Gothic was, he urged, the "only rational" architecture, for it could fit itself to every function. "Whenever it finds occasion for change in its form or purpose, it submits to it without the slightest sense of loss either to its unity or majesty." Can he really only have spent one afternoon glancing at Pugin when he said, "It is one of the chief virtues of the Gothic builders, that they never suffered ideas of outside symmetries and consistencies to interfere with the real use and value of what they did"? Ruskin explained that, "If they wanted a window, they opened one; a room, they added one; a buttress, they built one; utterly regardless of any established conventionalities of external appearance, knowing . . . that such daring interruptions of the formal plan would rather give additional interest to its symmetry than injure it . . . Every successive architect, employed upon a great work, built the pieces he added in his own way, utterly regardless of the style adopted by his predecessors."[26] This is a clear description of Pugin's "picturesque beauties" and a definition of architectural virtue adopted by the leading Arts and Crafts architects whether they worked with Gothic motifs or not.

No mid-Victorian architect could be untouched by Pugin and Ruskin. Three in particular, Butterfield, Street and Devey, were of great importance to the Arts and Crafts movement. William Butterfield was born in 1814, two years after Pugin, and died in 1900 the same year as Ruskin. George Edmund Street (1824–1881), like Butterfield, was an enormously successful church architect; but it is their secular buildings, less influenced by sectarian prejudices than their ecclesiastical work, that made the greater impact on Arts and Crafts people. George Devey (1820–1886) is a much more shadowy figure; he did not court publicity—a gentleman architect, most of his buildings were large country houses.*

In their parsonages and schools of the 1840s and '50s Butterfield and Street took domestic architecture further towards informality than Pugin. As early as 1844 (the year Pugin's Grange was finished), Butterfield designed his first vicarage at Coalpit Heath, Gloucestershire in local stone. In outline, it is simple with a high gable terminating the main elevation. The Georgian sash windows are asymmetrical in a most un-Georgian manner and the first floor fenestration does not follow the windows on the ground floor. An enormous chimney crashes through the eaves to balance the gable. The chimney breast is half pierced with the window of an inglenook, and the massive porch barges into the window. These are the sort of changeful accidents that occur in vernacular building—and in a young architect's work.

Street's first efforts were more controlled. In the little village school at Inkpen, Berkshire, completed in 1850, all the windows are flat-topped (at Coalpit Heath, many of the main windows have pointed arches). Gables in the tiled roof emphasize the principal windows, which are crowned with pointed arches flush with the bricks of the wall; the spaces between the arches and the flat tops of the windows are filled with a pattern of decorative tiles common in the district, and the upper floor of the attached school house is completely covered in plain red tiles.

Street's next major secular work, the vicarage and schools at Boyne Hill, Maidenhead, begun in 1854, is much more varied, with all sorts of gables, chimneys and buttresses, all in local red brick with blue brick bands and patterns. In the vicarage, windows are surmounted by shallow pointed arches but elsewhere Street used several variations, including quite steep pointed arches with brickwork between them and the heads of the flat-topped windows.

* Little is known of Devey, though scholars are bringing more to the surface all the time. For very many years the only description of his work was a series of articles in the 1907 *Architectural Review* (Vol. XXI), then still under Arts and Crafts influence. Mark Girouard's articles in *Country Life* (see reference 28) are the best modern account.

6 *Butterfield. All Saints, Margaret Street, London (started 1851)*

7 *George Edmund Street. Vicarage and schools, Boyne Hill, Maidenhead, Berkshire (started 1854)*

8 *Butterfield. Cowick Vicarage, Yorkshire (1854)*

Under the influence of Ruskin, Street had visited Northern Italy in 1853 and the strong patterning at Boyne Hill shows the influence of that trip to the striped churches of Lombardy, and of Ruskin's teaching that the "true colours of architecture are those of natural stone".[27] Street could not afford stone so the natural colours of brick were the next best thing.

Butterfield had already shown a grave gaiety in the elaborate brick and stone patterning on All Saints, Margaret Street, London (started 1849). But in a series of Yorkshire parsonages and schools started 1853, he adopted a much more restrained style. Cowick vicarage is typical: a four-square plain red brick house with a steeply pitched red tiled roof terminated at one end by a hipped gable which is balanced by a smaller gable further along. The walls are pierced by all manner of windows, mostly flat-topped narrow sashes, sometimes grouped and arranged higgledy-piggledy with, over the wider ones, pointed arches flush with the rest of the brickwork.

George Devey is quite a different kettle of fish. He too set up practice in the late 1840s, but he worked almost exclusively for large country landowners and produced at least twenty-five country houses, some of them very large, and innumerable estate cottages. His first important original work was restoring and adding to a group of cottages at the gate of Penshurst Place, Kent. With their red tiled roofs, half-timbering and roughcast, balanced over a ragstone ground floor, the cottages appear to be genuine vernacular buildings, yet only part of the delicately integrated group is truly old.

Devey trained as a watercolourist (under J. S. Cotman and J. D. Harding) as well as an architect; he never lost an exquisite sense of painterly picturesque, using native materials and techniques in a way Pugin would surely have admired. Devey's picturesqueness was much more locally based than that of the Gothick architects who built the *cottages ornés* of the early nineteenth century. As Mark Girouard has pointed out, "these had been deliberate excursions into fancy dress, but Devey's kind of rural archaeology had never been tried before".[28]

9 *George Devey. Cottages, Penshurst Place, Kent (1850)*

10 *Devey. Cottage, St. Alban's Court, Nonington, Kent (1860s to 1880s)*

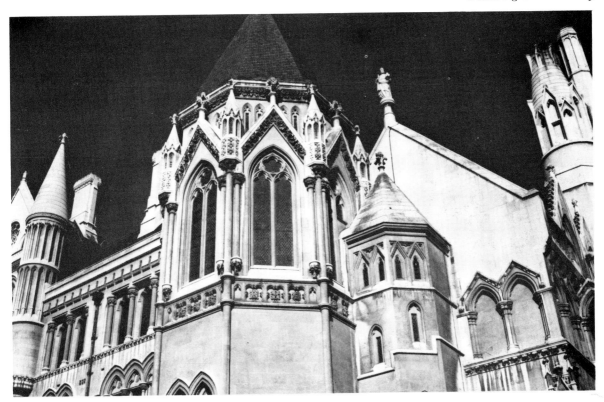

11 *High Victorian Gothic changefulness. George Edmund Street's Law Courts, Strand, London (designed 1866 completed 1882). Underlying symmetries are obscured by the clash of functionally generated forms*

Many of Devey's larger houses give the impression of having been built over many years, as indeed several were—St. Alban's Court at Nonington in Kent, for instance, was built from the 1860s to '80s. But with its Elizabethan and Jacobean styling it looks as if it had been built over two hundred years and finally finished two hundred years before Devey. He even used a ground floor of local ragstone which meets the brick of the upper storeys in a most haphazard and irregular line, giving the impression that a brick house had been built upon the ruins of a much older stone building.

This kind of complex artificial aging, which requires much reticence and humour on the part of the architect, was increasingly loved by clients (particularly those with new money) in the second half of the nineteenth century, and it became an important ingredient in Arts and Crafts thinking, which simultaneously embraced Pugin's principle of fidelity to

place and Ruskinian fidelity to function. The clash between the two approaches to design produced some of the most characteristic Arts and Crafts architecture.

Devey's love of local materials and techniques is clear, but there is no evidence that he was himself involved in practical work. Indeed, he almost certainly was not, for any obvious connection with trade would have caused him embarrassment with his grand clients. Butterfield is supposed to have been "engaged in practical smithery"[29]: Street certainly learned smithing so that he could design ironwork properly, and he painted murals in the Boyne Hill Church and believed that every architect "should himself be able to decorate his own building with painting and sculpture". But as his son remarked, "rapidly increasing press of work . . . convinced him, I think, of the inapplicability of such views in our modern times".[30] Street had, in effect, decided that he could not resolve Pugin's paradox of the relationship between designers and craftsmen in his own way of life and became noted for detailed control over the way in which his buildings were built.

Ruskin squarely faced this paradox: "the painter should grind his own colours; the architect work in the mason's yard with his men". Not that this should lead to equality "the distinction between one man and another [should] be only in experience and skill and the authority and wealth which these must naturally and justly obtain".[31]

Ruskin's early political views were a more harshly expressed version of the neo-feudalism Pugin had preached in *Contrasts* twelve years before. They gave him a rather peculiar view of freedom.

In *Stones* Ruskin avowed that "there might be more freedom in England, though her feudal lords' lightest words were worth men's lives . . . than there is while the animation of her multitudes is sent like fuel to feed the factory smoke".[32]

By the 1860s Ruskin had moved to a kind of state socialism, and in *Unto This Last*, he sketched out an ideal society almost as fierce as Utopia in which the old, sick and destitute are cared for, practical education is provided for all, there is a mixed economy, but the indigent are set "under compulsion of the strictest nature . . . to the more painful and degrading forms of necessary toil".[33]

In his last political stance, founding a society to pursue the ideals of the dignity of labour and fight against machines and their alienating effects, Ruskin anticipated the social experiments of the Arts and Crafts movement. In 1871 he founded the St.

George's Guild which aimed to give the example of a better life. Members were to be devoted "first to the manual labour of cultivating pure land . . . and secondly together with this manual labour and much by its means they are to carry on the thoughtful labour of true education, in themselves and in others".[34] Machinery was restricted to devices powered by wind and water—"electricity perhaps not in future refused". But "steam is absolutely refused as a cruel and furious waste of fuel to do what every stream and breeze are ready to do costlessly".[35]

The St. George's experiment failed after three ill starred communities were started at Barmouth, in Worcestershire and near Sheffield. Apart from Ruskin's progressive mental collapse, one of the main reasons for failure must have been his curiously contradictory attitude to authority. While embracing what he called socialism, Ruskin always stressed "the impossibility of equality". The St. George's Guild communities were under the charge of wise overseers imposed from above and so could never be the free groupings of husbandmen and craftworkers for which half of Ruskin longed. It was the guild socialism which William Morris preached in *News from Nowhere* which provided the logical answer to Ruskin's political dilemma.

1 *The Times* reprinted in the *Journal of Design*, 1851, quoted by Naylor, Gillian in *The Arts and Crafts Movement*, Studio Vista, London 1971, n. 18, p. 200

2 *The Illustrated Exhibitor* John Cassell, 1851, p. 91. The *Exhibitor* was published as a series during the course of the Great Exhibition.

3 Ferrey, Benjamin *Recollections of Pugin* 1861, Scholar Press 1978, p. 187

4 Pugin, A. W. N. *The True Principles of Pointed or Christian Architecture*, London 1841, p. 47, Academy Editions, London 1973, p. 47

5 Ferrey *op. cit.*, p. 65

6 Pugin A. W. N. *op. cit.*, p. 70

7 *Ibid.*, p. 1

8 *Ibid.*

9 *Ibid.*, p. 2

10 *Ibid.*, p. 27

11 *Ibid.*, p. 53

12 *Ibid.*, p. 72

13 *The Builder*, Vol. X, 1852, p. 605

14 Pugin, A. W. N. *op. cit.*, pp. 64–65

15 Pugin, A. W. N. *An Apology for the Revival of Christian Architecture in England*, London 1843, reprint 1969, p. 20

16 Ferrey *op. cit.*, pp. 470–473

17 Ruskin, John *Modern Painters*, Vol. III, Appendix 3, in Cook and Wedderburn *Works of John Ruskin*, London 1904, Vol. V, p. 429

18 Ruskin, John *The Stones of Venice*, Vol. I, Smith Elder, London 1851, Appendix 12, p. 372. (This appendix was dropped in the second and all subsequent editions, which were published after Pugin's death.)

19 *Ibid.*, p. 371

20 Ruskin, John *Stones, op. cit.*, Vol. II 1853, Chapter III "The Nature of Gothic", p. 161

21 Pugin, A. W. N. *Apology, op. cit.*, p. 41

22 Ruskin, John *The Seven Lamps of Architecture*, Smith Elder, London 1849, p. 48

23 Ruskin, John *Stones, op. cit.*, Vol. II, p. 165

24 *Ibid.*, pp. 165–166

25 *Ibid.*, p. 198

26 *Ibid.*, p. 179

27 Ruskin, John *Seven Lamps, op. cit.*, p. 47

28 Girouard, Mark "George Devey in Kent", *Country Life* 149, 1971, p. 745

29 Thompson, Paul *William Butterfield*, Routledge & Kegan Paul, London 1971, p. 501

30 Street A. E. *Memoir of George Edmund Street RA*, John Murray, London 1888, p. 13

31 Ruskin, John *Stones, op. cit.*, Vol. II, p. 169

32 Ruskin, John *Stones, op. cit.*, Vol. II, p. 162

33 Ruskin, John *Unto this last* 1862, in Cook and Wedderburn, *op. cit.*, Vol. XVII, p. 22

34 Quoted in Naylor, Gillian *op. cit.*, p. 93

35 *Ibid.*

3 The Prophet

Virtually all the critics agreed that the standard of work shown at the second international exhibition in 1862 had improved since 1851. But in the Medieval Court, the exhibits of one firm, Morris, Marshall, Faulkner & Co., were singled out for special hostility. The *Builder* denounced the firm's furniture as "unnecessarily rude and ugly".[1] The *Building News* was much more explicit: "If all modern inventions, luxuries, tastes and history are to be entirely ignored, and Medieval art is required in its mingled purity and impurity, then undoubtedly Messrs Morris, Marshall & Faulkner take and well merit the foremost rank. Their works are almost perfect; their hangings, their music stand, their sofa, their chests, would all suit a family which might suddenly be awakened after a sleep of four centuries, and which was content to pay enormous prices suitably to furnish a barn. Standing on the opposite side of the Court and looking at the hangings, the harmony is exquisite; there is scarcely a false tone throughout them. The design of the ornament is also in keeping with the workmanship of the material. And all are thoroughly medieval; but they are no more adapted to the wants of living men, than medieval armour would be to modern warfare, middle-aged cookery to civic feasts, or Norman oaths to an English lady's drawing room. They would be all very well as curiosities in a museum, but they are fit for nothing else . . . The two doors of the lacquered cabinet are beautifully painted with single figures on a punctured gilt background. These pictures are decidedly the best of Messrs Morris, Faulkner & Marshall's work. If we possessed the cabinet, we should cut them out and put the rest behind the fire, *because* it gives us perfectly the rude execution and barbarous ornament of centuries ago. Messrs Morris, Faulkner & Marshall's works are the most complete, and the most thoroughly medieval of any in the Court. They are consequently the most useless."[2]

Morris, Marshall Faulkner & Co was the furnishing wing of the pre-Raphaelite movement, which explained both the Ruskinian savageness of execution of the woodwork and the quality of the painting. The firm, which was to have a prodigious effect on late nineteenth-century design,* had been founded only a year before the exhibition by a group of artists brought together by William Morris.

Morris (1834–1896) was born in Walthamstow, the son of a wealthy City businessman. In 1840, when Morris was six, his father acquired a fortune by speculating in a Devon copper mine, and the family moved to Woodford Hall on the fringe of Epping Forest, a world which had not changed greatly for hundreds of years. The household "brewed its own beer and made its own butter; as much a matter of course as it baked its own bread."[3] Morris rode his pony in the forest (sometimes clad in a specially made suit of armour): he fished and shot, gardened and learned the beauty of plants and birds. The Epping period ended when Mr. Morris died in 1847 and his family, though still well off, had to move back to Walthamstow.

All his life, Morris tried to recreate the idyllic, almost medieval life of Woodford Hall: self-sufficient, financially secure, practical, in close contact with nature. But in Morris's vision, the ideal was to be shared by everybody, not just those who happened to own great houses in the country.

Love of medieval beauty was fostered by his undergraduate years in an Oxford little changed since the fifteenth century. It was confirmed when, with Edward Burne-Jones, his greatest university friend, he read the newly published *Stones of Venice*. The

* For all the magazine's hostility, the firm was awarded two medals by the exhibition's jury—public acclaim enough to set the company on the track of prestigious commissions (for instance rooms in St. James's Palace and the South Kensington Museum).

effect of "The Nature of Gothic" on the two young men was dramatic and made them resolve to give up their common ambition to take the cloth. Burne-Jones decided to become a painter and Morris resolved to be an architect.

At twenty-two, after obtaining a pass degree, Morris took articles with Street, then architect to the Oxford diocese. Morris described Street as "a good architect as things go now, and he has a good deal of business, and always goes for an honourable man."[4] The relationship lasted only nine months, for Burne-Jones, who was already studying under Dante Gabriel Rossetti, introduced him to his master and Morris "made up my mind to turn painter and studied the art but in a very desultory way for some time."[5]

In 1857, he took rooms with Burne-Jones at 17 Red Lion Square, and, being unable to find suitable furniture, he sketched some designs, massive pieces which were made up by a local carpenter and painted with scenes from Chaucer and Dante by Rossetti and Burne-Jones. Savage furniture was born.

In the same year Rossetti offered to paint the walls and roof of the new Oxford Union Building. A gang of painters including Morris and Burne-Jones took part in creating a now lost Pre-Raphaelite masterpiece. (Rossetti had no real knowledge of how to work in fresco, and the paintings began to fade almost as quickly as they were done.) Morris had chosen as his subject "How Sir Palimydes loved La Belle Iseult with exceeding great love out of measure and how she loved not him again but Sir Tristram."

Morris's story was hidden behind a great mass of sunflowers and his figures were so ill proportioned that they caused Rossetti to burst into sarcastic laughter. But, behind the vegetation, Morris had found his own Iseult, Jane Burden, a groom's daughter, a "stunner", with a long neck, vast dark eyes and a great mane of dark hair, who had been persuaded by Rossetti to sit as a model for the frescoists. William and Jane were engaged in 1858, and in the same year Morris's friend from the Street days, Philip Webb,

12 *The great settle which moved from Morris's Red Lion Square lodgings to the Red House*

was commissioned to design a house for the couple. This was the Red House at Bexley Heath which is described in the next chapter. It was as difficult for a convinced Ruskinian to furnish his new home as it had been to fit out Red Lion Square. Webb had to design much of the furniture, and the interior was decorated by Morris and his friends.

The experience determined Morris's final choice of career. He was to be a designer and interior decorator. In April 1861, the firm of Morris, Marshall, Faulkner & Co. was set up with, as partners, Morris, Burne-Jones, Webb, Rossetti, Ford Madox Brown (the Pre-Raphaelite painter who had already dabbled in furniture design), Charles Faulkner (one of Morris's Oxford friends, a mathematics don), and Marshall (a surveyor friend of Brown). Morris was general manager. The Firm was set up at 8 Red Lion Square and offered furniture, wall paintings, stained glass, embroidery, table glass, metalwork, jewellery and sculpture. Although its work had received such a drubbing from the critics at its first public appearance in the 1862 exhibition, the Firm quickly secured work: the partners bought things for themselves; Webb persuaded his clients to commission decorative schemes, and Gothic church architects like Street, White and Bodley ordered stained glass and wall decorations. It was on these ecclesiastical commissions that the Firm survived the '60s to blossom into domestic success in the '70s.*

As a Ruskinite, Morris was bound to become involved in craft work as well as design. He explained to an admirer, "almost all the designs we use for surface decoration, wallpapers, textiles and the like, I design myself. I have had to learn the theory and to some extent the practice of weaving, dying and textile printing: all of which I must admit has given me and gives me a great deal of enjoyment."[6]

His own designs for wallpapers, textiles, tapestries, embroideries and carpets are too well known and well loved to need description here. Their power emerged from a creative tension between Pugin's rule that the designer should be truthful to his materials (for this reason Pugin argued that the patterns of wallpaper

must always be flat, with no hint of perspective) and Ruskin's doctrine of naturalism under which the (imperfect) designer should struggle as hard as possible to depict (imperfect) nature. Of all Morris's splendid designs, the most joyous combine Pugin's stiff heraldic structure and a loving, delicate observation of leaves, fruits and flowers.

For all his skill as a designer, Morris never tried architecture. His experience in Street's office had not been happy: he had been set to copying a drawing of a doorway in St. Augustine's church, Canterbury (by Butterfield) and "suffered much tribulation in delineating the many arch mouldings 'and at last the compass points nearly bored a hole through the drawing board'."[7] The mechanical nature of architectural work did not at all suit Morris's temperament, but he was quite clear that architecture was the mother of the arts and crafts, that it should be a "union of the arts mutually helpful and harmoniously subordinated to one another."[8]

His ideal was an architecture altogether free of imposed style, one which would grow unselfconsciously from its surroundings and the needs of ordinary people. "If the old cottages, barns and the like, are kept in good repair from year to year, they will not need to be pulled down to give place either to the red-brick, blue-slated man-sty, or the modern Tudor lord-bountiful cottage. And where . . . new buildings must be built, by building them well and in a common sense and unpretentious way, with the good material of the countryside, they will take their place alongside of the old houses and look, like them, a real growth of the soil."[9] He hoped that "it will be from such necessary, unpretentious buildings that the new and genuine architecture will spring, rather than from our experiments in conscious style, more or less ambitious or those for which the immortal Dickens has given us the never-to-be-forgotten adjective 'Architectooralooral'."[10]

A clean simplicity should be the aim, for "simplicity of life, even the barest, is not misery, but the very foundation of refinement." The choice was between "a sanded floor and white-washed walls, and the green trees and flowering meads and living waters outside; or a grimy palace with a regiment of housemaids always working to smear the dirt together so that it may be unnoticed."[11]

If the Arts and Crafts architects had ever felt the need to write a manifesto, these passages might well have formed its core, so widely were their principles accepted. Their work is often accused of being back-

---

* Success and Morris's declining private income caused the dissolution of the original partnership. In 1875 Morris, whose money and energy had carried the company, reorganized it under his sole proprietorship as Morris & Co. This caused a split with Rossetti and Brown, but Burne-Jones and Webb remained faithful friends and continued to contribute designs. The quarrel between the original partners was later made up with the help of Edwina Burne-Jones, Edward's wife.

13 *Bibury, Gloucestershire. This Cotswold hamlet was described by Morris as "surely the most beautiful village in England." The ageless domestic architecture of England held by Morris to be a model for future building*

Author's opinion

ward looking and, of course, it often was so. Yet for those who took the teachings of Ruskin and Morris really seriously, classical architecture was forbidden as were experiments with machine-made products like steel and cast iron. They were restricted to a range of traditional materials, used in a more or less traditional way but without classical rules. So, even if they had not wanted affinities with pre-classical late medieval and Tudor building, it would have been almost impossible to have escaped them, just as William Morris could envision the post-industrial, post-hierarchical society of *News from Nowhere* only through a translucent screen of idealized medievalism as painted by Carlyle, Walter Scott and Ruskin. No architect can be free of influences from the past and most Arts and Craftsmen welcomed and exploited the obvious connections with late medieval architecture

→ What is the News of Nowhere

in their own work.* At the same time some of the more adventurous spirits were prepared to experiment with new materials like concrete which could be adapted to craftsmanly techniques (see p. 64 and p. 77).

Morris's vision of the town as it might be was as potent as his ideas on architecture. It foreshadowed the Garden City movement of the turn of the century (chapter 13). Cities, he believed, should be quite different from "our great sprawling brick and mortar country of London . . . the centre with its big public buildings, theatres, squares and gardens; the zone round the centre with its lesser guildhalls grouping together the houses of the citizens; again with its parks and gardens; the outer zone again, still its district of public buildings, but with no definite gardens to it because the whole of this outer zone would be a garden thickly besprinkled with houses and other buildings. And at last the suburb proper, mostly

* At first occasionally, then increasingly, Georgian architecture, classical building's relaxed little brother, was also seen as a native architecture, and a suitable source of inspiration.

fields and fruit gardens with scanty houses dotted about till you come to the open country with its occasional farm-steads."[12]

If the new architecture and planning were to draw their inspiration from the old, preservation of old work was vitally important—not just as a model but as a reminder of the continuity of the past, present and future. In 1877, Morris was outraged by a proposal by Sir George Gilbert Scott to restore Tewkesbury Abbey. Earlier restorations by High Victorian architects which were honestly but ruthlessly intended to return buildings to their original state had, in Morris's eyes, ruined much fine medieval architecture, partly through ignorance and partly through having to use nineteenth-century methods of work, under which it was impossible for stonecarvers to express true Gothic savageness.

The Tewkesbury project caused Morris to found the Society for the Protection of Ancient Buildings, which, with Morris's crusading zeal and Philip Webb's quiet technical competence, popularized the doctrine of honest repair rather than wholesale restoration to a state of perfection which often had reality

not in history but in the architect's imagination. In the late nineteenth century SPAB saved many old buildings from the process of skimming off the accretions of time normally practised by the High Victorians. Many Arts and Crafts architects were members of SPAB, and the Society's gentle, honest approach did much to form their attitudes to old work which, whenever the occasion demanded, was lovingly and honestly incorporated into new construction.

In the SPAB manifesto, Morris urged his contemporaries "to treat our ancient buildings as monuments of a bygone art, created by bygone manners, that modern art cannot meddle with without destroying.

"Thus, and thus only . . . can we protect our ancient buildings and hand them down instructive and venerable to those that come after us."[13]

The understanding that the heritage of the past belonged to everyman was one of the mileposts on Morris's long march towards communism. The impetus came very largely from Ruskin. Ruskin had seen the imperative of allowing every craftsman freedom to make his own contribution, no matter how ham-fisted. He had understood the importance of creative work and the need to give nobility to the degraded lives of the Victorian poor by offering everybody the chance of creativity. And he had stressed the need for beauty and health in the lives of the

14 *Great Coxwell Barn, Gloucestershire. Morris thought it "unapproachable in its dignity, as beautiful as a cathedral, yet with no ostentation of the builder's art." He believed that such structures could be the pattern of new public buildings*

15 *Kelmscott, William Morris's country house. A medieval manor growing unselfconsciously from its surroundings. Paradoxically, the realization that buildings like Kelmscott were the inheritance of everyman helped direct Morris towards Communism*

whole community. Morris believed that Ruskin, "by a marvellous inspiration of genius . . . attained at one leap to a true conception of medieval art . . . The essence of what Ruskin taught us was simple enough . . . It was really nothing more recondite than this, that the art of any epoch must of necessity be an expression of its social life, and that the social life of the Middle Ages allowed the workman freedom of individual expression, which on the other hand our social life forbids him."[14] But Ruskin, as the St. George's Guild showed, had refrained from the last logical step—acceptance that if everyone could be creative, society must be reorganized in a way that would give everyone an equal chance to create.

William Morris took this step in 1883 when he joined the Social Democratic Federation, the only socialist body then in existence. It was the start of a commitment to the socialist movement to which, through numerous vicissitudes, he remained faithful to the end of his life. He was never just a passive supporter but:

"When I joined the Communist folk, I did what
in me lay
To learn the grounds of their faith. I read day
after day
Whatever books I could handle, and heard about
and about
What talk was going amongst them; and I
burned up doubt after doubt,
Until it befel at last that to others I needs must
speak."[15]

By 1889 Morris was prepared to declare that "I call
myself a Communist and have no wish to qualify that
word by joining any other to it. The aim of Communism seems to me to be the complete equality of condition for all people; and anything in a Socialist direction which stops short of this is merely a compromise
with the present conditions of society; a halting place
on the road to the goal."[16]

Morris believed that the only way of resolving the
Puginian paradox was by revolution—bloody if need
be*—for "if people were once to accept it as true,
that it is nothing but just and fair that every man's
work should have some hope and pleasure always
present in it, they must try to bring the change about
that would make it so."[17]

Morris inherited Ruskin's hatred of machines but
he was far from the popular picture of a late Victorian
intellectual luddite trying to smash machinery with
single stick, carpenter's chisel and embroidery needle
that has been painted by some historians. Morris did
not hate machines as such—just the way in which
they were used by Victorian capitalism. For him,
Victorian machinery, like classical architecture,
reduced workers to slavery as machine minders or
carvers-to-rote.

Morris's ideal society ressembled that of his friend,
the anarchist Peter Kropotkin. Creative work would
be offered to everybody but, concomitantly,
everyone would have to take his turn at the essential
but unpleasant jobs like cleaning sewers or coal min-
ing. He could not conceive, as we can, of machines
that would accomplish these tasks, but he would
undoubtedly have welcomed them, for he argued that
"if the necessary reasonable work be of a mechanical
kind, I must be helped to do it by machine, not to
cheapen my labour, but so that as little time as possible may be spent upon it and that I may be able to
think of other things while I am tending the
machine."[18]

"Yet for the consolation of the artists I will say that
I believe that a state of social order would probably
lead at first to a great development of machinery for
really useful purposes, because people will still be
anxious about getting through the work necessary to
holding society together; but that after a while they
will find that there is not so much work as they
expected . . . and if it seems to them that a certain
industry would be carried on more pleasantly as
regards the worker, and more effectively as regards
the goods, by using hard work rather than machinery,
they will certainly get rid of their machinery, because
it will be possible for them to do so . . . I have a hope
. . . that the elaboration of machinery in a society
whose purpose is not the multiplication of labour as it
now is, but the carrying on of a pleasant life, as it
would be under social order—that the elaboration of
machinery . . . will lead to the simplification of life,
and so once more to the limitation of machinery."[19]

Morris was well aware that he was in a contradictory predicament. When he was working on Philip
Webb's house, Rounton Grange, in 1874, the client
Sir Lowther Bell heard Morris "talking and walking
about in an excited way", and went to inquire if
anything was wrong. "He turned on me like a wild
animal—'It is only that I spend my life ministering to
the swinish luxury of the rich.'"[20] Morris was a
capitalist who preached communism; a designer of
mass produced art who believed in the freedom of
individual craftsmen; a manufacturer of machine-
made ornament who preferred utter simplicity.

These contradictions, which echo through the
whole Arts and Crafts movement, were the product
of a visionary trapped by circumstances in a very
different world from the one he wanted to see. William's daughter May recalled that when preparing to
visit a client to discuss some elaborate scheme of
decoration "he would often remark laughing that it
would not answer, in the interests of the Firm, if he
were to say what he really liked—white walls and no
furniture and no pictures or stuffy curtains: that is for
ordinary houses; for fine arras tapestry was the one
decoration for stately buildings in our northern countries, 'Wall papers are a poor makeshift' said the
designer of them many a time."[21]

This seems cynical and reinforces the view of contemporaries like Norman Shaw who believed that
Morris was a money grubbing hypocrite (p. 59). But
the alternative of fully enacting his social ideals in his

---

* In Chapter XVII of *News from Nowhere*, Old Hammond relates
that the change in society came about through "war from beginning
to end: bitter war, till hope and pleasure put an end to it."

own way of life would not only have impoverished his family without changing society in the least, but it would have deprived Morris of the time and energy he needed to set the example of what the world could be like, freed from the fetters of capitalism.

Paul Thompson has analysed Morris's predicament. "Morris had in fact considered a complete scheme of profit sharing . . . Morris calculated that in 1884 his own income from the firm was £1,800 while Wardle [the manager] received £1,200 and four others about £500 each. Two of the foremen were given bonuses. The rest, except for two or three 'lame dogs', were paid by piece work, rather above their trade rates. If he paid himself a foreman's wage he could distribute £1,600 a year to the other workmen, £16 a year each. But the utmost this income could do would be to help 'a few individuals more creep out of their class into the middle class'. True co-operation could never be organized within capitalism; and the gesture itself would cripple the support he now gave the socialist cause."[22]

Morris's communism was that of a man freed by his membership of the upper middle class. His intense individualism would never have allowed him to accept collectivism. The man whose volcanic energy caused him to gnaw the dinner table and twist the tines of his fork in his mouth when thwarted* was not likely to accept consensus quietly. Morris was never much at home with groups of people of any sort. George Bernard Shaw, who, though a non-revolutionary Fabian socialist, sometimes appeared with Morris at street corner meetings, recalled that "he was an ungovernable man in a drawing room. What stimulated me to argument, or at least repartee, made him swear."[24]

Yet Morris knew that, if working people got power in his lifetime, his privileged vision was unlikely to be accepted. "I have always believed that the realization of Socialism would give us the opportunity of escaping from that grievous flood of utilitarianism which the full development of the society of contract has cursed us with; but that would be in the long run only; and I think it quite probable that in the early days of Socialism the reflex of the terror of starvation, which so oppresses us now, would drive us into exces-

ses of utilitarianism . . . So that it is not unlikely that the public opinion of a community would be in favour of cutting down all the timber in England, and turning the country into a big Bonanza farm or market garden under glass. And in such a case what could we do?"[25]

C. R. Ashbee, a young apprentice architect toying with socialism, was introduced to Morris in 1886. He "received us kindly and invited us all in to supper. Everything in his house is beautiful—such Rossettis, and such a harmony of colours and tones! Miss Morris in a plain crimson velvet dress with red glass beads and a silver ornament, looked like an Italian chatelaine of the fifteenth century. Sitting at table one felt like one of the people in Millais's Pre-Raphaelite picture of Isabella. Everything was harmonious . . .

"Old Morris was delightful, firing up with the warmth of his subject, all the enthusiasm of youth thrilling through veins and muscles; not a moment was he still, but ever sought to vent some of his immense energy. At length banging his hand on the table: 'No,' said he, 'the thing is this; if we had our Revolution tomorrow, what should we Socialists do the day after?'

"'Yes . . . what?' we all cried. And that he could not answer. 'We should all be hanged, because we are promising the people more than we can ever give them.'"[26]

In fact, Morris was regarded as safely respectable by the class he spent so much energy in trying to overthrow. So much so that, in spite of having been twice arrested at Socialist demonstrations, he was seriously canvassed for the Lauriateship when Tennyson died in 1892. He smartly turned down the offer —though he derived some pleasure from receiving it.

It is this respectable Morris who presides in bronze over the Pantheon of the Arts and Crafts movement, the Hall of the Art Workers' Guild; his ebullient rug of curly hair is tamed and his douce expression can rarely have been worn in life. Below are written in letters of gold the names of the members. They gave him the place of honour because his example, in art and in life, had inspired them all: more than any other single man, Morris shaped the nature of the Arts and Crafts movement.

* The strength of Morris's teeth occasionally had odd repercussions. Visiting, on behalf of SPAB, a church which was in the process of destructive restoration Morris saw some vile new oak stalls about to be installed. "Call that carving," he shouted, "I could gnaw it better with my teeth."[23] The vicar was not impressed.

1 *Builder*, Vol. XX 1862, p. 420
2 *Building News*, Vol. IX 1862, p. 99
3 Mackail, J. W. *The Life of William Morris*, Longmans Green, London 1922 (5th edition), p. 9
4 Lethaby, W. R. *Philip Webb and His Work*, Oxford 1935, p. 14

5 Letter to Andreas Scheu; quoted in Morris, May *William Morris, Artist, Writer, Socialist*, Vol. II, Basil Blackwell, Oxford 1935, p. 10
6 *Ibid.*, p. 12
7 Lethaby, W. R. *Philip Webb*, *op. cit.*, p. 15
8 Morris, William "The prospects of architecture", Lecture to the London Institution 1881. Printed in May Morris *Works of William Morris*, XXII, p. 119
9 Morris, William "On the external coverings of roofs", Lecture, 1890, *Works*, op. cit., XXII, p. 408
10 Morris, William "Address to Birmingham Art Students" 1894, *Works*, *op. cit.*, XXII, p. 429
11 Morris, William "The prospects of architecture", *op. cit.*, p. 149
12 Morris, William "Makeshift" (1894), in May Morris *William Morris*, *op. cit.*, II, p. 474
13 Morris, William *SPAB Manifesto*, 1877. Still required to be signed by every recruit to the Society today.
14 Morris, William "The revival of architecture", Lecture, 1888, *Works*, *op. cit.*, XXII, p. 323
15 Morris, William *The Pilgrims of Hope* section VI. Quoted by E. P. Thompson in *William Morris: Romantic to Revolutionary*, Merlin Press, London 1977, p. 270
16 Morris, William Letter in *Commonweal*, 18.5.89. Quoted in May Morris *William Morris*, *op. cit.*, II, p. 313
17 Morris, William "The prospects of architecture", *Works, op. cit.*, XII, p. 140
18 Morris, William "How we live and how we might live" (1885), *Works* XXIII, *op. cit.*, p. 20
19 *Ibid.*, p. 24
20 Lethaby, W. R. *Philip Webb*, *op. cit.*, p. 94
21 Morris, May *William Morris*, *op. cit.*, III, p. 616
22 Thompson, Paul *The Work of William Morris*, Quartet Books, London 1977, p. 50
23 Morris, May *William Morris*, *op. cit.*, II, p. 621
24 Shaw, G. B. in May Morris *William Morris*, *op. cit.*, II, xviii
25 Morris, William in May Morris *William Morris*, *op. cit.*, II, p. 315
26 Ashbee, C. R. *Memoirs*: typescript in the Victoria and Albert Museum Library, Vol. I, p. 19

William Morris. Tile panel c. 1877

4 Lamplighters

When Morris entered Street's Oxford office in 1856, the chief clerk was a tall, thin rather serious young man called Philip Webb. They were to be lifelong friends, committed alike to the causes of art and socialism.

Phillippe Speakman Webb (1831–1915) was the son of a country doctor. He grew up in an Oxford almost untouched by the industrial revolution: a virtually medieval city in an idyllic landscape. Looking back, he wrote, "I was born and bred in Oxford and had no other teacher in art than the impressive objects of the old buildings there, the effect of which on my natural bent have never left me."[1] His teacher in the business of architecture was John Billing, a Reading architect whom he served from 1849 to 1852 after which he spent an unhappy period as clerk in Wolverhampton.

Street's invitation to return to Oxford must have been a godsend to Webb who was never happy unless surrounded by old buildings. From Street, Webb imbibed iron self-discipline and a love of the craft of building. But it was Morris who ignited the fire. Webb was always withdrawn yet Morris could bring him out—to the extent of taking part in a battle of soda syphons when the two, with Faulkner, rowed down the Seine from Paris to St. Opportune in 1858. On the back of one of the maps in the Murray guide used by the three on the Seine trip was a sketch by Webb for his first large commission, a house for Morris.

Both had gone to London when Street moved his practice from Oxford in 1856. Morris drifted away from architecture and into the arms of the Pre-Raphaelites in the next two years. Webb remained with Street until 1858 and, in the early months of the next year, he designed the Red House at Bexley Heath for the newly married Morris—it turned out to be the only house Morris ever built for himself. In it

both owner and architect began to work out their theories in practice, to such effect that when, fifty years later, Lawrence Weaver published *Small Country Houses of Today*, which contains a virtual roll call of Arts and Crafts architects, he felt bound to include the Red House because "It stands for a new epoch of new ideals and practices. Though the French strain which touched so much of the work of the Gothic revivalists is not absent, and the Gothic flavour itself is rather marked, every brick in it is a word in the history of modern architecture."[2]

The Gothic flavour is to be seen in the very steeply pitched roof topped by the French leaded lantern and in the pointed arches over the loggia and the windows. These are virtually the only motifs directly copied from Gothic. Yet the house is Gothic in spirit, in direct descent from the domestic work of Street and Butterfield (who was one of Webb's few heroes).

Its windows are sized and proportioned and placed to suit what goes on inside the house and are not arranged regularly to suit some imposed style. The red bricks and tiles, which made the house so unusual to contemporaries, used to stucco, were carefully chosen to give variation of colour and to avoid any impression of mechanical perfection. Outside there is virtually no ornament except for the pointed arches over the doors and sash windows, an echo of Butterfield's parsonages and Street at Boyne Hill. Overt Gothicism is fading away, for the arches are flush with the rest of the brickwork as if they are trying to disappear—as they do in most of Webb's more mature work.

In plan, the house was revolutionary. The most logical layout for an architect wanting to fulfill the ideal of Ruskinian changefulness is a long thin strip of rooms in which the functions of each can be clearly shown on the outside. Webb adopted this chain-like plan with the addition of a corridor down the side

16 *Philip Webb. The Red House, Bexley Heath, Kent (designed 1859)*

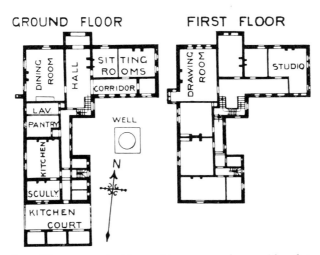

17 *Red House, plans. The prototypical long, thin, room-and-a-corridor Arts and Crafts plan*

which connected all the rooms and obviated the need for walking through one room to get to another, common in medieval planning, but potentially embarrassing for nineteenth-century Britons (though not, apparently, for their American contemporaries).

Webb bent this one-room-and-a-corridor strip into an L shape forming a courtyard round the well (necessary because no mains water was available). The result is like a Butterfield parsonage cut down the middle with the two halves set at right-angles to each other. Butterfield himself had occasionally experimented with L-shaped plans but never honed them down to the room and a corridor width. For this, there were precedents in the vast castellated country houses of architects like Anthony Salvin, but Webb was one of the first to apply the scheme to a quite small house; it was to be echoed in innumerable Arts and Crafts plans before the end of the century though Webb himself never re-used it.

If the layout was a powerful precedent, the orientation was not. All the principal rooms faced north in the Georgian fashion; the kitchen faced west (which gave it the maximum amount of heat from the sun just when dinner was being prepared) and the garden round the well was faced by no more than the long thin corridor. Later, as his friend and assistant George Jack recorded, "Webb often said that he never wanted to see [the Red House] or hear about it again, and that no architect ought to be allowed to build a house until he was forty."[3]

The interior was restrained but greatly enlivened by Burne-Jones and Rossetti murals. There was massive furniture designed by Morris and Webb, including a settle from Red Lion Square: a mad and splendid combination of cupboard, bookshelf and sitting bench, very plain joinery but illuminated with panels designed by Rossetti. There was stained glass in the leaded lights of the corridors and above the staircase in its corner tower was what Weaver called a "tall pyramidal roof left open on the inside and patterned in blue and green, a little Persian in feeling".[4] Besides his furniture, Webb contributed designs for table glass and metal work, none of which Morris could find on the market to fit his exacting standards. There is no evidence to show how much influence each of the collaborators had on the design of the Red House, but it is probably safe to say that the dark glowing interiors owed more to Morris while the rather austere exterior had more of Webb in it.

While Morris was fierce, ebullient, febrile, and eloquent, Webb was his alter ego. Gentle, modest,

18 *Webb. Number 1 Palace Green, Kensington, London (1869)*

19 *George Frederick Bodley and Philip Webb. Abermule, Montgomeryshire (1869)*

20 *Webb. 19 Lincoln's Inn Fields, London (1869)*

patient and deeply reserved in public, he refused to
have his buildings published, and virtually the only
light so far shed on Webb is by his disciple and
biographer William Lethaby. Yet in private he was
affectionate and kindly, fond of jokes, good claret and
snuff which in moments of stress he would take in
enormous quantities. He was generous—for instance
though he did not smoke, he always had an inexhaustible supply of cigars for his friends. George Jack,
writing of Webb after his death said, "it is like trying
to remember past sunshine—it pleases and it passes,
but it also makes things to grow and herein Webb was
like the sunshine, and as little recognized and
thanked."[5]

Unthanked he may have been, but his buildings
were enormously influential. Of his largest town
house, number 1 Palace Green, Kensington, built in
1869 for the future Earl of Carlisle, Lethaby wrote
that it was remarkable "as having furnished precedents for fashionable house builders for a whole generation. Here first, so far as I know, cut-and-rubbed
brickwork forming moulded and dentilled cornices
was used in recent times.* Here too, are pilaster strips
in brickwork, 'aprons' under the window sills, a
coved cornice, a carved panel, ornamental arrangements of brickwork, silver-grey slating, wrought-iron
balconies, big sash windows with wide wood-frames,
some little circular windows and a firm lead-covered
dormer. All these things came in naturally in their
places and grew out of the circumstances without
effort, but this house furnished a pattern-book of
'features' for architects who designed by compilation
from cribs."[6]

Webb himself had a horror of copying. Yet he was
unwilling to divorce himself entirely from the past.
The Palace Green house has great Gothic pointed

---

* Lethaby was wrong, as Gavin Stamp has pointed out to me.
Bodley and Nesfield, for instance, had both used rubbed brick
cornices earlier. George Frederick Bodley (1827–1907) was one of
the greatest later Victorian ecclesiastical architects. He was one of
the early (1863) and constant patrons of the Morris firm for stained
glass. His career was crowned, a year before his death, with the
commission for the Episcopal Cathedral, Washington (still building
to modified designs).

His domestic architecture was often a blend of brick-and-gabling
with symmetrical planning and windows with Georgian sashes.
Bodley and Webb were close—so much so that when, for instance,
Bodley fell temporarily, but seriously, sick, he asked Webb to
complete Abermule, Montgomeryshire (1869), a house that had
much in common with Webb's architecture of the next decade,
with severe rubbed brick detailing, virtually symmetrical main
fronts, Georgian windows and interior detailing. Changefulness
was confined to the less important elevations and the stable block.

arches as well as eighteenth-century sash windows.
Number 19 Lincoln's Inn Fields, designed in the
same year, is much more Georgian in feeling (it was
after all set in an eighteenth-century terrace), but
with its gable-hooded porch and central stone bay
projecting from the reserved brickwork on either
side, it is very far from being a neo-Georgian building.

During the '70s, Webb elaborated the symmetry
first seen in Lincoln's Inn Fields. Houses like Rounton Grange near Northallerton, Yorkshire (1872–
1876), Joldwynds near Dorking, Surrey (1873) and
Smeaton Manor, Yorkshire (1876) were all variants of
symmetrical planning, with the main accommodation
crammed into a big rectangular block. The exteriors
of this period were all more or less derived from
Georgian—but the details were much simplified and
were used with the same kind of austere insouciance
that makes Lincoln's Inn Fields so distinctive.

Much of the '80s was taken up with designing and
building Clouds at East Knoyle near Salisbury which
was burnt down soon after completion and then
rebuilt. Now half destroyed and much mutilated, the
house was partly symmetrical but, on a much larger
scale, it showed a move back towards the relaxed
planning of the Red House.

Clouds was a foretaste of the freedom of Webb's
masterpiece, Standen, near East Grinstead, Sussex,
designed in 1891 and completed by 1894. Unlike
many of the houses of the '70s and '80s, Standen was
not designed for a landed family but for J. S. Beale, a
successful solicitor, which may explain its lack of
formality. There is no tinge of symmetry about Standen, which has a long, thin L-shaped plan two rooms
deep with a corridor in the middle. This allowed all
rooms to be orientated in the way late Victorians
preferred, main family spaces: conservatory, drawing, dining rooms face south; the morning room
and kitchen face east and the servants' hall looks
west.

Outside, the building is a monument to Ruskinian
changefulness and Puginian fidelity to place. The
existing old farm house was incorporated into the
complex at Webb's insistence. Its traditional tile
hanging is echoed in the new work and complimented
by all sorts of local materials and techniques: roughcast, clapboard, brick and stone, each of which
enabled Webb to emphasize different functions. Even
the windows are carefully differentiated, with leaded
lights to show the circulation spaces (hall, corridor
and so on) and big sash windows to indicate the

21 *Webb. Joldwynds, Surrey (1873—now destroyed)*

22 *Webb, Smeaton Manor, Yorkshire (1876)*

23 *Webb. Clouds, East Knoyle, Wiltshire (1880s)*

24 *Webb. Standen, Sussex (1891–1894)*

rooms. Apart from these windows, all references to past styles have disappeared; the only mouldings are the minimum needed to keep the building waterproof. The result is a big house that looks as if it grew up in stages over many years—the effect that Devey tried so hard to produce, but without any of Devey's curious picturesque jumbles of materials—each change of material is sharp, showing exactly where internal arrangements stop and start.

Standen dramatically illustrates Webb's abiding passion for traditional building and local materials which was strong even in his most classicizing days—the roof of Rounton Grange for instance was a north Yorkshire combination of pantiles and stone slates; Joldwynds, like Standen, was in a mixture of local brick, hung tiles and weatherboarding; at Smeaton Manor the bricks were fired from clay found near the site.

Webb was passionate about good building; he spent much time discussing technique with the craftsmen of his day who still built as their forebears had done for hundreds of years. Lethaby remembered that "He was deeply interested in limes and mortars, the proper ways of laying roof tiles and forming chimneys, of finishing plaster ceilings and mixing whitewash. He forced himself to become an expert in ventilation and drainage."[7]

As important to Webb as right building was the necessity of relating his building to the site and to local traditions of building. In a letter to a client at Arisaig, Argyll (1882) he urged: "if you should fail in getting whin stone of sufficient size to do the memorial from stone got from your own ground, it would seem hardly to the purpose to get that sort of stone from elsewhere—unless it could be got from somewhere near by. Still, I think, in the rude little churchyard, with its ancient ruins standing by, the native stone would look more congruous than any imported stone would; but if the whin stone is not to be come at I think *unpolished* granite would be the next best, though in that case I should have to make a fresh design as the design you have is quite unsuited to the working of granite."[8] Truth to materials and respect for locality could not go much further.

To get the effects of traditional craftsmanship that he wanted, Webb could be as stubborn as Pugin. Building the house at Arisaig twenty years earlier, he found that few of the men could understand English. "He managed however, to make them understand one thing—that he meant to have his own way; for he set them to building experimental slabs of walling, in order to settle the kind of facing the house was to have . . . The old traditional way of using this stone had died out in favour of imported stone and fancy surfaces. Webb got his way, however, more or less, as he always did, for he was an obstinate man. He taught the masons their business, much to their disgust at the interfering foreigner."[9] He could be autocratic with clients too and would threaten to reduce the size of the drawing room if a client would not allow enough space for the servants.

But the autocracy was not aimed at building monuments to himself—or, apart from his symmetrical gestures, to his clients. In everything he did, including the beautiful animals and birds drawn for Morris's designs (the originals of which have a tenderness and accuracy which recall Dürer), Webb was concerned to let the object speak for itself and to withdraw his own personality as much as possible. Jack recalled, "I remember one design he did for a house that was never built, wonderfully elaborate and interesting. As the days went on, I found he had been using his india rubber very freely and he made the remark to me 'Whatever you do, cut out, cut out.'"[10] He wanted to achieve the commonplace, to be at one with the old craft traditions. Like Morris, he saw that this was only possible after a social revolution. Like Morris, he was condemned by the contradictions of his ideals to serving the luxury of the rich and to dictating design to his workmen. His last years of practice before he retired in 1900 to a country life of increasing poverty and cheerfulness, were much devoted to the Society for the Protection of Ancient Buildings which, under Webb's gentle tutelage became "a real school of practical building—architecture with all the whims which we usually call 'design' left out."[11]

Almost his last commission was for memorial cottages to William Morris at Kelmscott. The little grey houses, true in every detail to Cotswold tradition, varied only by a relief carved by Jack, are a fitting monument to Morris and to his architect—"the best man that he had ever known".[12]

Influential though he was on W. R. Lethaby and the next generation, Webb left no direct architectural descendants. Of his very few assistants, only Jack made a career for himself and that was as furniture designer for Morris & Co. rather than as architect. It was Richard Norman Shaw (1831–1912)—Webb's almost exact contemporary—whose office became the most prestigious nursery of Arts and Crafts talent. Shaw followed Webb as Street's chief clerk in 1859 and he shared some of his predecessor's reserve. Yet he was free of Webb's puritanism and he never shunned publicity. His prodigious volume of ever changing work figured large in the magazines of the '70s and '80s, while Webb's relatively small output of buildings was only rarely seen and had to be searched out by devotees.

Webb survived on the patronage of a few sympathetic clients. Shaw set himself up to cater for the taste of the *nouveaux riches*, initially producing a neo-medieval world for a generation raised on Walter Scott, then changing to take in new fashions of the class (p. 157). Webb he respected, but he could not stomach his austerity. Webb was, he thought, "a very able man indeed, but with a strong liking for the ugly."[13]

Before joining Street, Shaw had trained under William Burn, an eclectic Scottish classicist, and under the last great Gothick country house architect, Anthony Salvin. His work owed much to his early years under these two masters of the picturesque.

A digression is worthwhile to see the office that Shaw entered as an assistant at 28, an unusually late age for an up and coming Victorian architect. It shows the pattern of training of many Arts and Crafts people. Shaw told Street's son: "We worked hard—or thought we did—we had to be at the office at nine o'clock and our hour of leaving was six o'clock—long hours—but he never encroached on our own time and as a matter of fact I am sure I never stayed a minute past six o'clock.

"There were some interesting men in the office, and we were thoroughly happy. I am sure we were loyal, and believed in our master entirely, so that our work was really a pleasure; [Street] was our master—and let us know it—not by nagging or in an aggressive spirit, but by daily showing that he knew more than any of us and could in a given time do about twice as much. When a new work appeared, his custom was to draw it out in pencil in his own room—plans, elevations and sections—even putting in the margin lines and places where he wished the title to go; nothing was sketched in; it was *drawn* and exactly as he wished it to be, so that really there was little to do except to ink in his drawings and tint and complete them."[14] Street's own T square rattled long into the night. Shaw's chief assistant, W. R. Lethaby remembered him saying, "Street, you know, would not let us design a keyhole."[15]

So if a mid-Victorian architect was to rise above being a tracer and a copier of his master, he had to seek further inspiration. Immediately after leaving Street in 1862, Shaw went on sketching trips to west Kent and Sussex with his old friend from Burn and Salvin days, William Eden Nesfield (1835–88). They sketched Devey's work at Penshurst Place and, like Devey, extensively studied local vernacular cottages. As Andrew Saint, Shaw's biographer, records "immediately the 'Old English' style emerges."[16]

"Old English" was a Deveyan mixture of half-timbered or tile-hung upper storeys surmounting brick or stone ground floors with mullioned windows and leaded lights, all dominated by tall clusters of decorative brick chimneys. The style is both savage and changeful in Ruskin's sense. The first example of Shaw's personal style is a tiny cottage design of 1862 which in its crashing juxtaposition of porch and gable has the studied clumsiness of Butterfield's Coalpit Heath parsonage of nearly twenty years before. And it was from Butterfield, not Devey, that Shaw learned his use of fake timbering and of the hipped gable, both of which were to become ingredients of "Old English".

By 1864, Shaw felt sufficiently confident to submit an entry for the Bradford Exchange competition. It started off on the ground floor as a sort of Gothic with pointed arches and gradually rose through a carefully controlled series of irregular windows punched in a plain stone wall to a complex of hips, gables, balconies and half-timbering on top. The whole is dominated by a picturesquely irregular tower capped by a series of pitched French hats. Old English tried to come to town but was not acceptable; the design was placed sixth in a field of eight.

But the style *was* at home in the country. By the late '60s, Shaw was building really large country houses, Glen Andred and Leys Wood at Groombridge in Sussex, for instance, which show the Old English style at its purest and most confident. In both, a masonry lower storey is topped with a medley of tile-hung walls and roofs terminating in a riot of gables and dormers. The wall planes project and recede, and the levels subtly change. The great intricate mass is held together by the mullioned windows and pinned down by the gigantic vertical shafts of the great chimneys.

Like Webb, Shaw began to adopt a free classical style in the '70s, particularly for the London work he was then beginning to attract. Webb's use of renaissance motifs was always extremely idiosyncratic but Shaw was a much more clear-cut exponent of the Queen Anne style which had been pioneered by, among others, Nesfield, Shaw's partner of the early

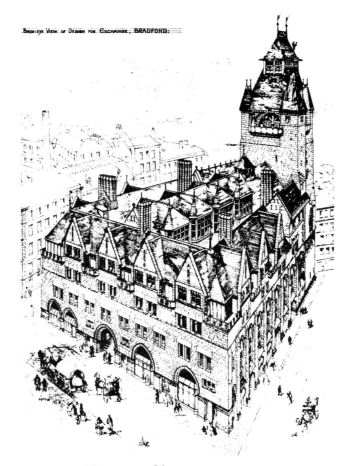

BIRD-EYE VIEW OF DESIGN FOR EXCHANGE, BRADFORD.

25 *Shaw. Bradford Exchange competition entry (1864)*

26 *Shaw. Leys Wood, Groombridge, Sussex (1867–1869)*

years. Mark Girouard, the style's historian, defines it as "a kind of architectural cocktail, with a little genuine Queen Anne in it, a little Dutch, a little Flemish, a squeeze of Robert Adam, a generous dash of Wren and a touch of Francois 1er."[17]

With its great range of expression, Queen Anne was eminently suitable for use by architects who continued to believe in Ruskinian changefulness but who wanted to enrich the diet of Gothic and vernacular models. Shaw's own house at 6 Ellerdale Road, Hampstead, designed in 1874, is largely composed of renaissance elements but they are assembled in such a free manner that it would have made the hair of even the most uncultivated eighteenth-century country builder stand on end. The main elevation starts off being apparently symmetrical under a cornice and two gables, but from there down everything is free. The up-hill end with its oriel windows is, almost perversely, four storeys high, while the lower end, with its brick bay, has only three main floors, dominated by the great one-and-half storey dining room window. Between the oriels and bay are a series of windows of several shapes and sizes disposed round a big staircase light to maximize the clash between the two series of floor levels.

27 *Shaw's own house, 6 Ellerdale Road, London (1874)*

28 *Shaw. Bedford Park. Shaw house types arranged on a typical avenue (Building News, 21 December, 1887)*

The dining room, Saint says, is "the house's *pièce de résistance*. It is almost a cube, a storey and a half in height. It has high panelling, quarry tiles round the carpet and a massive inglenook to the west, the first to be used in town ... Above it accommodates the precious workroom or 'den' where Shaw's drawing was done".[18] This was reached by a little private stair; it had a porthole window looking down the road and another internal window so that Shaw could communicate with his family.

In 1877, when Shaw was alternating between Old English and Queen Anne, he got what to him must have been one of his least important commissions, yet it was to have a profound effect on domestic architecture of the next four decades. In the mid '70s, a speculator called Jonathan Carr bought an estate, Bedford Park,[19] near the new railway station at Turnham Green and asked E. W. Godwin and the firm of Coe & Robinson for house designs for a development of small detached and semi-detached villas.

Godwin's designs were attacked in the *Building News* and Carr turned to Shaw for a new set of standard drawings. Shaw produced standard house designs and did not supervise the works. He started with tile-hung variants of Old English, echoing Godwin, but moved towards the cheaper Queen Anne as the economics of speculative building began to bite. Only for the Tabard, a mixture of pub, coffee house and department store, was enough cash available to do a more or less pure Old English job.

The cultural impact of Bedford Park was tremendous; writers and artists flocked to live in the jolly red houses along tree lined streets, and the new suburb was given the widest publicity. Its (quite) low density pattern of basementless brick houses in a bosky setting became the pattern for the late nineteenth-century suburb and eventually for the Garden City movement.

By the mid '80s, Shaw was still working in both the Old English and the Queen Anne styles. His house for the illustrator Kate Greenaway at 39 Frognal, a few hundred yards from Shaw's own house, is tile-hung on a brick base with a gable and mullioned windows: it is a cottage compressed into a small tower with, on top, a studio ingeniously diagonally orientated to obtain north light and to complicate the outline. The

29 *Shaw. The Tabard Inn, Bedford Park, the suburb's Old English pub (1879–80)*

30 *Shaw. Kate Greenaway's house, Frognal, London (design 1884)*

31 *Shaw. 180 Queen's Gate, Kensington, London (design 1883, now destroyed)*

32 *Ernest George. Market Hall, Moreton in Marsh, Gloucestershire (1887)*

design of the Greenaway house started in 1884, and the year before Shaw had designed 180 Queen's Gate, a mighty, full-blown example of Queen Anne, much more obviously organized than the Ellerdale Road house but still very free, with the main rooms emphasized by a bay and by an arch-covered recess. Terminated with symmetrical tall pillaster-clad chimney stacks and great scrolled gables, the house fore-shadowed Shaw's transition to a much more orthodox formality in the decades around the turn of the century.

As the Frognal and Queen's Gate houses show, Shaw's work was still extraordinarily free and full of variety in the mid '80s. At the time, his office was staffed by men who were to become leading figures of the next generation. But before going on to them, it is worth glancing at a couple of Shaw's contemporaries whose practices were breeding grounds for Arts and Crafts talent.

Ernest George (1839–1922) set up on his own at the age of twenty-two, after training under the obscure Samuel Hewitt. His extremely successful practice, which continued virtually until his death, handled work of all kinds but the bulk was country houses, some of which were based on local traditions of building, handled with gentleness and sympathy by George and his succession of partners: Thomas Vaughan, Harold Peto and Alfred Yeates.

But George was by no means a convinced vernacular revivalist. He was a picturesque architect with a great armoury of styles, and he would as happily adopt the romanesque for a crematorium as French renaissance for a music school. Lutyens, one of his many distinguished Arts and Crafts pupils and assistants,* remembered that in the '80s George was "a distinguished architect who took each year three weeks' holiday abroad and returned with overflowing sketch books. When called on for a project he would look through these and choose some picturesque turret or gable from Holland, France or Spain and round it weave his new design. Location mattered little and

---

* Others included Robert Weir Schultz, Herbert Baker and Guy Dawber.

33 *Thomas Graham Jackson. Design for cottages at Sevenoaks, Kent (before 1897)*

no provincial formation influenced him, for at that time terra cotta was the last word in building."[20]

Thomas Graham Jackson (1835–1924) had a distinguished Oxford career before being apprenticed to Sir George Gilbert Scott like Street and Bodley. From that High Goth, Jackson acquired a passion for medievalism, on which he wrote a spirited apologia *Modern Gothic Architecture.* His secular Gothic buildings, for instance the Oxford Examination Schools and the Brasenose Master's house, were highly regarded by contemporaries for their toughness and masculinity, earning him the nickname of Anglo-Jackson. Yet he could be delicate and charming as his design for workmen's cottages at Sevenoaks shows.

Jackson had a remarkably flexible definition of Gothic "I regard all buildings which conform to the conditions of English climate, material and habit as Gothic."[21] This allowed him to adopt a wide range of elements, including Flemish gables and even, when he was feeling particularly perverse, large chunks of renaissance architecture. As the *Architectural Review* remarked censoriously, "his work seems to us varied to the verge of eclecticism."[22]

It was from the eclectic work of men like Shaw, George and Jackson that the Arts and Crafts architects set out to find a new direction.

1 Lethaby W. R. *Philip Webb and his Work*, Oxford 1935, p. 7. The book is a collection of articles first published in *Builder* during 1925.

2 Weaver, Lawrence *Small Country Houses of Today*, Vol. I, Country Life, London n.d., p. 180

3 Jack, George "An appreciation of Philip Webb", *Architectural Review* Vol. XXXVIII, p. 1915, p. 3

4 Weaver, L. *op. cit.*, p. 182

5 Quoted in Lethaby *Philip Webb, op. cit.*, p. 194

6 Lethaby *Philip Webb, op. cit.*, p. 88

7 *Ibid.*, p. 122

8 *Ibid.*, p. 129

9 Jack *op. cit.*, p. 4

10 Quoted in Lethaby *Philip Webb, op. cit.*, p. 137

11 Lethaby, W. R. *Ernest Gimson, his Life and Work*, Stratford London and Oxford 1924, p. 3

12 S. C. Cockrell quoted in Lethaby *Philip Webb, op. cit.*, p. 230

13 Lethaby *Philip Webb, op. cit.*, p. 75

14 Quoted in Street, A. E. *Memoir of George Edmund Street RA*, John Murray, London 1888, p. 283

15 Lethaby *Philip Webb, op. cit.*, p. 75

16 Saint, Andrew *Richard Norman Shaw*, Yale 1976, p. 28

17 Girouard, Mark *Sweetness and Light: the Queen Anne Movement 1860–1900*, Oxford 1977, p. 2

18 Saint *op. cit.*, p. 179

19 Saint *op. cit.* gives a detailed explanation of the development of Bedford Park on pp. 201–210

20 Quoted in Hussey, Christopher *The Life of Sir Edwin Lutyens*, Country Life, London 1950, p. 17

21 *Architectural Review*, Vol. I, 1897, p. 140

22 *Ibid.*

5 The Guilds are Forged

"Early in 1883, the pupils of R. Norman Shaw, RA, formed a Society for the discussion of Art and Architecture. Its members," recalled Edward Prior, "though trained as Architects took the name of Art for the Association, and called themselves the 'St. George's Art Society' as meeting under the shadow of St. George's Church Bloomsbury"[1]—and perhaps under that of Ruskin's St. George's Guild.

Shaw's Bloomsbury Square office was the main nursery of the young men who founded the Arts and Crafts movement, and they owed much to his training. Shaw was much more liberal than his own master Street. W. R. Lethaby, who was Shaw's chief assistant from 1879, recalled, "Mr Shaw was extraordinarily generous to his clerks, sometimes letting them 'design' minor matters, not because of any gain to him but because he thought it would make their work more interesting and be a training."[2] However much Shaw's own style changed, his assistants remained fondly indebted to him for their grounding in the craft of architecture.

The St. George's Society was the first association to emerge from the fizzing and often rumbustious atmosphere generated by four of Shaw's pupils. Lethaby at twenty-six was senior to the thirty-one year old Edward Prior, Mervyn Macartney, thirty, and Gerald Callcott Horsley, twenty-one. The four were made five by Ernest Newton in whose Hart Street rooms they met. Newton had been Shaw's chief clerk until 1879, when Lethaby took over.

By October 1883, the Society had become aware that meetings of young architects were not enough. Prior recalled, "Art and Architecture were drifting asunder. Was it possible to bring them together again? Close connection had been historically necessary to both. Was this now to be accepted as mere ancient history?"[3]

On one hand, the Royal Academy was "now giving its favour almost entirely to oil painting", selecting members "more often on the basis of culture or professional success, than in view of the merit of their art. On the other there was the Institute of British Architects, whose theory of architecture had driven from its doors most of those architects whose art was acknowledged; which had forbidden to Artists a personal interest in their handicrafts and had opened its doors so widely to business interests that Surveyors had become the largest element of its body."[4]

Macartney and Horsley were deputized to ask Shaw for advice. Prior reported his reply that "In France, Architects, Painters and Sculptors were trained together in one common school of the Arts. If Architecture in England was missing its way, it was for the young men to bring her back from professionalism. The Architects of this generation must make the future for themselves and knock at the door of Art until they were admitted."[5]

This is worth a digression. In the '80s and '90s there was a great row about whether architecture should, as the RIBA hoped, be put on a professional footing, like law, medicine or divinity, with a central professional body setting educational standards or whether it ought to remain essentially a craft—taught by masters to apprentices in a way little changed since the middle ages.

Not surprisingly, Shaw and his pupils took the side of art and craft. In 1891 the imbroglio was brought to the attention of the public by a manifesto in *The Times* opposing a move to make architecture "a close profession" by law with entry regulated by examination which "by raising artificial barriers, would have a tendency still further to alienate"[6] painting and sculpture from architecture. Among the manifesto's signatories were Shaw and contemporaries such as Webb, Jackson, and Bodley; Lethaby and his generation, Macartney, Newton, Prior, Horne and Ricardo;

and among the non-architects, Morris and the Pre-Raphaelites: Madox Brown, Burne-Jones and Holman Hunt were for once prepared to make cause with academicians like Alma-Tadema.

Shaw and Jackson edited a book, *Architecture, a Profession or an Art*, published a year later, in which essays by the editors and Lethaby, Prior, Newton Bodley and others aired the argument further. Their objection to the examination system was explained to be not only that it would sever architecture from the other arts, but that it would also give the training of architects an entirely wrong bias towards business and theory. The proposals of the RIBA and its allies to allow architects to practice only after examination, would, they believed, actually reduce standards of design and competence for "if he cannot properly direct the execution of his design, discriminate between good and bad materials, and judge of the qualities of workmanship, [no-one] has claim to be looked on as an architect however much he knows of law, surveying, 'business' and all the routine of professional practice".[7]

The objectors to the proposed law had nothing against formal architectural education. Indeed Jackson and Shaw both taught in the Royal Academy Schools, and the men of Lethaby's generation attended classes there or at the Architectural Association. And they recognized the difficulties of part-time education. Shaw wrote to a friend, "by the time they have worked in their respective offices from 9.30 to 5.30, and then three days a week from 6 to 8 in the schools, getting home about 9, you could hardly expect them to throw themselves with much ardour into the study of 'descriptive geometry applied to scientific masonry'."[8]

In the end, the breach between the RIBA and the protagonists of architecture as an art (and craft) was

34 *John Brett. "The Stonebreaker" (1857–8). Ruskin's call for truth to nature, faithfully followed by painter members of the Art Workers' Guild, conflicted with his axioms on changefulness and savageness, followed by the architects and craftsmen*

largely healed when, in 1906, the RIBA set up a board of inspection for schools (on principles agreed by the two sides) and encouraged design work in school studios. But for Shaw, there was no forgiveness and, after an early resignation from the Institute, he twice turned down the royal gold medal for architecture which was (and is) in the RIBA's gift.* Now, after the results of nearly eighty years of Institute-supervised examinations, it is difficult not to think that Shaw and his co-signatories of the manifesto really had a great deal of right on their side. The trouble was that they gave no indication of how an aspirant of talent and appropriate experience should set up as an architect. But then, apart from offering a few letters after his name, nor did or does the RIBA.

Back in 1883, after Macartney and Horsley had got their answer from Shaw, the Five canvassed their friends and acquaintances and, at eight o'clock on January 8, 1884, twenty-one architects, artists and designers met in the Board Room of the Charing Cross Hotel under the chairmanship of John Belcher (1841–1913), an architect of the generation between Shaw and his clerks. As well as the Five, the meeting included architects such as John Dando Sedding (1838–1891) who, like Shaw, had been with Street, and Basil Champneys (1842–1920) another late Gothic Revival architect. There were painters, Alfred Parsons and J. McLure Hamilton, sculptors Hamo Thornycroft and Blackall Simonds and one designer, Lewis F. Day.†

The meeting agreed to set up a society which should consist of "Handicraftsmen and Designers in the Arts" aimed at reuniting the arts and crafts. There was a good deal of controversy about whether the society should seek publicity, with Macartney and Ernest Newton calling for a series of public exhibitions. Lethaby was vehement for "the institution of a National Gallery of Representative Modern Painting and Sculpture." But Prior and Horsley carried the day with the motion that "at present the proposed Society shall not aim at publicity." It was a temporary proviso of great permanence: through its period of influence in the decades around the turn of the cen-

tury to today, the society has always shunned publicity.

By the end of 1884 the society had acquired a name—the Art Workers' Guild—and had agreed to meet for practical demonstrations of craft techniques, discussions and for small private exhibitions. Of its first fifty-five members, twenty-six were painters, four sculptors, eleven craftsmen and fifteen architects.* It was a strange blend of academic artists with revolutionary architects and designers, between whom the only theoretical link was Ruskin.

Ruskin had called for a new relationship between designer and craftsman with the craftsman's mistakes being welcomed as a sign of honesty. But, virtually simultaneously, he had demanded the most scrupulous naturalism in painting and sculpture: "no artist [can] be graceful, imaginative or original, unless he be truthful".[10] The marriage between Ruskin's theories of architecture and painting attempted by the Art Workers' Guild created confusions that were never resolved.

A much more straightforward realization of Ruskin's Gothic principles had been proposed a couple of years before by Arthur Heygate Mackmurdo (1851–1942), an architect of the same generation as the famous Five but from a completely different background.

Mackmurdo, the son of a wealthy chemical manufacturer, trained under T. Chatfield Clarke but left in 1869 "as ignorant of architecture as when I entered this architect's office."[11] He persuaded James Brooks, whose Gothic Revival churches he had admired when involved in social work in East London, to take him as an assistant. Brooks was as hard a taskmaster as Street and designed "every single incidental object and ornament", but there were "constant failures in getting these designs carried out with any degree of artistic sympathy" which "well nigh drove the man mad."

"I realized that in the same way I should suffer did I not build a bridge to overreach the void. I must become personally acquainted with the technique of those arts most naturally acquainted with architecture. Some knowledge might enable me to design with that technical propriety essential for the complete marriage of the imagination and the material."[12]

Mackmurdo's determination to achieve the consummation of design and craft so compellingly urged

* On the first occasion, the only previous refusee had been Ruskin, and the wits remarked that the one "had turned it down because he was not an architect, the other because he was."[9]

† The last two, with Sedding, and Walter Crane (the illustrator) belonged to a group called "the Fifteen" who had been meeting since 1880 in each others' houses to discuss papers on the decorative arts.

* The figures—and total—are Prior's.

in the "Nature of Gothic" must have been reinforced by a trip to Italy with Ruskin himself in 1874, after which Mackmurdo stayed on to study in Florence. Travelling with the arch-priest of the Gothic had a strange effect on Mackmurdo. He returned with a strong taste for the Italian renaissance which he never abandoned, and the conflict between the two ideals frequently doomed Mackmurdo's architecture to quirky mediocrity; but his allegiance to Ruskinian architectural principles bore far more impressive fruit.

After he returned from Italy, Mackmurdo taught with Ruskin at the Working Men's College. In 1882, he started the Century Guild of Artists, "to render all branches of art the sphere no longer of the tradesman but of the artist." He had previously schooled himself in the "technique of modelling and carving, trying my hand at some ornamental stonework for the first house I built. I learned to do repoussé work in brass and mastered sufficiently the elements of embroidery to enable me to design for this art. Under a skilful cabinet maker, I learnt enough about materials and constructive processes to enable me to design pieces of furniture, with one or two of which I took a hand in making."[13] He had become the perfect Ruskinian architect.

But even this formidable combination of skills was not enough, and he decided that for the execution of design "which I was not capable of" he must attract "young men who were already working in their applied arts."

The Century Guild was founded by Mackmurdo, aged thirty-one, and Selwyn Image, thirty-three, designer of stained glass, book illustrations and embroidery. They were joined by the eighteen year old Herbert Horne (later to become architect, typographer and biographer of Botticelli), Clement Heaton, a stained glass artist and Benjamin Creswick whom Gillian Naylor describes as "the self taught sculptor who as a boy had worked in a Sheffield knife factory."[14] Designer Heywood Sumner was also associated with the Guild, and William de Morgan, already established as a distinguished ceramicist, Mackmurdo said off-handedly "assisted me by executing my designs for tile work."

Workshops were set up for metal work and furniture and, in 1884, the Guild contributed a complete music room to the Health Exhibition in London. The

35 *Arthur Heygate Mackmurdo. Century Guild stand at the Liverpool Exhibition of 1886*

36 *Mackmurdo. Writing table (1886)*

37 *Mackmurdo. 8 Private Road, Enfield, Middlesex (1883)*

same room, with small variations, was seen at the Liverpool International Exhibition of 1886 and the Manchester Jubilee show of 1887.

The room was distinguished by thin columns capped by a series of wafer-thin squares, one of Mackmurdo's hallmarks. Another was in some of the furniture: the sinuous intertwined forms of vegetation fretted into the backs of chairs and the brackets of shelves and printed on wallpapers and fabrics. The sinuous motifs had some influence on the Arts and Crafts work—particularly on Voysey's early textile designs. But most members of the movement preferred stiffer patterns derived from heraldry; Mackmurdo's interlaced curves are supposed to have had a formative influence on Art Nouveau, the continental contemporary of Arts and Crafts.*

Mackmurdo's thin square-topped columns had more influence; Voysey adopted them in his furniture and, through him, they were picked up by Mackintosh. Mackmurdo used similar elongated effects in his most original architecture: they appear for instance in his curious house, 8 Private Road, Enfield (1883). The building is in a stripped classical style but in Mackmurdo's masterpiece, 25 Cadogan Gardens, London (1899), they are used with great delicacy in a sort of elegant Queen Anne style which is neither classic nor Gothic. Mackmurdo's last buildings, for instance his own house Great Ruffins in Essex (1904), are in a complicated and clumsy classicism—sadly disappointing after such an extraordinarily promising beginning.

In 1884, the Century Guild had started the *Hobby*

---

* Northern architects had been bidden to eschew the relaxed, sinuous line by Ruskin, one of whose definitions of Gothic was *rigidity*: "the Gothic ornament stands out in prickly independence and frosty fortitude, jutting into crochets, and freezing into pinnacles . . . alternately thorny, bossy, and bristly, or writhed into every form of nervous entanglement; but, even when most graceful, never for an instant languid, always quickset: erring, if at all, ever on the side of brusquerie."[15] But Ruskin warned against excessive rigidity.

38 *Mackmurdo. 25 Cadogan Gardens, London (1899)*

Horse, a magazine devoted to a revival of arts and crafts which, itself, did much to re-awaken the art of printing. The first issue was edited by Mackmurdo with woodcut illustrations involving curved plant forms designed by Image and Horne cut by Arthur Burgess. Image and Horne took the editorial chair in later editions.

The magazine was intended by Mackmurdo to publicize Ruskinian ideals of design and production and its early editions are studded with articles by a carefully chosen cast of nineteenth-century progressives: Ford Madox Brown, the Rossettis, May Morris (William's embroiderer daughter), Matthew Arnold, G. F. Watts and Oscar Wilde. Whatever the direct impact of the words (which seems to have been little), the image of the magazine was, according to Mackmurdo, so powerful that it inspired William Morris to begin printing and set up the Kelmscott Press.

The Century Guild was a commercial venture, rather like the Morris Firm, and a different kind of association from the Art Workers' Guild in which architect Edward Warren (Guild master in 1913) explained that "we neither seek public recognition, nor try to teach the world, nor even, definitely to teach each other; yet we are not without aims. Each member learns from each."[16]

T. G. Jackson remembered the AWG's meetings: "Morris once giving us an evening on paper-making, and bringing his paper-maker, Bachelor, who made a sheet for us in the room, showing how by a dextrous handshake, difficult to acquire and sometimes, strange to say, lost again, the workman secures that interlacing of the linen fibres which makes the durable hand-made article . . . The great feature of these evenings were the demonstrations by which the papers were illustrated. When enamelling was the subject there was a gas-stove in the room and enamels were prepared and burned. When plaster work was under discussion modelling and casting were going on before our eyes. I remember reading a paper on Intarsiatura, which was afterwards published, and showing a large number of tracings from old examples and also having one of Bessant's men cutting out and mounting veneers in the room. We also had exhibitions of all kinds of art and for some years an annual display of the members' own work in various crafts. This was superseded by the Arts and Crafts Exhibition which grew out of the Guild."[17]

C. R. Ashbee recalled less formal evenings. At one of these in the '90s, the Guild "held a mock trial, Mrs. Grundy *v* the AWG. Mrs. Grundy was indicting the

Society for indecency and for flaunting Art in divers colours in the Voysey manner—Prior was Council for the Defence; Selwyn Image for the Prosecution—Voysey himself was Mrs. Grundy and Cecil Brewer was her little boy . . . Cecil with his cheeks rouged, with short white stockings and panteloons sat on a cornice in the Hall at Cliffords Inn sucking oranges with the peel of which he occasionally pelted his friends, and as he dangled a pair of long spindly legs he shouted mimic childish satire in his high pitched voice."[18]

Such behaviour was not the only reason why the Guild was reluctant to appear in public. There were fundamental differences between members. In 1891, Mackmurdo (who had joined in 1888) tried to get the Guild to take corporate action against decorations being carried out in St. Paul's. The trouble was that the scheme was being carried out by painter W. B. Richmond, Master of the Guild for that year. Two contradictory Guild resolutions were sent to the Dean, and, to avoid similar embarrassments, the Guild's rules on public action were gradually tightened.

As early as 1885, members of the Art Workers' Guild who believed in a Ruskinian fusion of art and craft realized that a new organization which did not include the academic painters and sculptors was needed if the message was to be carried to the public. W. A. S. Benson, metal worker and cabinet maker, and one of the members of the Guild, produced a scheme for the "Combined Arts". This took shape as the Arts and Crafts Exhibition Society which held its founding show in autumn 1888, when the term "Arts and Crafts" (reputedly coined by bookbinder J. T. Cobden-Sanderson) first entered general currency.

The Society quickly collected the progressive element of the Art Workers' Guild and attracted new blood, some of which was transfused back into the Guild, for relations between the two associations were cordial and the membership overlapped (for instance, Walter Crane was simultaneously Master of the Guild and President of the Society in 1888).

Most notable amongst the new recruits was William Morris himself, who, after doubts about the financial success of the Society, threw himself into the project. (He was elected to the Art Workers' Guild at the same meeting as Mackmurdo on November 2, 1888.) By the early 1890s, the Society combined the talents of the Five and their group, Mackmurdo's Century Guild people and Morris's circle of Pre-Raphaelites (including non-academic painters like

Holman Hunt and Ford Madox Brown) and a large number of craftsmen. The only obvious omissions from this extraordinarily rich gathering were Shaw, Ruskin (who was by then going mad, and was not a designer), and Webb, who though he had faithfully soldiered through the nightmare maze of late nineteenth-century Socialist associations with Morris, was congenitally anti-corporate.*

The first exhibition brought a very favourable notice from the *Builder* which reported that "it represents the views and tastes of a sect; but the amount of beauty and variety in the work exhibited says a great deal for the talent and artistic feeling in the ranks of the sect, and it is impossible to go over it without reflecting what real progress has been made in decorative design during the last quarter of a century.

"Twenty-five years ago, such an exhibition as this—so full of fine colour and outline, and so devoid

* Both Shaw and Webb's work was exhibited in the shows though.

of anything which can be regarded as vulgar, or in bad taste, would have been impossible."[19] The Society's shows (held at the New Gallery, Regent Street) were not simply exhibitions of work but included lectures and demonstrations as well; in every sense, it was an extension of the Guild.

Cobden-Sanderson remembered "William Morris, on a raised platform, surrounded by products of the loom, at work on a model loom specially constructed from his design . . . to show how the wools were inwrought, and the visions of his brain fixed in colour and in form; Walter Crane, backed by a great black board, wiped clean alas! when one would have had it for ever still adorned by the spontaneous creations of his inexhaustible brain . . . Selwyn Image . . . with sweet reasonableness depicting . . . the bright new Jerusalem; Lethaby entrancing us with the cities which crowned the hills of Europe."[20]

The Society's aims were expressed in a series of papers, many of which had previously been published in its catalogues, collected in 1893 as a small, stout book edited by Morris. His introduction set the theme: "we can expect no *general* impulse towards the fine arts till civilization has been transformed into some other condition of life . . . Our business as artists [is] to supply the lack of tradition by diligently cultivating in ourselves the sense of beauty, . . . skill of hand, and niceness of observation, without which only a *makeshift* of art can be got." The Society's exhibitors, he believed, showed that "there is still a minority with a good deal of life in it which is not content with what is called utilitarianism"; they called attention to that "most important side of art, the decoration of utilities by furnishing them with genuine artistic finish in place of trade finish."[21]

Morris's contribution to the first Arts and Crafts Exhibition Society's exhibition was hailed by *Today*, the Fabian magazine, as one of his "best services to Socialism."[22] But by 1893 he was a tired man with only three years of crowded activity to live. His somewhat bathetic conclusion was expanded by Walter Crane in sentiments which rivalled those of Morris at his height in an essay "On the Revival of Design and Handicraft": "The movement . . . represents in some sense a revolt against the hard mechanical conventional life and its insensibility to beauty (quite another thing to ornament). It is a protest against that so-called industrial progress which produces shoddy wares, the cheapness of which is paid for by the lives of their producers and the degradation of their users. It is a protest against the turning of men into

39 *John Dando Sedding. Holy Trinity, Sloane Street, London (designed 1888)*

machines, against artificial distinctions in art, and against making the immediate market value, or possibility of profit, the chief test of artistic merit. It also advances the claim of all and each to the common possession of beauty in things common and familiar."[23]

Industrialization was reluctantly accepted by Crane, but, "we have reached the *reductio ad absurdum* of an impersonal artist or craftsman trying to produce things of beauty for an impersonal and unknown public ... Under such conditions it is hardly surprising that the arts of design should have declined".[24] The aim of the Society's exhibitions was to break this vicious circle. "At present, indeed, an exhibition may be said to be but a necessary evil; but it is the only means of obtaining a standard, and giving publicity to the works of Designer and Craftsman".[25] And it asserted "the principle of the essential unity and interdependence of the arts".[26]

This ferment of Arts and Crafts activity quickly had results in buildings, one of the first and most magnificent of which was Holy Trinity, Sloane Street, Chelsea, (1888 on) by John Dando Sedding (1838–1891), finished by his pupil Henry Wilson. Sedding had worked in Street's office with Webb and Shaw and was a very early member of the Guild and the Society. Horsley commented that the two associations "were the means of bringing Mr. Sedding into touch with many artists and prompted him to gather round him to help him in his last work, the Great church of the Holy Trinity in Upper Chelsea, some of the foremost craftsmen of the day."[27] The most important artists (apart from Sedding and Wilson) were all members of both associations: Harry Bates, sculptor; F. W. Pomeroy, sculptor; Nelson Dawson, metal worker; and Burne-Jones (a member of the Guild fleetingly and an early exhibitor at the Society).

Those who visit the church now, expecting it to be encrusted with Arts and Crafts gems, are initially disappointed. Of the thousands who pass it every day, few must notice its recessed dusky brick facade in which two thin towers frame a giant clear glass win-

40 *Sedding. Holy Trinity, west front*

dow which is contained by an ogee arch. The only relief is a certain luxuriance in the tracery of the window and a jolly, almost jangling, fussiness in the stone strap-work above the top of the arch and in the stone frills at the top of the towers.

Inside, the first impression is of equal austerity. The nave and chancel are formed into one great room, wide and high and very light from the mighty west window. The pale stone columns soar towards the vaults* with scarcely a break, only corbelled angels where, in traditional Gothic, the capitals would be. The simplicity is due to lack of money and to Sedding's early death (the church was started only a couple of years before). For instance, a Burne-Jones frieze which was to have run between the arcade and clerestory was never executed. Nor was the banded masonry Sedding originally intended for the nave and aisles. But Gerald Horsley's perspective of the design shows that Sedding's intention was to create a simple big well-lit space in which the plain structure dominated and knit together the contributions of individual artists—the effect we get today.

Throughout the '90s, Arts and Crafts artists contributed to the church—wherever you look, the details are exquisite. Burne-Jones designed (and the Morris firm made) the east window with panel after panel of elegant Pre-Raphaelite saints. Richmond was responsible for the windows of the north aisle and Christopher Whall those of the south with their linear naturalistic scenes above abstract chevrons of coloured glass, equal to anything produced by Mackintosh or Wright in the same period (1904–23). Pomeroy did the angels on the chancel columns. Sedding and Wilson as well as Dawson were responsible for the metal work—which ranges from delicate, Italianate tracery in the chancel gates (by Sedding who had strong affections for Renaissance detail) to robust, heraldic gilded strap-work in the organ screen (by Wilson and Dawson).

Of course, the whole effect is Gothic—but of a special kind. It was stripped to its structural essentials. The carefully placed ornament was not executed by ordinary craftsmen, as it should have been according to the theories of Pugin, Ruskin and Morris, but

* Rebuilt after destruction in the Second World War.

by fellow members of the Guild and of the Exhibition Society, who were enlightened and agreeable enough to be trustworthy and avoid the potential catastrophies of real Ruskinian savageness.

Sedding at Holy Trinity got as near to resolving the Puginian paradox as any Arts and Crafts architect. The church was a precursor of many simple yet rich, rather introverted Arts and Crafts ecclesiastical buildings built in the two decades around the turn of the century.

1 Prior, E. S. "The origins of the Guild", lecture to the Guild 6, December 1895. Printed in H. J. L. J. Massé *The Art Workers' Guild 1884–1934*, Oxford 1935, p. 6
2 Lethaby, W. R. *Life of Webb*, op. cit., p. 75
3 Prior op. cit., p. 7
4 *Ibid.*
5 *Ibid.*
6 *The Times* 3.3.1891, quoted in *Architecture a Profession or an Art*, eds. Shaw, R. N. and Jackson, T. G., John Murray, London 1892, p. xxxiii–xxxiv
7 Shaw, R. N. and Jackson, T. G., *ibid.*, p. 7
8 Saint, A. *Richard Norman Shaw*, Yale, New Haven and London 1976, p. 316. The quotation is from a letter from Shaw to Frederic Eaton 9.11.90.
9 *Ibid.*, p. 318
10 Ruskin, John *Modern Painters*, Vol. I, p. 47
11 Mackmurdo, A. H. *History of the Arts and Crafts Movement*, typescript in William Morris Museum, Walthamstow, chapter VIII
12 *Ibid.*
13 *Ibid.*
14 Naylor, Gillian *The Arts and Crafts Movement*, op. cit., p. 117
15 Ruskin, John *Stones of Venice*, op. cit., Vol. II, p. 204.
16 In Massé op. cit., p. 4.
17 Jackson, T. G. *Recollections*, ed. Basil H. Jackson, Oxford 1950, p. 218
18 Ashbee, C. R. *Memoirs*, typescript in the Victoria and Albert Museum library, Vol. II, p. 59
19 *Builder*, Vol. LV, 1888, p. 241
20 Cobden-Sanderson, J. T. *The Arts and Crafts Movement*, Hammersmith Publishing Society, 1905, p. 17
21 *Arts and Crafts Essays* by members of the Arts and Crafts Exhibition Society, Rivington Percival & Co., London 1893, p. xii
22 Quoted in Thompson, E. P. *William Morris*, op. cit., p. 540
23 Crane, W. "Of the Revival of Design and Handicraft" in *Arts and Crafts Essays*, op. cit., p. 12
24 *Ibid.*, p. 10
25 *Ibid.*
26 *Ibid.*
27 Horsley, G. C. "The Unity of Art", in Shaw, R. N. and Jackson, T. G. (eds.) *Architecture: a Profession or an Art*, John Murray, London 1892, p. 202

6 The Guide

Amongst all the intense talk of Art and Beauty in the Guild and the Exhibition Society, no one seems to have had much time to think out what the words meant. William Richard Lethaby (1857–1931) set himself the task of producing definitions for the late nineteenth century.

In the summer of 1879, Norman Shaw went into his assistants flourishing a copy of *Building News* in which some of Lethaby's drawings had appeared, asking "What do you think of this? I am going to write and ask him to come here."[1] Shaw was taking a gamble: up to then Lethaby had spent his whole life in the provinces and had no academic training of any kind.

He was the son of a Barnstaple frame maker and was apprenticed to a local man, Alexander Lauder, painter turned architect, who must have had much influence on Lethaby's early years, for Lauder was an inventor of new technical devices such as ventilators and drainage systems, as well as being a vigorous artist craftsman who, as his grandson recalled, "would decorate many of the houses he built with huge sgraffito murals, terracotta friezes and high-relief ceramic tiles, all carved and modelled with his own hand."[2] And "he used to insist that all the men working on his own buildings should have an understanding of one another's craft, so that each might feel that he was building a house and not just practising carpentry, bricklaying or plumbing."[3]

Leaving Lauder, Lethaby worked briefly in Derby and Leicester before entering the Shaw office at twenty-one. It was another world: the big, fashionable metropolitan practice in which older, university educated men like Edward Prior and Mervyn Macartney were at home. The shock must have increased Lethaby's natural diffidence and modesty, but in a very short time he was a leader in the larking which so surprised Robert Weir Schultz when he joined the firm in the early 1880s after apprenticeship in the dour Glasgow office of Rowand Anderson.[4] One singularly dull afternoon Shaw and Lethaby held a cricket match in the office with T squares and an india rubber;[5] it was a very different place from Shaw's own nursery in Street's office.

But it was Lethaby's talent that made him Shaw's chief clerk—and perhaps more: an acquaintance once referred to Lethaby as Shaw's pupil " 'No', said Shaw, 'on the contrary it is I who am Lethaby's pupil'."[6]

For all his prolific artistic talent, it was as a teacher that Lethaby made his impact. In *Architecture, Mysticism and Myth* published in 1891, two years after he had left Shaw, Lethaby set out to ask "what . . . are the ultimate facts behind all architecture which has [sic] given it form? Mainly three: *First*, the similar needs and desires of men; *secondly* on the side of structure, the necessities imposed by materials, and the physical laws of their erection and combination; and *thirdly* on the side of style, nature. It is of this last that I propose to write."[7]

In *Cosmos* (Lethaby's nickname for the book), he expanded Ruskin's concept of "naturalism" and put it forward as the origin of style in architecture: "if we trace the artistic forms of things, made by man, to their origin, we find a direct imitation of nature."[8] From a vast magpie's nest of myths drawn from peoples as different as the Byzantines and the Abyssinians, the Chinese and the Incas, Lethaby pulled out what he believed to be the guiding principles of symbolism and form of all previous architecture, for instance the sun as the sign of going out and coming in, "pavements like the sea" and "ceilings like the sky".

But Lethaby was quite clear that man's past perceptions of the macrocosmos should not be a guide to the future of architecture. The high architectures of

56

41 *William Richard Lethaby. Window, Church of St. John the Baptist, Symondsbury, Dorset (early 1880s). An example of Lethaby's early design work*

42 *Lethaby. Avon Tyrell, Hampshire (completed 1893), south front*

past ages were the products of tyranny, "each stone cemented in the blood of a human creature . . . such an architecture is not for us, nor for the future.

"What then will this art of the future be? The message will still be of nature and man, of order and beauty, but all will be sweetness, simplicity and freedom, confidence and light; the other is past, and well is it, for its aim was to crush life: the new, the future is to aid life and to train it 'so that beauty may flow into the soul like a breeze'."[9]

This vision is virtually identical with that of *News from Nowhere* (first published in instalments in the *Commonweal* the year before). By the early '90s Lethaby was very much under the influence of Morris and Webb and was drawing away from Shaw, who was by then becoming increasingly formal and classical.

In his earliest years as a practitioner in his own right, Lethaby filled in his time and augmented his income by making drawings and designs for Morris & Co.[10] And his rooms were near to Webb's in Gray's Inn. Lethaby had met Morris and Webb through SPAB and, while still in Shaw's office, had become converted to their view of society. Shaw distrusted Morris whom he regarded as "just a tradesman, whose only object was to make money, and as for his Socialism, that was just a pose. He thought that instead of producing expensive textiles and wallpapers . . . Morris as a Socialist should devote himself to the manufacture of cheap chests of drawers and wallpapers at 10½d a piece."[11] But for Lethaby's socialism, Shaw had a good humoured tolerance; the father of one of his pupils with whom Lethaby had agreed to go on a sketching tour "rushed up to see Shaw in a great state: 'I hear my boy is going sketching with a socialist', to which Shaw replied, 'he's perfectly harmless, I assure you, perfectly harmless'."[12]

Lethaby's architecture must also have seemed harmless to Shaw, for the first building Lethaby completed by himself, Avon Tyrell near Christchurch, Hampshire (the commission was Shaw's setting-up present), is a very Shavian house. Completed in 1893, its main rooms face south and are

43 *Avon Tyrell, west front*

divided from the entrance and servants' quarters by a long internal corridor running from east to west, which is intersected at right angles by a huge hall that cuts across the house from north to south—in essence very similar to some of Shaw's large country house plans of the 1880s. Similarly Shavian are the great mullioned windows and the three Queen Anne bay windows on the south front. These are not unlike the oriel windows in Shaw's own house (p. 40) with leaded lights, timber frames, a curved transom over the centre and bands of moulded plasterwork between the glazed areas (now replaced at Avon Tyrell by tiles). But at the top of the same elevation is a row of four projecting gables, not so very different from those which Lethaby's neighbour Philip Webb was designing for Standen in the same years.

With what seems conscious idiosyncracy, Lethaby placed the bays, not centrally under the gables, but—almost but not quite—under the valleys between them, emphasizing the difference between the Webbian top hamper and the Shavian base. The back of the house is much less formal, with windows of all sizes and shapes arranged over a series of receding planes closely mirroring the functions within.

Lethaby's next house, the Hurst, at Four Oaks near Birmingham, was much smaller, but it also had many Queen Anne motifs. For instance, on the south front, two large bays with segmentally headed sash windows rose up through the pitch of the roof. But the plan was remarkably different, much more like Webb's Red House—L shaped and one-room-and-a-corridor deep. Lethaby's client, Colonel Wilkinson, was plainly more fond of sun than Morris, for the Hurst's orientation was the reverse of the Red House, with the main rooms facing south and west. Sadly the effect of this orientation on the open space enclosed by the two wings cannot now be seen, for the house has been demolished. It was one of only six major buildings put up by Lethaby.*

* Apart from the ones discussed in this chapter, there were the Eagle Insurance Company offices, Birmingham (chapter 10) and High Coxlease, a house near Lyndhurst, Hampshire.

44 *Lethaby. The Hurst, Four Oaks, Birmingham (1893—now demolished)*

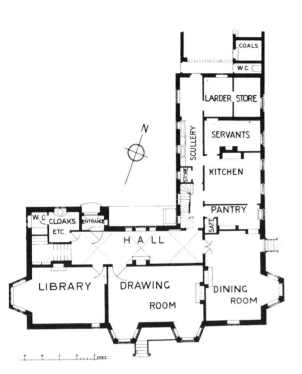

45 *The Hurst, ground floor plan*

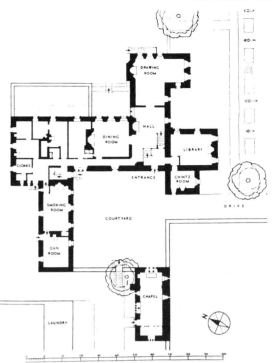

47 *Melsetter House, ground floor plan*

46 *Lethaby. Melsetter House, Hoy, Orkneys (completed 1898)*

His next commission was for another Birmingham businessman, Thomas Middlemore, who had retired to Hoy in the Orkneys. Melsetter House was completed in 1898. Its plan is a most sophisticated development of Webb's additive layout. Two thin, interlocking Ls ingeniously incorporate, at half levels, an existing small farmhouse and allow the main spaces—drawing room and library—to obtain both the main views and sunlight from the south and west.[13] The exterior is as closely modelled on local tradition as even Webb would have wished, with white harled (roughcast) walls, crow-stepped gables and greenish Caithness flags on the steeply pitched roofs. (Orkney shares a tradition of building with the north-east coast of Scotland.) The fenestration, with bold stone surrounds to the small paned sash windows, resembles that of an eighteenth-century Scottish vernacular mansion, but with Ruskinian changefulness in its disposition.

May Morris described Melsetter as, "a sort of fairy palace on the edge of the great northern seas, a wonderful place, this building which was remotely and romantically situated with its tapestries and its silken hangings and its carpets, which came from my father's workshop. It seemed like the embodiment of some of those fairy palaces of which my father wrote with great charm and dignity. But, for all its fineness and dignity, it was a place full of homeliness and the spirit of welcome, a very lovable place. And surely that is the test of an architect's genius: he built for home life as well as dignity."[14]

Lethaby's last work is the tiny church at Brockhampton in Herefordshire, and it is his most curious. Built in 1901 and 1902, it is constructed like no other church on earth. The thick walls are plain, of local red sandstone, and the roof is carried on simple, great pointed stone arches that spring virtually from floor level. But the slope of the roof is made of unreinforced concrete, which outside is covered by thatch in the local tradition. This stone-thatch-and-concrete structure* is topped by a tower over the south door, the upper half of which is clap-boarded and capped by a pyramid covered in shingles.

Spatially, the church is like a minute cathedral, with a big square crossing tower that shoots light diagonally downwards and, in the nave, square-

---

* The mixture of concrete and thatch, bizarre as it seems at first, was not simply picturesque. As well as giving visual reminders of local buildings, the thatch was an excellent water-proofing material and provided very good thermal insulation. Combined with the high thermal mass of the concrete, the insulative thatch gave the roof properties (for instance slow response to sudden changes of external conditions, absence of condensation) that are still being pursued today: indeed a mixture of thatch and concrete would still be an excellent combination if thatching were not now so expensive. Thermally, the Brockhampton roof was one of the most sophisticated constructions of its day—and more so than many of our own.

48 *Lethaby. Brockhampton Church, Herefordshire (built 1901–1902), from south-west*

49 *Brockhampton Church, interior*

topped windows in deep embrasures which give an ever varied play of horizontal light. Simple though the building is externally, though quietly relieved by much arcane Cosmos-like symbolism, the interior is rich with finely carved choir stalls, Burne-Jones tapestries and Christopher Whall's stained glass.

The church is one of the greatest monuments of the Arts and Crafts movement. Yet it nearly broke Lethaby, who had insisted on being master builder as well as architect. John Brandon-Jones says that "So much responsibility was thrown on Lethaby himself that the strain brought him to the verge of a breakdown and he never repeated the experiment."[15]

A parallel career had opened to Lethaby in 1896 when he was appointed first Principal of the LCC's Central School of Arts and Crafts. Lethaby the teacher began to emerge. The school was described by Esther Wood shortly after it opened. Studios were open during the day but "teaching is done entirely in the evenings . . . the students assemble in their various departments; each branch of study being open to men and women equally, with the exception of the life class for men. Some curious varieties of personality and character may be seen in almost every room. Young and middle aged men, strong manual labourers, refined and scholarly-looking craftsmen, quiet, earnest girls and smart little lads scarcely out of their fourth standard, are gathered together round the tables and desks or thinking out their designs plodding steadily on at some set task."[16]

This was the realization of Lethaby's ideal of a school for everyone involved in building, which he described in a 1904 essay on architectural education. "The highly artificial separation of the present system is obviously most disastrous to progress in building, and I feel most strongly that up to a stage all who are to be engaged in building in any skilled capacity should meet in schools common to all."[17]

But what was progress in building? Where was that future that Lethaby left undefined at the end of *Cosmos*? Gradually Lethaby evolved the answer.

In 1896 he was a disciple of Morris, decreeing that "beauty can only be brought back to common life by our doing common work in an interesting way".[18] This thesis was gradually refined: "All work of man bears the stamp of the spirit with which it was done but this stamp is not necessarily 'ornament'. The unadorned indeed can never stand as low as that which is falsely adorned in borrowed, brazen bedizenments. High utility and liberal convenience for the noble life are enough for architecture . . . Consider

any of the great forms of life activity—seamanship, farming, housekeeping—can any-one say where utility ends and style, order, clearness, precision begin?"[19]

Utility and need for Lethaby were the key: "there is . . . a brown-bread and dewy-morning ideal of beauty, and a late champagne-supper ideal. Who would say which was the right one were it not for Necessity's 'You must'? We have to love the health ideal, or cease to exist."[20] To fulfil this ideal in architecture, "experiment must be brought back once more into the centre of architecture and architects must be trained as engineers are trained . . . The modern way of building must be flexible and vigorous, even smart and hard. We must give up designing the broken-down picturesque which is part of the ideal of make-believe."[21] Yet innovative as the new architecture should be, "no art that is only one man deep is worth much; it should be a thousand men deep. We cannot forget our historical knowledge, nor would we if we might. The important question is, can it be organized or must we continue to be betrayed by it? The only agreement that seems possible is agreement on a scientific basis, on an endeavour after perfect structural efficiency. If we could agree on this we need not trouble about beauty for that would take care of itself."[22]

The thousand men had come to Lethaby's elbow when he led the cohorts of the Arts and Crafts movement to produce a design for the Liverpool Cathedral Competition (1902). Lethaby, Henry Wilson, Halsley Ricardo, R. W. Troup, Weir Schultz were joined by sculptor Stirling Lee and Christopher Whall, the stained glass artist. The building was to consist of a gigantic nave-and-choir, roofed by a series of concrete vaults folded together in a curved corrugated carapace. The walls were buttressed by a series of chapels surmounted by concrete semi-domes, and the whole composition was dominated by a stupendous, tapering detached campanile. If one ignores this entirely original feature, the effect is curiously middle-eastern, and, as John Brandon-Jones has pointed out, it "must have been based on the Byzantine studies made by Lethaby and Weir Schultz".[23]

Lethaby later said of concrete that it "is only a higher power of the Roman system of construction. If we could sweep away our fear that it is an inartistic material, and boldly build a railway station, a museum, or a cathedral, wide and simple, amply lighted, and call in our painters to finish the walls, we might be interested in building again almost at

50 *Lethaby* et al. *Liverpool Cathedral competition design (1902–3), produced by a team of Arts and Crafts workers captained by Lethaby*

once."[24] But the assessors of the competition, Shaw and Bodley, were not impressed, and the scheme was not even placed.

Liverpool Cathedral was Lethaby's last venture into designing buildings. He not only found himself in emotional difficulties organizing the work on Brockhampton as he believed it ought to be done, but he believed himself too ignorant to continue. "It is absurd . . . that the writer should have been allowed to study cathedrals from Kirkwall to Rome and from Quimper to Constantinople; it would be far better to have an equivalent knowledge of steel and concrete construction."[25]

The rest of his life was devoted to teaching at the Central School, then at the Royal College of Art, and to looking after Westminster Abbey, to which he was appointed surveyor in 1906, after which for twenty years Lethaby looked "upon myself here as the family butler"[26] and cared for the fabric according to the strictest SPAB principles.

It was writing rather than building that made him one of the most influential architects of the turn of the century. And it was through his essays that Lethaby, talented, kindly, erudite, persuasive, perceptive and forward looking, yet always prepared to temporize, became one of the betrayers of the gospel of Ruskin and Morris. As he became more and more divorced from the realities of ordinary building, his theories became increasingly opposed to many of the original Arts and Crafts ideals. By 1915, perhaps because of the pressures of the War and the example of Germany's successful industrial use of some of these ideals, Lethaby was preaching that "We must bring our new Chippendales, Flaxmans and Cranes into our industrial commerce."[27] The Puginian paradox of the relationship between designer and craftsman was to be resolved firmly in favour of the designer and the machine.

Ideologically, Lethaby had removed one of the two basic objections to machines raised by Ruskin and Morris. For the Ruskinian objection to machine production of grotesque facsimiles of craftsmanship could be countered by Lethaby's argument that ornament was no longer necessary in ordinary building and, where it was necessary, it would be a natural outcome of everyone living the good Arts and Crafts life. Yet Lethaby's "brown-bread and dewy-morning" ideal could scarcely be enjoyed by factory hands, roused in the dark by the mill hooter and required to spend nine or ten hours a day labouring intensely as appendages to machines. This was the reality of most industrial life in the first decades of this century and nowhere did Lethaby come to terms with the objection of Ruskin and Morris that minding a machine reduced the minder to slavery.

Certainly, he had an excuse, for, as the comprehensive historians of technology have written, "scientific industry, even during the second half of the nineteenth century, did much to diminish danger, hardship and squalor".[28] But the relationship of man and machine had not fundamentally changed.

To change that relationship, a revolution was necessary—either social (which Lethaby, socialist though he was, would not accept) or technological (which he could not foresee). His acceptance of the early twentieth-century industrial *status quo* was a reversal of his early ideals, in which a young architect would "associate with himself, not thirty draftsmen in a back office (a number which I understand has [in 1892] been exceeded) but a group of associates and assistants on the building itself and in its decoration."[29]

It is unfair to suggest that Lethaby was the Iscariot of the Arts and Crafts movement, for, being the most articulate of the generation which succeeded Morris, he provided a mirror to the development of the movement, and his later essays were the reflection of a revolution which had lost its impetus.

He had, after all, been one of the leaders of the movement: in setting up the associations, in carrying forward the messages of Ruskin and Morris, in producing innovative buildings, in methods of work and teaching. His leadership was of the best, most natural kind. On Lethaby's death, Alfred Powell recollected, "he was about the jolliest companion anybody could dream of, always full of life. It seemed as though his five wits were multiplied by eight or ten, he had so much sensation, and his senses were all so continuously alive. It was that which made him so sympathetic to everybody; there was no kind of person he could not sympathize with."[30] Mackail, (Morris's biographer) recalled that Lethaby lived, "not with his head in the clouds, but with his head in air which had something superterrestrial about it; and when he descended to the ordinary levels of earth he was often like someone who had strayed into darkness."[31]

Lethaby had lived long enough to know that the new architecture of the twenties had no more achieved real functionalism and escaped from iconographic imperatives than had Pugin fully succeeded when he found in purest Gothic the answer to his search for a truly practical architecture. The Modern Movement, he said, was "only another design humbug to pass off with a shrug—ye olde modernist style—we must have a style to copy—what funny stuff this art is."[32]

Lethaby's life, for all its turns and twists, was totally devoted to art. On his grave is the epitaph "love and labour are all", yet a truer memorial is perhaps to be found in the hall of the Art Workers' Guild, where Lethaby looks across the ranks of the Arts and Crafts movement to confront William Morris at the other side. Morris's shaggy majesty gazes at a rather sad Pooterish face, walrus moustached and close cropped, with deep-set, kindly thoughtful eyes. It is the confrontation of idealism and disillusion.

51 *Lethaby. High Coxlease, Lyndhurst, Hampshire (1900–1901)*

1 Weir, Robert W. Schultz "William Richard Lethaby", paper read before the Art Workers' Guild on 22nd April 1932 and published by the Central School of Arts and Crafts in 1938. This architect's name is confusing. Before the First War, he called himself Robert Weir Schultz, which he then changed to Robert Weir Schultz Weir.
2 Thomas, Brian *RIBA Journal*, Vol. LXIV, 1957, p. 218
3 *Ibid.*
4 Weir *op. cit.*
5 Robert Shaw quoted in Saint, A. *Richard Norman Shaw* p. 187
6 Weir *op. cit.*
7 Lethaby, W. R. *Architecture Mysticism and Myth*, republished by The Architectural Press, London 1974, p. 3
8 *Ibid.*, p. 4
9 *Ibid.*, p. 8
10 Brandon-Jones, John *RIBA Journal*, Vol. LXIV, 1957, p. 220
11 Blomfield, Sir Reginald *Richard Norman Shaw*, Batsford, London 1940, p. 12. Blomfield is here paraphrasing notes by Robert Shaw, the son of R.N.S.
12 Weir *op. cit.*
13 The plans were first published by John Brandon-Jones in *AA Journal*, March 1949, p. 168–169. Brandon-Jones, who was stationed in Orkney during the Second War, gives a beautifully evocative description of the house.
14 Morris, May, in *RIBA Journal*, Vol. XXXIX, 1932, p. 303. She was speaking at the memorial symposium in the year after Lethaby's death.
15 Brandon-Jones, John *RIBA Journal*, Vol. LXIV, p. 220
16 Wood, Esther *Architectural Review*, Vol. II, 1897, p. 241
17 Lethaby, W. R. "Architectural Education", in *Architectural Review*, Vol. XVI, 1904, p. 161
18 Lethaby, W. R. "Arts and the Function of Guilds", first published in the *Quest*, Birmingham 1896; reprinted in Lethaby, W. R. *Form in Civilization*, Oxford 1957, p. 162
19 Lethaby W. R. "Architecture as Form in Civilisation" (1920), in *Form and Civilization, op. cit.*, p. 7
20 Lethaby, W. R. "What shall we call beautiful?" Originally published in *Hibbert Journal* 1918; reprinted in *Form in Civilization, op. cit.*, p. 121
21 Lethaby, W. R. *Architecture*, Williams and Norgate, London 1911. The quotation comes at the end of Lethaby's beautiful succinct little history of architecture for laymen.
22 *Ibid.*, p. 249
23 Brandon-Jones, John *RIBA Journal*, Vol. LXIV, p. 220
24 Lethaby, W. R. *Architecture, op. cit.*, p. 249
25 *Ibid.*, p. 247
26 Quoted by Powell, Alfred, in *Times Literary Supplement*, 17th April, 1973
27 Lethaby, W. R. "Design and Industry", an address delivered to the Design and Industries Association in 1915. Reprinted in *Form in Civilization, op. cit.*, p. 44
28 Singer, Charles et al *A History of Technology*, Vol. V, Oxford 1970, p. vii
29 Lethaby, W. R. "The Builder's Art and the Craftsman", in *Architecture a Profession or an Art*, ed. Shaw, R. N. and Jackson, T. G., John Murray 1892, p. 168
30 Powell, A. H. *RIBA Journal* Vol. XXXIX, 1932, p. 311
31 Mackail, J. W. *op. cit.*, p. 312
32 Quoted in Macleod, Robert *Style and Society*, RIBA, London 1971, p. 67

7 The Explorer

There is a legend that when Lethaby was confronted by an irate woman client saying, "I cannot see, Mr Lethaby, that you have done a single thing that I asked you to do", he replied, "Well, you see, my first duty as an artist is to please myself."[1] If even the diffident and mild mannered Lethaby could take such a high-handed aesthetic line, the lady could count herself lucky that she was not dealing with the much more fiercely independent Edward Schroder Prior (1852–1932), a co-founder of the Art Workers' Guild with Lethaby and perhaps the most brilliantly original of all Shaw's pupils.

At first sight, Prior appears to be a typical late Victorian hearty. A Harrovian and son of a barrister, he was a Cambridge blue (high jump, long jump, hurdles) and was amateur high jump champion before entering Shaw's office in 1874. There he joined in the horse-play with more than ordinary vigour. "He could take off his trousers one day in the office because they were wet, or on another occasion he could tie up O'Neill, one of the dimmer pupils, in a brown paper parcel and leave him in the lobby."[2]

The tough, bullying manner never left him: the *Architect and Building News* commented when he died, "He could be something of a grizzly bear at times for he was pertinacious, and his opinion, once formed was hardly to be changed ... Yet it was a kindly bear withal, that would emerge, honours divided, from a wordy warfare with a joyous twinkle in its eye; and for any small personal attention or service, it would be immensely grateful and appreciative."[3]

Inside the bear's skin was a scholar and artist. His books on Gothic architecture and sculpture, widely acclaimed in their day, helped him achieve the Slade Professorship of Fine Art at Cambridge in 1912, a post which he used to found the Cambridge school of architecture.

By then his creative life was virtually at an end. It had started thirty years earlier with a series of essays in Norman Shaw's styles: Carr Manor in Meanwood, Leeds (1879–82), a remodelling of an original house, has touches of Old English half-timbering and big plastered coved eaves a bit like those Shaw was using fifteen years before; High Grove, Harrow (1880–1) is Queen Anne at its most formal, and the Red House, Harrow (1883–4) is an example of half-timbered Queen Anne.

Shaw had been right when he wrote to Prior's mother about Edward that "it really does not matter when a man begins. He is certain to do but little for a year or two, barely perhaps making both ends meet, and the sooner he gets over this dull period the better ... but once he gets a bit of a start, he won't want much help from anyone."[4] Prior's start was at Carr Manor, but even at this early stage there is evidence of the mature architect. Shavian touches are kept to the stables and cottages. The main block is a many gabled, irregular composition in local stone, pierced by long rows of leaded windows, which are divided by stone mullions. One of its sources is plainly the Old English style, but the dark stone severity is all West Riding—owing much to local seventeenth-century halls like those at Riddlesden and Sowerby. In this, Prior's earliest work (it seems to have been Shaw's setting-up commission to him), he showed a tremendous Puginian affection for local materials and techniques which distinguished all his later work.

In 1885, at West Bay, near Bridport, Dorset, Prior built Pier Terrace along one side of the harbour. He took up local themes: squared warm limestone rubble for the lower two storeys with, on the second floor and round the bay windows of the first, slates cut to an almost (but not quite) hexagonal pattern which can be seen on many other buildings in the area. The whole is topped by a mansard of Roman tiles, under

52　*Edward Schroder Prior. Carr Manor, Leeds, West Yorkshire (1879–1882), the main front*

53　*Prior. Pier Terrace, West Bay, Dorset (1885). The two bays nearest the camera are not by Prior.*

which the fenestration, at first appearing to be regular, moves up and down and changes in shape according to the dictates of slope and internal need.

Not very much later (1885–1887), Prior was building the Henry Martyn Hall, Cambridge, an impeccably Gothic building but one which, again, showed much knowledge of local building techniques. Pugin would have been pleased with its strung courses of ashlar separating broad bands of pebble, flint and stone, mixed higgledy piggledy in the manner of Cambridgeshire churches. The stair in the turret is made visible by allowing its treads to emerge on the outside; it is a building of great savageness and changefulness in which the effect is as much due to the craftsman as the architect.

Prior, for all his belief in the individuality of the artist, was perhaps closer to Ruskin's ideal of the building designer than any other Arts and Crafts architect of the first generation. He made his position quite clear in 1901 when discussing the Liverpool Cathedral competition. He advocated that the client (the Church of England) should decide on the overall dimensions, lighting, access and furniture requirements and then the building should be produced by a team of craftsmen working together under the direction of an administrative ("planning") architect who, at all costs, must not design himself. For Prior believed that "there are now no Gothic architects, but no Classic either—or any of other designation able to impress upon building that individuality of earnestness which the great architects of the nineteenth century achieved."[15] An architect of some sort was necessary to cope with "the complexities of modern life, the varied requirements of denser population, the by-laws of controlling authorities".[6]

But he should make it his business only "to find and quarry the best stone, make the best brick, forge the best iron, cut the best timber, so season and dress and build as will make the best construction . . . Cannot an architect be found who will so consent to be builder without thought of design?"[7] The execution and design of the work would be left to "masons skilled to work and lay stone, bricklayers to build, carpenters, plumbers and ironworkers expert in the crafts to make a building."[8] Never, in any of his work, did Prior achieve this easy, direct relationship between architect and craftsman, so perhaps his Liverpool manifesto was not supposed to apply fully to ordinary building but was particularly intended for a great cathedral where Prior, quoting Matthew Paris,

54 *Prior. Henry Martyn Hall, Cambridge (1885–1887). There was originally a spire on top of the Gothic oriel*

urged that *"congregati sunt artifices"*—or at least they ought to be.

The highest flowering of architecture, Prior believed, happens when "instead of art being the province of a sect, the whole people combines in the pursuit of beauty and becomes endowed with the faculties of artists."[9] Yet in the imperfect late Victorian world, where this revolution had not yet occurred, Prior was totally opposed to the growing practice of "professional" architects employing collective platoons of assistants who did the real work. In *Architecture: a Profession or an Art*, Prior's essay on "The profession and its ghosts" was scathing about such architects, in whose practices the problems of keeping the organization running meant that "little time can be left for even that directorate of architectural 'designing' which is the ostensible groundwork of all this business . . . Pecksniffs go unabashed in these days."[10]

"So the mechanical look of our architecture is readily explained. The world, by employing the professional architect, does not admit of Architecture being an art."[11] The architect must be an artist (except when designing cathedrals) but Prior had nothing but contempt for the nineteenth-century concept of the artist: "our art is always the expression of strong individuality; so that each artist is a school of himself—with a rise, a flourish, perhaps a decadence—and then complete extinction: he can hand on no torch to his successor."[12]

The way forward, for Prior, was not traditionalism. He was sure that "the 'styles' are dead . . . such things are gone by. The saviour of his art to the architect is no longer in knowledge but in experiment, in the devices of craftsmanship, in going back to the simple necessities of Building and finding in them the power of beauty."[13]

Prior, the individual artist who wanted to be simply the chief supervisor of craftsmen, the traditionalist who believed the future lay in experiment,

emerged as an integrated architect when he designed the Barn on a hill overlooking Exmouth in 1896.

The plan was revolutionary. Prior took the basic long, thin Arts and Crafts layout, one room and a corridor deep, and broke it like a chicken's leg, snapping back the two limbs to 90°. They are joined by the cartilage of the entrance hall and the knuckles, the drawing room and dining room, stick out at either side. The intentions were to obtain wide views of the sea from the principal rooms, to provide a sun trap in the angle between them and to reduce the amount of circulation space necessitated in the long thin plan by keeping the corridor on the inside of the angle. It is said by some historians[14] to have been modelled on Norman Shaw's Chesters (1891–3), a mighty classical house in Northumberland which has elements of an X plan but which had (partly because it was a late great nineteenth-century palace) none of the virtues of prospect or economy which Prior achieved in the Barn.* Prior's butterfly plan was to have great influence in the next two decades.

* An equally probable source was a house by the French architect Hector Horeau in Avenue Road, near Prior's St. John's Wood house. Built in 1856, it had two wings set at 45° to the central irregular hexagon containing the drawing room and circulation spaces. The house (demolished in the 1950s) was published in the *Builder* (1859).

55 *Prior. The Barn, Exmouth, Devon (designed 1896)*

56 *The Barn, texture of the walls: savage building realized*

57 *The Barn, entrance front*

Externally, Prior expounded his beliefs in Puginian fidelity to place and Ruskinian savageness in a
great, soft tea-cosy roof of local thatch supported by
walls of local stone. Warm grey ashlar is mixed
haphazardly with passages of red boulders and little
arpeggios of sea pebbles, all combined to give a wonderfully varied texture that could never had been
exactly specified by the architect but which must have
come at least as much from the craftsman's sen-
sibilities as from the drawing board. Sadly, there are
no records of Prior's relationships with his masons,
but letters from the local estate office show that Prior
was fiercely living up to his ideal of the architect as
specifier of good materials and was closely supervising the works from his father-in-law's rectory at Bridport.[15]

Prior, the experimental architect, tried two novel
techniques at the Barn: a concrete first floor reinforced by tree trunks (an eminently sensible fire-
proofing and sound deadening technique in an area
where tree trunks were cheap) and, to obtain approval
from the local council, he treated the thatch with an
"incombustible solution". Neither was of much help
when the Barn burnt down on 4th October, 1905. It

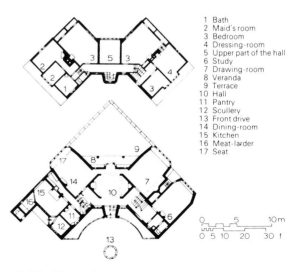

1 Bath
2 Maid's room
3 Bedroom
4 Dressing-room
5 Upper part of the hall
6 Study
7 Drawing-room
8 Veranda
9 Terrace
10 Hall
11 Pantry
12 Scullery
13 Front drive
14 Dining-room
15 Kitchen
16 Meat-larder
17 Seat

58 *The Barn, plans*

was re-roofed in slate and refloored in timber, but the main lines of the house (now a private hotel) can still be seen; the rather run-of-the-mill Queen Anne fenestration was restored and the texture of the literally unique walls was unaffected. And unchanged too was the house's relationship with its garden.

Through William Morris, the Arts and Crafts garden inherited an affection for English cottage plants, such as sunflowers and stocks, but to anyone imbued with the attitudes of Ruskin and Morris it seems remarkably formal: terraced, pleached, pergolaed, clipped and axial, the gardens of Prior, Voysey and Mackintosh seem in direct contradiction to the naturalness and changefulness their authors so carefully created in their buildings.* Prior explained his attitude in a series of essays in the *Studio* on garden making. He attacked the natural garden which pretended to look "more beautiful than anything that man can make. Such should go by the name of the unnatural garden—for, since man is a part of Nature, his natural garden will be that which shows itself his, not by its wildness, but by the marks of order and design which are inseparable from his work."[16]

The necessity of putting humanity's stamp on nature was clear: "the formality of the enclosure gives

---

* The Arts and Crafts Garden inherited from the High Victorian Italian fashion a love for terraces, topiary and little trees in tubs. But most Arts and Craftsmen rejected the Italianate taste for carpet bedding; their middle class clients could not afford the cost.

59, 60, 61, 62 *Thomas Mawson. Garden designs*

indeed the true garden motive, that of a plot separated for a man's fancy . . . made to be another chamber of a man's house".[17] Axiality and regularity, he believed, are "not set forth here as being rules or recipes of art but only as the examples of that direct common sense which should govern all garden operations".[18] Yet he was urgent that no commercial, machine-made products be used in gardens—only hand cut stone flags and hand made stock bricks and, amongst these, he would allow to grow "harebell and fragile toadflax [which] may year by year spring up in zigzags of delicate greenery, and seem not out of place"[19] as they do now under the feet of the High Court judges who alone stride the terraces of Carr Manor. (These terraces have remained virtually untouched, though the remaining grounds of the Leeds Judges' Lodging have been turned into a miniature landscaped park which would have made Prior sick.)

This disgust with "natural" gardening was partly a reaction to the eighteenth-century ideal in which the house, a perfect artefact, was set in an idyllic Claudian landscape. The Arts and Crafts ideal was almost exactly opposite, with a "natural" house set in a formal landscape. The original Arts and Crafts formality in garden making* was gradually broken

---

* Beautifully catalogued by Thomas Mawson in *The Art and Craft of Garden Making*.[20]

63 *Prior. Home Place, Holt, Norfolk (1903–1905)*

down, but never by Prior's generation; Gertrude
Jekyll and William Robinson* brought changeful
principles to gardening—yet ironically Miss Jekyll
worked hand in hand with Lutyens, the great convert
to classical architecture. Jekyll enjoyed direct contact
with the soil: "to the diligent worker its happiness is
like the offering of a constant hymn of praise".[21] She
was "strongly for treating garden and wooded ground
in a pictorial way, mainly with large effects . . . I try
for beauty and harmony everywhere especially for
harmony of colour." And she made "no parade of
conscious effort."[22]

Prior would have despised the informality but he
would certainly have agreed with the large effects. As
he got older, the formality of his gardens began to
invade his houses. His next butterfly house, Home
Place (1903–1905) near Holt in north Norfolk was
symmetrical not only at front and back but on the
entrance side as well. Each of these symmetrical ele-

* Since 1883 William Robinson had been inveighing in *The English
Flower Garden* against "styles" of gardening and arguing for a
horticulture responsive to the needs of topography and natural
growth of plants. Jekyll, who contributed regularly to his magazine
Gardening Illustrated, integrated Robinson's Ruskinian gardening
naturalism into the practice of design by late Ruskinian architects
like Lutyens.

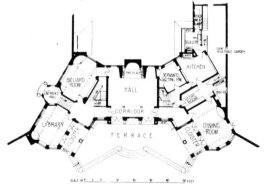

64 *Home Place, ground floor and garden plans*

vations faced an axially arranged garden. The house showed Prior in his most savage mood. It was built of solid concrete* faced with pebbles found on the site, zigzag patterns of thin tiles (showing their edges only) and, at the corners, cut local stone. The effect is aggressively restless, almost hiding the symmetrical formality of the plan and even overwhelming the horrid modern porch which has been slapped onto the main front and the standard metal window frames that have replaced many of Prior's casemented leaded lights. The result is confusing because, though all the materials were local (including the Norfolk pantiles on the roof), and the patterns used all had precedents in local vernacular building, the whole effect had a strangely foreign exuberance, compared by Pevsner to Gaudi's daring.[24]

It was in technique of building that Prior got nearest to the Ruskinian ideal. Instead of a contractor, Prior used Randall Wells as site clerk; Wells must have been a concrete expert for he also supervised Lethaby's Brockhampton church. He hired labour and bought materials as they were needed and he saw to it that the services subcontractor fitted his work in with the rest. The aggregates for the concrete and the pebbles for the exterior were found by excavating a flower garden an acre in extent and six feet deep in front of what was to be the main elevation. (Prior believed that by using his own materials, the client had virtually covered the cost of digging this enormous hole.) The construction of the concrete walls was Roman fashion, "without planking"[25] and the concrete upper floors were reinforced by "iron chainage" instead of the then common steel joists. The roof timbers and the rest of the carpentry were of oak, which "for this use could be obtained locally at a cost hardly above that of good deal." Prior claimed with glee that by not using a builder "the expenditure . . . has been kept to the sum of the estimate, £8,000" but warned readers of the *Architectural Review* that his direct labour system had some disadvantages—principally not having a contractor to blame for the size of the final bill. Yet Prior's toughness was not daunted by such problems, as Lethaby's gentler nature had been after his similar experiment at Brockhampton, and he went on to complete his finest church: St.

* Both Prior and Lethaby were interested in concrete, which became quite a popular Arts and Crafts material. They must have learned about it in Shaw's office, for in the '70s and early '80s Shaw was experimenting with concrete in various ways, following his own master, Street, who had used Roman concrete for economy as far back as 1870.[23]

65 *Prior. Bothenhampton Church, Dorset (1887–1889)*

Andrew, Roker, County Durham, in 1907.

Prior had started his church building career with Holy Trinity, Bothenhampton, Dorset, built between 1887 and 1889. It is a small church, built very simply. From the outside, it seems quite conventional, a quiet nineteenth-century exercise in Early English Gothic with lancets in the chancel and narrow coupled windows between the buttresses of the nave. Inside, the space is very simple, with the unadorned timber roof of the nave supported on three plain stone arches which follow the external buttresses and which spring smoothly out of the walls very low down.

The chancel is a little more complicated, with similar stone arches springing high up between strange corbel-like structures which are virtually the only decoration: there is scarcely a moulding to be seen anywhere.

As at Lethaby's Brockhampton church, the effect is of great serenity: because the arches spring so low, just above waist height, the space is comfortably enclosing, like a big kindly cave. The cave-like feeling is enhanced by the very deep embrasures of the windows through which light ripples, muted and never

66 *Prior. Roker Church, Northumberland (1907)*

67 *Roker Church, interior*

glaring, across the warm limestone. Then, beyond is the narrow high chancel in which the eye is drawn heavenwards by the corbels and the little trefoil window over the lancets at the east end.

The Roker church, designed with Randall Wells, is a much bigger affair. Prior reused his theme of a comparatively wide nave with a simple timber roof supported on great plain arches springing low down.* At Roker, though, the buttresses are almost completely on the inside, which means that the arches spring from quite deep within the church. At the bottom ends, the buttresses are cut off just above head height and their inner edges are supported on simple paired hexagonal columns allowing a passage way between the columns and the wall—the cave effect is enhanced by these little tunnels under the buttresses which allow access to the north and south ends of the pews.

Prior again had a narrow, high chancel to which the wider nave is spliced in typically robust fusion by a pair of arches angled in plan, giving a canted entrance to the transepts. The chancel is curious because it sits under the massive tower which was placed at the east end to make it visible far out to sea. Over the chancel and under the tower is a ceiling painted like the sky† in a way Lethaby would have approved. Though the building itself is very plain, its furnishings are sumptuous examples of high Arts and Crafts work, including a tapestry reredos by Burne-Jones, an altar cross of wood with ebony and metal inlay by Ernest Gimson and a stone font carved by Randall Wells.

Externally, the building looks pretty Gothic until you get close up and realize that all the curves of traditional tracery have been straightened out to become simple diagonals of stone supported on unadorned polygonal mullions. The relationship of chancel and tower is particularly strange. Instead of firmly siting the tower at the east end, Prior allowed the chancel to project a few feet to the east, retaining the ridge height of the nave so it seems that the church has been punched through its tower from west to east—a true if rather wilful expression of Ruskinian changefulness. Needless to say, the whole building was constructed in local stone, grey and rough from a neighbouring hillside.

For his last big church, St. Osmond's at Parkestone in Poole, Dorset (1913–16), Prior must have been

---

* At Roker the arches are of concrete reinforced with iron rods, and the ridge and purlins are in concrete reinforced with steel.

† Painted in 1927 by Macdonald Gill to a programme by Prior.

68 *Prior. St. Osmond's, Parkestone, Poole, Dorset (1913–1916), west front*

69 *St. Osmond's, interior*

is an echo of Prior's use of overt stylism in the Cambridge Medical Schools (finished in 1904, only three years after his polemic on the Gothic principle for Liverpool had been published in the *Architectural Review*). In 1904 the same magazine* reported of the Cambridge building that "classic forms have been used to ornament the fronts, but the work is plain towards the courtyards, upon which the large microscope rooms look."[27]

The heavily rusticated street fronts of the building are inexplicable within Ruskinian cannons—though the plan is changeful, with the medical museum darting out at an angle to the main body of the work, and the classicism of the elevation is full of wit and surprise. The only possible Arts and Crafts justification for the building's style is its context: a neo-classical street in central Cambridge, which therefore possibly deserved the grand classical manner.

Perhaps classical formality was important to Prior when he was working for official clients. His design for the government medical school at Netley in Hampshire (1900), in no way subject to a classical

* Presumably the article was written by Prior himself or by prior agreement.

puzzled to find a suitable material, for he was building round an existing brick structure in the Byzantine style by G. A. B. Livesay. In the end he "persuaded makers of simple pottery by the shores of Poole harbour to turn their clay to bricks of every colour from purple to vivid orange".[26] Again Prior (who was working with Arthur Grove) used simple arches, round this time, to roof the nave. But they are supported on mighty columns topped by terracotta Byzantine capitals and flanked by aisles covered by concrete barrel vaults. The simple interior (so kind to Livesay's work that you cannot see the join) is of roughcast relieved by terracotta. Outside, the building wears a fantastic but muted coat of many colours and patterns in which Prior's special bricks are made to dance in diapered and patterned work. The lines are as usual simple, with windows topped by semi-circular arches and roundels in the clerestory. The great west rose window consists of two concentric circles connected by straight glazing bars—an echo of the straightened Gothic of Roker.

The overt use of (ideosyncratic) Byzantine motifs

70 *Prior. Cambridge Medical Schools (1904)*

context, was to have been executed in most rigorous neo-classical symmetries. Was symmetry (itself always dear to Prior) the generator of Prior's later urban style?

After the War, Prior's practice evaporated, partly because of his academic commitments. Yet he never lost his early inspiration. An ex-student recalled, "His ideal to make the Cambridge School in fact what it was called—a school of architectural studies—, had something in it deeper and wider than any dallying with the crafts. It aimed, through cultural training, at a recognition of the whole field of art as *practice*, not theory; the production of a world of builders (not architects) who would build with direct knowledge of working conditions, controlling workmen (not contractors), yet fully cognisant of the business of building and the implications of a contract with the client. An impossible ideal, perhaps [but] with him it was the conviction of a lifetime."[28] It was this unyielding adherence to an ideal that made Prior the man he was and gave all his architecture such an individual stamp.

To his excessively successful classical contemporary Reginald Blomfield, Prior "of all Shaw's men . . . was the strongest personality. Somehow I think his real ability should have taken him further than it did; perhaps he was too unyielding, constitutionally incapable of accepting the *via media*".[29]

Yet in the end, which went further? Every one of Prior's buildings repays study with delight and interest. Can anyone say that of the endless acres of Blomfield's work?

1 Saint, A. *Shaw, op. cit.*, p. 145. Saint is quoting from notes left by Robert, Richard Norman Shaw's son.

2 *Ibid.*, p. 186. Again from Robert Shaw's notes.
3 *Architect and Building News*, Vol. CXXI, 1932, p. 23
4 Blomfield, R. *Richard Norman Shaw, op. cit.*, p. 88
5 Prior, E. S. "The New Cathedral for Liverpool", *Architectural Review*, Vol. X, 1901, p. 145
6 *Ibid.*
7 *Ibid.*, p. 146
8 *Ibid.*
9 Prior, E. S. *A History of Gothic Art in England*, George Bell & Sons, London 1900, p. 7
10 Prior, E. S. in Shaw and Jackson *Architecture—a Profession or an Art, op. cit.*, pp. 107–108
11 Prior, E. S. "Church building as it is and as it might be", *Architectural Review*, Vol. IV, 1898, p. 108
12 *Ibid.*, p. 106
13 *Ibid.*, p. 158
14 For instance Franklin, Jill "Edwardian Butterfly Houses", *Architectural Review*, April 1975, pp. 220–225
15 The correspondence between Prior and the Rolle estate is extensively quoted in Hoare, Geoffrey and Geoffrey Pyne *Prior's Barn and Gimson's Coxen*, privately published by the authors, Seaforth, Little Knowle, Budleigh Salterton 1978.
16 Prior, E. S. *Studio*, Vol. XXI, 1901, p. 28
17 *Ibid.*, p. 31
18 *Ibid.*, p. 94
19 *Ibid.*, p. 182
20 Nowhere better shown than in Mawson, Thos H. *The Art and Craft of Garden Making*, Batsford, London 1907
21 Jekyll, G. *Wood and Garden*, Longmans, 1904, p. 2
22 *Ibid.*
23 Saint, A. *Norman Shaw op. cit.*, p. 165–171 gives an interesting description of Shaw's use of concrete
24 Pevsner, N. *Buildings of England: North East Norfolk and Norwich*, Penguin, Harmondsworth 1973, p. 169
25 This and the following short quotations on construction are taken from *Architectural Review*, Vol. IXX, 1906, pp. 70–82
26 Huges, H. C. *RIBA Journal*, Vol. XXXIX, 1932, p. 859. Huges was one of Prior's earliest students at Cambridge.
27 *Architectural Review*, Vol. XV, 1904, p. 159
28 Fyfe, Theodore *RIBA Journal*, Vol. XXXIX, 1932, p. 814
29 Blomfield, R. *Richard Norman Shaw, op. cit.*, p. 90

8 The Pathfinder

Sometime during 1894, Prior, then living in Melina Place, St. John's Wood, acquired a new next door neighbour who was just as fiercely independent and incapable of taking the *via media*.

Charles Francis Annesley Voysey (1857–1941) was one of the few major Arts and Crafts architects born in the '50s who did not belong to the apostolic succession of Street and his pupils: Morris, Webb and Shaw and through Shaw to his pupils, Lethaby, Prior, Newton and Macartney. But, the same age as Lethaby, Voysey was an early member of the Art Workers' Guild (elected in December 1884, the Guild's first year), and he must have known Prior for several years before they became neighbours.

Though similar in their fierce independence and strength of character, and in their reverence for Pugin and Ruskin, Prior and Voysey were unalike in almost every other way. Prior had been through the mill of conventional English upper middle class education; Voysey was almost completely privately educated. Prior, as far as his political opinions can be discerned, seems to have been a Whig; Voysey was definitely a high Tory—but of libertarian temperament. Prior was a conventional Anglican; Voysey was fervently religious. Prior always attempted great fidelity to local materials and building traditions; Voysey evolved a style which, though susceptible of local variation, was applicable everywhere.

Voysey was born at Hessle in the East Riding of Yorkshire where his father, the Rev. Charles Voysey, was running a school. When Voysey was fourteen, his father was dismissed from the Church of England in one of the great ecclesiastical scandals of the nineteenth century; his heresy was that he did not believe in the doctrine of eternal damnation or, as his son put it, "he believed in a good God rather than an angry one".[1]

The influence of the Rev. Charles was always strong. Voysey was educated by him at home in the Yorkshire years and his father's kindly puritanism permeated his life. "If he had to punish any of his children", Voysey wrote, "he would creep up to the bedside before the culprit was asleep, and gently stroking the head, with tears in his eyes, would soften the little heart with a few kind words and leave it in peace. His suffering in causing pain in order to do good could not be doubted and is the experience of all noble parents, surgeons, doctors, dentists and others. And surely of the Creator likewise?"[2]

Voysey's early years must have been very happy, if strictly regulated, and, perhaps as a result, there is an element of what some have condemned as childishness in all his work: a delight in simple jokes such as designing an iron bracket to the profile of a client's face and a love of obvious symbolic imagery: hearts, bull's eye windows and big green water butts. Perhaps it is only in retrospect that his buildings themselves seem to have a childlike quality, but with their big roofs, wide doorways and low walls, they are models of what many children, particularly country bred ones, first draw when they make a picture of a house.

In 1871, the year of his trial in the Lords, Charles Voysey moved to Dulwich to set up his own Theistic church, and C.F.A. was sent to Dulwich College, where he stayed for only eighteen months. The tough régime of a public school did not suit him, and he was withdrawn to study under a private tutor.

Though his art master at Dulwich had dubbed him incompetent for any artistic profession, he was articled for five years to the Victorian Gothic architect J. P. Seddon in 1873. The relationship was a success, and Seddon introduced him to the writings of Pugin, who was to be one of Voysey's guiding stars. Of Ruskin he probably already knew something for Ruskin taught drawing at a school which Voysey's sisters attended. In 1879 he worked briefly for Saxon Snell, an innovator in sanitation techniques, before being asked to join the office of George Devey, a member of his father's church.

In 1880, Devey's practice was wide and flourishing. Voysey learned much from him about designing houses in the country—which, on a different scale, were to be Voysey's main contribution to architecture. And he learned a style—or rather two styles.

Voysey set up his own practice in about 1882, and supported himself on surveys, alterations and designs for furniture, fabrics and wallpapers. As a designer he was both influenced and helped by Mackmurdo, whose flat, sinuous designs of birds and leaves, and furniture with tall, tapering verticals topped by thin

square capitals were to re-echo through much of Voysey's work. But the architectural influence was Devey. In a design for a house, published in the *British Architect* in 1889[3] but probably designed some years before, Voysey seems to be trying to cram as many Deveyan idioms into as small a space as possible. The walls have a stone base course with brick on top. They are pierced by rows of stone mullioned windows, patterned in all kinds of diapers and chequers, and bulge out into square, polygonal and semi-circular bays. On top is an exuberant roof which heaves up and down, with hips, gables both Dutch (in masonry) and English (in half-timbering), and a series of little dormers. It was never built—perhaps because it would have been extremely expensive for

71 *Charles Francis Annesley Voysey. House design (published 1889)*

72 *George Devey. St. Albans Court, estate cottages (1870s–1880s)*

the amount of space it would have provided.

Devey had a quiet approach for cottages which was to be the foundation of Voysey's mature style. On the St. Alban's Court estate, where work was proceeding during Voysey's time in Devey's office, are several groups of cottages; they are the architectural forefathers of Voysey's small country houses. The floors are clearly delineated, usually by projecting the upper one; windows are in mullioned bands crammed up against the projection of the upper floor, the eaves or the projecting gables. Doors are simple, low and wide and the effect would be strongly horizontal but for the massive chimney stacks. The materials are quite different to the ones Voysey commonly used—Devey's cottages are covered in hung tiles, half-timbering and patterned brickwork. But imagine the effect of moving the mighty chimney stack round to the end of the cottage shown on p. 83, strip off the Old English clothing and replace it by roughcast and you have something very like a mature Voysey house.

Voysey's mature style began to emerge in 1888 when he published a design for a cottage in the *British Architect*. He had made the drawings in 1885 in the hope that he could build a house for himself and his new wife. The cottage was completely asymmetrical, long and low with its horizontality emphasized by recessing the ground floor. Its leaded windows were in long mullioned bands, the upper ones hard up against the wide eaves (themselves supported on delicate curved iron brackets) and the lower windows anchored visually between buttresses. The wide door (green in the original drawing) was recessed behind a Tudorish arch and balanced by a green water butt at the other end of the elevation. The whole composition is pinned down by a little tower over the stairs. The plan is economical; though long and thin, it is compact, with the major circulation space on the ground floor doubling as a "picture gallery and lounge".[4] It is the Arts and Crafts one-room-and-a-corridor plan in one of its most compressed forms.

All these themes were to be the basis of Voysey's later work*. His buildings were never symmetrical, for he was a firm believer in Ruskinian changefulness and praised Gothic architecture because "outside appearances are evolved from internal fundamental conditions; staircases and windows come where most convenient for use. All openings are proportioned to

the various parts to which they apply."[5] The horizontality of most of his work derived from a belief in the symbolic importance of long low straight lines: "When the sun sets horizontalism prevails, when we are weary we recline, and the darkness covers up the differences and hides all detail under one harmonious veil, while we, too, close our eyes for rest. What, then, is obviously necessary for the effect of repose in our houses, [is] to avoid angularity and complexity in colour, form or texture, and make our dominating lines horizontal rather than vertical."[6]

The buttresses of the lower floor were, so he claimed, the result of economy. In 1897, an article in the *Studio*, presumably published with his approval, explained that "Mr Voysey employs these buttresses to save the cost of thicker walls for the lower storey of his buildings. That they chance to afford pleasant-looking shelters for a garden seat and break up the wall-surface happily, giving the facade a certain architectural pattern of shadows he realizes, and is, beyond doubt delighted by the picturesque qualities . . . [But] Mr Voysey would no more dream of adding a superfluous buttress than he would add an unnecessary panel of cheap ornament."[7] The roughcast, too, was an economy. Horace Townsend explained in another *Studio* article (Voysey was a favourite of the magazine from its foundation) that "Mr Voysey's preference for [roughcast] . . . which is marked by the way—is based, so he tells me, mainly on its economy. He considers a nine inch brick wall faced with cement rough-cast is as warm and weather-tight as any much more expensive construction."[8]

The wide door had particular symbolic importance for Voysey who believed that doors should be "wide in proportion to height, to suggest welcome—not stand-offishly dignified, like the coffin lid, high and narrow for the entrance of one body only."[9]

And the long, thin Arts and Crafts plan was adopted partly because of his belief that servants should not be kept in dungeons as was common in many Victorian houses. "In offices for servants' use, let them be cheerful, and not shabby and dark, as if it did not matter how you treated your servants because you were paying for their services. Some day men will be ashamed to do ugly things and cheap and nasty treatment of servants will be regarded as dishonouring to the master."[10]

In 1888, the immediate result of publication of the design was Voysey's first important commission—for a similar cottage at Bishop's Itchington, Warwickshire which, when built, was quite like the original,

---

* I have been free in juxtaposing Voysey's opinions of different dates in the quotations which follow, because, once he had achieved maturity, his ideas and architecture changed little. The quotations are chosen as the most apt expressions of often uttered beliefs.

73 *Voysey. Cottage design (1885)*

74 *Voysey. Cottage, Bishop's Itchington, Warwickshire (1888)*

75 *Voysey. Walnut Tree Farm, Castlemorton, Hereford and Worcester (1890)*

76 *Voysey. Tower house, Bedford Park, London (1891)*

though the half-timbering was omitted, a projecting porch added and the eaves line was broken by hipped dormer windows over the principal upstairs rooms.

Voysey was off, and, during the next twenty years, he built a multitude of houses, most of which used the themes he had brought together at Bishop's Itchington. There were, of course, exceptions: a charming little tower house for a narrow site in Bedford Park (1891), some flats in Hans Road (see page 120), and there was a curious flirtation with classical detailing in the late '90s in houses like New Place, Haslemere (1897). But all these buildings bear a Voysey stamp.

The basic vocabulary was gradually added to and refined. Voysey's next commission after Bishop's Itchington was Walnut Tree Farm (now Bannut Tree Farm) at Castlemorton near Malvern (designed 1890), where the roof pitch is increased to 45° and the eaves are pulled down to the bottom of the first floor

77 *Voysey. Sketch for a house on the Hog's Back, near Guildford, Surrey (1896)*

windows, which are expressed as a series of gables. This gives a much greater expanse of roof and reduces the apparent height—a device used in many of Voysey's later buildings, in which steep sweeping roofs united quite complicated plans and sections, for instance in the beautiful Sturgis House (1896) on the Hogs Back near Guildford (ruined by Herbert Baker's 1913 additions). Tucked under the first floor at the east end of Walnut Tree Farm is the half octagonal bay of the morning room, the first of a series of octagonal, polygonal and semi-circular bays, often capped by the projecting horizontal of a first floor but sometimes allowed to crash up through the eaves to end up as a kind of dormer (for instance at Broadleys, Windermere, 1896). Walnut Tree Farm shows Voysey's last extensive use of half-timbering which he abandoned because "bureaucratic bye-laws" necessitated half-timbering to be executed as boarding on rendered brickwork which Voysey

78 *Voysey. Broadleys, Windermere, Cumbria (1896)*

79 *Voysey. Perrycroft, Colwall, Hereford and Worcester (1893–1894), garden front from south-west*

refused to use because it was a sham.[11]

Perrycroft at Colwall in the Malvern Hills (designed 1893–1894) was Voysey's first large commission and shows his mature style to perfection with buttresses rising the full height of the walls to the wide eaves which cover the shallow bays in front of the principal bedrooms. The hipped roof is of green Westmorland slates (a favourite Voysey material), penetrated by big, tapering rectangular chimneys (the chimney pots are modern).

The entrance side has an open porch shielding double doors with long strap hinges. Lighting the first floor corridor is a long band of small paned windows just under the eaves. The composition is pinned down by a little tower, capped by a lead covered ogee-shaped roof with a weathercock on a high slender spike.

The siting is very carefully considered with bays and seats built between the buttresses to take advantage of the magnificent views over the green hills to the south-west and north-west. Voysey was always very considerate of his sites. "The character of the site", he wrote, "will suggest many limitations and conditions as to aspect and prospect. The contour of the ground obviously controls the arrangement, and

the colour, shape and texture of hills and trees suggest the colour, form and texture of our building. That is, provided we have no preconceived notions of classical *façades*, or a deep rooted preference for a particular style of architecture."[12]

The remarks about the locality determining the colour and texture of the building may seem odd in a man who was prepared to bring Westmorland slates to Herefordshire, but Voysey, always a symbolist, was making a visual analogue with the smooth green shapes of the hills themselves. At least he avoided the paradox of Prior's Home Place—a building created out of materials from the very site itself but which manages to look extraordinarily foreign.

Yet after a while, Voysey became trapped by his own style. The *Studio* reported in 1904 that "it is a matter of regret to the artist should a client insist on having what he or she deems a thoroughly characteristic house instead of one more properly native to the soil."[13] He was certainly prepared to exploit local materials—for instance where he could get really good brick as in the Wentworth Arms, Elmesthorpe, Leicestershire (1895), he left it exposed. He made designs for houses in local stone (mostly unbuilt) and, at Hill Close near Studland, Dorset (1896), he used

80 *Perrycroft, north (entrance) front*

81 *Voysey. House at Glassonby, Cumberland (1898), unexecuted—Voysey would have liked to use local materials where they were suitable and the client could afford them*

rough-hewn Portland stone round the windows and large local stone flags on the roof.

Hill Close was designed for the Edwardian animal painter, Alfred Suto, and had a large studio with a great window (sadly now replaced by modern patent glazing) looking out over the magnificent view over Studland Bay and Poole Harbour. The studio itself was a high room with a little library gallery over the door.* Most Voysey rooms were much lower, like the Hill Close dining room, which is not much more than eight feet high and which looks lower because of its deep plaster frieze of stylized trees. Voysey believed that "an eight foot room may be better ventilated and more comfortable to live in than a room twelve or fifteen feet and high and is certainly more easy to light and warm"[14]—because the lower ceiling reflected more light to the back of the room and so obviated the need for large areas of glass. The cold from large windows could lead to unsightly horrors, "hot water pipes and various demonical contrivances for heating . . . like tombs to the memory of cremated air".[15] (Voysey usually relied on open fires for heating with special connections to the outside air to provide drafts for the chimneys and to avoid them in the rooms.)

Voysey's objections to central heating were largely aesthetic. He believed that most contemporary commercial artefacts were hideously ugly, and, given a chance, he would, like Webb, design everything for a house from the forks to the door hinges. His ideal was "a well proportioned room, with whitewashed walls, plain carpet and simple oak furniture, and nothing in it but necessary articles of use, and one pure ornament in the form of a simple vase of flowers."[16]

This image of a white box containing a few exquisite objects seems strange from the man who was one of the most successful wallpaper designers of the turn of the century. He explained that "a wallpaper is of course only a background, and were your furniture good in form and colour a very simple or quite undecorated treatment of the walls would be preferable; but as most modern furniture is vulgar or bad in every way, elaborate papers of many colours help to disguise its ugliness."[17] Voysey was rather less extreme in practice and, for instance, used his wallpapers in the house he designed for his wife at Chorleywood (1899), where, presumably, he did like the furniture.

To achieve the simple effects he wanted, Voysey had to go to some trouble, particularly at first. In the Bedford Park tower house, "it was found necessary, in order to prevent the builder from displaying the usual 'ovulo mouldings', 'stop chamfers', fillets, and the like, to prepare eighteen sheets of contract drawings to show where his beloved ornamentation *was to be omitted* . . . Great pains have to be taken to prevent the workmen from unconscious 'decoration' as is their wonted habit".[18]

Voysey had firmly resolved the Puginian paradox in favour of the designer rather than the craftsman and he was also prepared to accept the machine—but tentatively, rather as Pugin himself had accepted it. "The human quality in familiar objects has in many cases been driven out by the machine. Nevertheless, the machine has come to liberate men's minds for more intellectual work than was provided for them by the sawpit."[19] But he was insistent that "we are far too keen on mechanical perfection. That love of smooth, polished surfaces is very materialistic [a quality that Voysey abhorred]; it can be produced without brains and in most cases can only be produced by the elimination of all human thought and feeling."[20]

From the earliest years, Voysey enlivened the austerity of his houses with occasional jokey details: the brackets bent to form his clients' profiles, and little grotesque finials, caricatures of the architect or his client. They were the echoes of Ruskinian savageness in the work of a man who designed every detail.

As he grew older, he became increasingly hostile to machine production. John Betjeman, who as a young editor of the *Architectural Review* rediscovered Voysey in virtual retirement in the early '30s, recalled that "he disliked machinery as 'unnatural' and would always advocate the use of craftsmen—from the craftsman who made his pipes to those who built his houses."[21]

But Voysey rarely had an opportunity to use craftsmanship lavishly. He was, after all, building houses that "compare favourably in cost with the miserable shams of the jobbing builder,"[22] and, as a Tory, he believed that there were certain qualities that were "essential to all classes of homes, but there are certain other qualities like grandeur, splendour, pomp, majesty and exuberance which are suitable only to comparatively few. In the category of general need, we should put repose, cheerfulness, simplicity, breadth, warmth, quietness in storm, economy of up-keep, evidence of protection, harmony with surroundings, absence of dark passages or places, even-

---

* Alexander Hamilton Fletcher has pointed out to me that the original gallery has been replaced with woodwork taken from Austin Reed's shop in Exeter.

82 *Voysey. Hill Close, Studland, Dorset (1896)*

83 *Hill Close, dining room. The frieze is original; the furnishings (including the light fitting) are modern*

84 *Voysey. Charles Voysey's House, Platt's Lane, Hampstead, London (1895)*

85 *Voysey. Spade House, Sandgate, Folkestone, Kent (1899), for H. G. Wells.
The nearest bay is a 1903 addition by Voysey*

ess of temperature."[23] But where he did have what he believed to be an appropriate client, Voysey was prepared to indulge in some splendour and exuberance—for instance in his design for a house for the Earl of Lovelace (1894–5), where the white walls are relieved by a bay with carved ornament. It was not built, nor did he ever build a big house for a grandee.

His clients were generally comfortably off members of the middle class like his own father, for whom he built a house in Platt's Lane, Hampstead (1895), and H. G. Wells, then a rising young left wing novelist, who, in 1899, chose Voysey as the "pioneer in the escape from the small snobbish villa residence to the bright and comfortable pseudo cottage."[24] In Wells, incidentally, Voysey for once had a client as strong minded as he was about some aspects of design. "Voysey wanted to put a large heart shaped letter plate on my front door [by then virtually a Voysey trademark], but I protested at wearing my heart so conspicuously outside and we compromised on a spade"[25] (i.e., by turning the heart upside down). Despite disagreements, the two must have remained on good terms, as Voysey was asked to add an extra bay in 1903.

Voysey's way of building could cope with almost any problem. The Platts Lane house shows how his style could be accommodated to a small suburban plot (by running an L-shaped plan along the north and east sides of the site and by putting the entrance facing south-west in the angle so that all the rooms had a sunny orientation). Wells's Spade House, on the cliff top at Sandgate in Kent, reveals how Voysey could run his buildings up a quite steeply sloping site.

He could even, without too much difficulty, adapt his style to a factory for Sandersons, the wallpaper

86 *Voysey. Factory for Sanderson & Sons, Chiswick, London (1902)*

manufacturers, at Chiswick (1902), with white glazed brick piers taking the place of buttresses and big small-paned windows with white spandrels between them. (The tops of the piers, which also act as ventilation shafts, are reminiscent of Voysey's furniture, complete with little Mackmurdoish capitals.)

And the technique could be adapted to quite large housing schemes—for example the row of cottages at Whitwood, Yorkshire (1904–1905) in which pairs of cottages with low walls and hipped dormers in the roof are set in a terrace between seven cottages with big gables facing the road. The planning is extremely economical in circulation space and yet commodious in living area; the cottages must have been extremely desirable miners' residences (the complex was built for Briggs & Sons colliery). The terrace is dominated by the tower of the miners' institute, which is topped by simple crenellations.

This was one of the first instances of overt Gothic detailing which developed after 1905 in Voysey's work, perhaps as a counter-blast to the growing popu-

87 *Voysey. Miners' cottages, Whitwood, Yorkshire (designed 1904–1905)*

88 *Voysey. Coombe Down, near Bath, Avon (1909)*

larity of the classical styles that were becoming popular. By 1909 he was designing a stone courtyard house for Coombe Down near Bath in which almost every detail was taken from Tudor precedents. But there, the client, T. S. Cotterell, had particularly requested something to remind him of his old college, Merton, and Voysey's white houses continued in a thin trickle until they ceased with High Gault, St. Margaret's-at-Cliffe, Kent in 1914. Voysey, though he lived to 1941, built nothing after the First War apart from a couple of alterations and some war memorials. Yet he continued to design, in Gothic and Tudor; and even produced an unbuilt Tudor tower block scheme in 1923.

Increasingly, he thought of himself as one of the last disciples of Pugin and Ruskin. He echoed Pugin (p. 12) in calling for a real English architecture. "Why . . . should England turn her back on her own country and pretend that she is such a born mongrel she can have no truly national architecture? Has she no national climate? Are her geological and geographical conditions the same as all other countries? Is there no difference between English and Italian men? . . . No one denies strong national character to the British people. Why, then, do we so persistently try to ape the manners of foreigners?"[26] But, at the same time, he was a total individualist who despised excessive reverence for tradition, believing that "if we are to try and harmonize with the laws of Nature and help her to progress we must leave the door perpetually open to progress and welcome (critically if you like) all attempts to improve our traditional modes and methods, whatever they may be."[27]

His was such a strong character that he was accused of not allowing his clients' personalities to influence their houses. There is some truth in the allegation. Voysey wrote to his client, Cecil Fitch, "all artistic questions you must trust me to decide. No two minds ever produced an artistic result."[28] But he was loved; in reply to a wounding article about his relationships with his clients published after a retrospective exhibition of his work organized by Betjeman in 1931, Voysey wrote to the RIBA librarian, "out of two hundred and forty-six clients I have worked for, fifty-three have returned with fresh commissions, and I have built a hundred and eight private houses, only one of which I should care to live in, and that is the house I built for my wife."[29] It was an unusually good record.

His last years were fraught with money worries. (As early as the First War he had to approach James

Morton, who printed many of his fabrics, for financial assistance.[30]) But he ended life as a Civil List pensioner and a pensioner of the Royal Academy and of the RIBA,[31] which, with fees and royalties for his designs, helped him keep afloat.

Gordon Russell remembered him in the early '20s. Voysey had only one job: "It's a house for a lunatic", he said, "such a nice man, and his doctor thought he might take an interest in the building of it. But I find it difficult. None of my friends can tell me how to deal with a client who, when the contract should be signed, gets under the table and refuses to come out."[32] Not surprisingly, the commission came to nothing.

His spirit was unimpaired. Betjeman gave a beautiful obituary picture of a man who changed little once he reached maturity. "He was a little below middle height and with an ascetic, clean shaven countenance . . . His dress was of his own design. He wore dark suits with no lapels to the coat, blue shirts and collars and a tie through a gold ring. He was always scrupulously neat and clean and his appearance never altered for all the time I knew him. He took snuff and smoked clay pipes that were made at a curious old pipe hospital in Soho."[33] Robert Donat, who married Voysey's niece, recalled, "You may have got the impression that butter wouldn't melt in his mouth. It certainly wouldn't unless it happened to be the very best butter. But if there was the slightest defect in the butter I'm afraid, without more ado, he would have spat it out. He liked only the best of everything."[34]

Kindly, austere, witty, argumentative, childlike, Voysey believed to his dying day in his father's good God and that "simplicity, sincerity, repose, directness and frankness are moral qualities as essential to good architecture as to good men."[35]

1 Much background information on Voysey is given in two essays by Brandon-Jones, John, in "C. F. A. Voysey: a memoir", *Architectural Association Journal*, London, 1957 (the pages are unnumbered) and in *C. F. A. Voysey: Architect and Designer*, Lund Humphries, London 1978. The latter is the catalogue of the 1978 exhibition held in the Brighton Art Gallery and Museum.
2 Quoted by Brandon-Jones, J. in *Architectural Association Journal, op. cit.*, p. 241
3 *British Architect*, Vol. XXXI, 1889, p. 248
4 *British Architect*, Vol. XXX, 1888, p. 407
5 Voysey, C. F. A. "The English Home" in the *British Architect*, Vol. LXXV, 1911, p. 60
6 Voysey, C. F. A. *Individuality*, Chapman & Hall, London 1915, p. 111
7 *Studio*, Vol. XI, 1897, p. 20
8 Townsend, Horace "Notes on country and suburban houses designed by C. F. A. Voysey" in *Studio*, Vol. XVI, 1899, p. 158

9 Voysey, C. F. A. "The English Home", *op. cit*, p. 70
10 *Ibid.*
11 *Studio*, Vol. XXXI, 1904, p. 128
12 Voysey, C. F. A. *Reason as a Basis of Art*, Elkin Matthews, London 1906, p. 11
13 Vallance, Aymer "Some recent work by Mr C. R. A. Voysey", *Studio*, Vol. XXXI, 1904, p. 127
14 Voysey, C. F. A. "Remarks on domestic entrance halls", *Studio*, Vol. XXI, 1901, p. 243
15 *Ibid.*, p. 244
16 Voysey, C. F. A. "The English Home", *op. cit.*, p. 69
17 "An interview with Mr Charles F. Annesley Voysey, architect and designer", *Studio*, Vol. I, 1893, p. 233
18 *Studio*, Vol. XI, 1897, p. 25
19 Voysey, C. F. A. "Ideas in things", one of a series of essays in *The Arts connected with Building*, ed. Davison, Raffles, Batsford, London 1909, p. 107. The essays were a series of lectures given to the Carpenters' Company.
20 *Ibid.*
21 *Architects' Journal*, Vol. CXIII, 1941, pp. 193–194
22 *Studio*, Vol. XI, 1897, p. 16

23 Voysey, C. F. A. "The English Home", *op cit.*, p. 69
24 Wells, H. G. *Experiment in Autobiography*, Victor Gollancz, republished 1966, p. 638
25 *Ibid.*
26 Voysey, C. F. A. "The English Home", *op. cit.*, p. 60
27 Voysey, C. F. A. "Tradition and individuality in art" 1928, unpublished paper in RIBA Library
28 Voysey to Cecil Fitch, December 4th, 1899. Published by John Brandon-Jones in a collection of correspondence in the *Architect and Building News*, Vol. CXCV, 1949, pp. 494–8.
29 Voysey to Edward Carter, October 21st 1931. Manuscript in the RIBA library
30 Morton, Jocelyn *Three Generations in a Family Textile Firm*, Routledge & Kegan Paul, London 1971, p. 286
31 *The Times*, 13 February, 1941
32 Russell, Gordon *Designer's Trade* Allen and Unwin, London 1968, p. 126
33 Betjeman, John *Architects' Journal*, Vol. XCIII, 1941, pp. 257–258
34 Donat, Robert *Architects' Journal*, Vol. XCIII, 1941, pp. 193–194
35 Voysey, C.F.A. "The English Home", *op. cit.*, p. 69

89 *Voysey. High Gault, St. Margaret's-at-Cliffe, Kent (1914)*

9 Into the Country

"There is still much of the peasant in every Englishman", wrote Muthesius, "although in England, of course, the peasant as a class has practically disappeared from the scene. But the natural, unaffected intelligence, the generous dose of common-sense, that we find in the Englishman, his fondness for his native place with its fields and ploughed land, his love of fresh air and open country—all this shows that some of the best qualities of the country-dweller have persisted in him. In no country in the world has so strong a sense of the natural and the rural been passed down to modern times as in the land of the greatest traditional wealth . . . Naturalness makes up the best part of the Englishman's character. And we see this character in its present-day form reflected in the English house more truly and clearly, perhaps, than in any other manifestation of English culture."[1]

Nowhere is Muthesius's idealized portrait of the English country house as the flower of national culture more true than in the work of Lethaby, Prior and Voysey, their contemporaries and followers. Their patrons were the upper middle classes; they rarely built big houses for really grand aristocracy or for the most flamboyant members of the new plutocracy. Nor were they often hired by the burgeoning late Victorian public and private institutions. The irony of Morris and Webb, both convinced socialists, being forced to work solely for the rich was echoed in the lives of their disciples, however much some of the younger men lacked their masters' political commitment.

They had to work for the most economically free people. For late Victorians one of the greatest freedoms was cheap and efficient public transport which had enabled the middle classes to move away from town centres, so their architects were usually required to build in the country or the suburbs. It is most unusual to find an Arts and Crafts house more than a couple of miles from a Victorian railway station. When Holmes and Watson were not wheeling up to a real medieval house in the station fly, they were approaching an Arts and Crafts version.

For the landed class, employing an Arts and Crafts architect to modernize country houses was a matter of course, unless a big ostentatious splash was wanted. For instance, in 1888, when Lord Redesdale, the grandfather of the Mitfords, decided to renovate his country seat, he employed Arts and Crafts forerunner Ernest George. But in his exhaustive memoirs, in which no opportunity of dropping a name was lost, Redesdale merely remarked, "I was now a free man, and . . . I sold my London house, took possession of Batsford and made up my mind to become a country squire."[2] There is no mention of the architect or his works.

Yet for less grand people, the image of the Arts and Crafts house with its calm, uncluttered interiors and rambling, steep-roofed exterior, quietly fitting into the countryside, was more important. It was exactly appropriate for a middle class aspiring to the landed values of the aristocracy. Vera Ryder was brought up in Copseham at Esher, a house which her father, a wealthy city businessman, had ramblingly altered by Guy Dawber.* A new nursery wing [was] added, with schoolroom, pantry and servants' hall. The old dining room and the drawing room . . . [were] made into one big dining-room. Finally a music room . . . was built at right angles to the drawing room and gave an imposing delightful finish to the place.

"The music room was a good room for sound with its high vaulted ceiling, and it was the focal point of our activities, both solemn and frivolous. Mother had no use for a drawing room as such, it would have

---

* Dawber was incidentally Sir Ernest George's site clerk at Batsford before starting his own practice (p. 103).

cramped her style. For Mother . . . had big ideas; there was nothing immature about her inspirations. She needed a place to entertain her friends with no restrictions and no cluttering up with the usual drawing room knick-knacks."[3]

Another, less relaxed aspect of middle class Arts and Crafts living was satirized by E. F. Benson in his description of the home of his heroine, super-snob Lucia Lucas, whose house, The Hurst, was in a village which suspiciously resembles Broadway in the Cotswolds. It "presented a charmingly irregular and picturesque front". It was formed of three cottages: "Two were of the grey stone of the district, and the middle one, to the door of which led the paved path, of brick and timber. Latticed windows with stout mullions gave illumination to the room within [which had panelled walls and a white-washed ceiling with exposed beams] . . . To the original windows certain new lights had been added; these could be detected by the observant eye, for they had a markedly older appearance than the rest. The front door, similarly, seemed amazingly antique, the fact being that the one which Mrs Lucas had found there was too dilapidated . . . She had therefore caused to be constructed an even older one made from oak planks in a dismantled barn, and had it studded with large worn nails of antique patterns fashioned by the village blacksmith . . . Over the door hung an inn-sign, and into the space where once the sign had swung was now inserted a lantern, in which was ensconced, well hidden from view by its patinated glass sides, an electric light."[4] Lucia Luca's rich husband was, incidentally, the founder of a hand printing press at "Ye Sign of Ye Daffodil" on the village green which existed mainly to print his prose poems "in blunt type on thick yellowish paper". This kind of behaviour was enough to give the Arts and Crafts movement a bad name; for several decades after the First War, "Arty Crafty" was synonymous with twee gentility.

The Arts and Crafts country house image was immensely influential on the upper middle class, and not only at home. In America, the great nineteenth-century cities all have their complement of Arts and Crafts suburbs. In 1904, Langford Warren commented in the Boston *Architectural Review* that "it is not too much to say that no other nation has succeeded in developing a domestic architecture having the subtle and intimate charm which in the English country house makes so strong an appeal to the love of home as well as to the love of beauty." Warren's article, which showed the work of Ernest George,

Voysey and other contemporary English architects, praised the "notable revivication of the old traditions and . . . application of the old forms to the needs of modern domestic life."[5] And he was quite clear that "our own best work, like that of England, will be done by founding it on the sound traditions of England's past, modifying these traditions frankly and fearlessly in the spirit of the old work to meet our new wants and new conditions."[6]

The blend of English tradition and modernity had its adherents on the Continent too. Muthesius worked for years on his monumental book which so thoroughly expounded British domestic architecture to the German speaking world. The book's influence can be seen all over northern Europe in country houses reminiscent of England.

Even in provincial little Switzerland, industrialist Theodor Bühler was so impressed with the style that he hired the English architect Baillie Scott to create a house which "should have the charm of a country seat . . . the general aspect of the house I should like to be simple, quiet and yet artistic, the facade not too irregular."[7] The result was a perfect Arts and Crafts manor complete with gables, half-timbering, roughcast, ashlar, leaded lights and a tall tiled roof which still stands at Uzwil today, a piece of turn-of-century England transported to east Switzerland.

At home, the relaxed changeful Arts and Crafts country houses eventually became so closely identified with the values of the upper middle class that they became anathema to anyone with a claim to being in the forefront of taste. When H. G. Wells commissioned Voysey to design what Henry James called his "stately treasure house on the sea shore"[8] in 1899, it was as a rebellion against the "small snobbish villa residence". But, a dozen years later, when Roger Fry, the critic and art impressario who mounted the first post-impressionist exhibition in London, was showing Viginia Woolf the Surrey landscape, he burst out, "My house is neighboured by houses of the most gentlemanly picturesqueness, houses from which tiny gables with window slits jut out at any unexpected angle." Their path "avoided these gentlemanly residences, but his talk did not altogether avoid the inhabitants of those houses—their snobbery, their obtuseness, their complacency and their complete indifference to any kind of art."[9]

If the clients were obtuse and indifferent, the architects did not follow them. Quietly they fostered the ancient traditions of craftsmanship; faithfully they followed Ruskin's injunction to let appearance be determined by the plan; sensitively they obeyed Pugin's dictum that architecture should reflect its locality.

If between 1900 and 1910 you had taken a balloon from Brighton and floated north-west above England, you would have seen drift after drift of Arts and Crafts buildings: first the large houses of wealthy City men on the Surrey ridge between Guildford and Redhill, then, passing the metropolis, there was another belt of brick and tile houses in south Hertfordshire and Middlesex. Further north, a pattern emerged, each large town had a crescent of suburbs, usually running from south-west to north to take advantage of the prevailing winds which blew urban smoke away to the east. In north Oxford, the more adventurous dons were living in Arts and Crafts houses, and little Naomi Mitchison was envying the newest houses "with lower ceilings and more bay windows with smaller panes which I thought much nicer than our own big sash windows."[10]

In Birmingham, rich business men were building some of England's most beautiful suburbs at Four Oaks and Sutton Coalfield. Away to the east, a strong telescope might have picked out the summer cottages of Leicester magnates built on the edge of the Charnwood forest. Near Manchester, there was Middleton and in Leeds the newly developed suburbs of Adel and Roundhay. Then north again to the wastes of the Scottish border with a glance at the retreats of rich Lancashire cotton men in the Lakes. Beyond, in Glasgow, the same pattern was repeated, with new, adventurous houses springing up to the north west and on the banks of the Clyde.

Between these major cities, and always near to the knots of the Victorian railway network which knitted the country in a ravelled pattern, were the larger country mansions, the artists' houses and the estate cottages from which so many Arts and Crafts architects derived their income. Here and there was a new church or a village hall, the public works of the richer private house patrons.

In this chapter, the balloon, taking a much more errant course in space and time, descends now and then to give closer glimpses of the country work of the Arts and Crafts men. Ernest Newton leads, partly because his career, as a founder-member of the Art Workers' Guild who developed a flourishing practice, shows the pattern for many successful architects of his generation, and partly because his work is brilliant and its delicacy, respect for tradition and gentle innovation are typical of Arts and Craftsmen in the country. After Newton, the glimpses are alphabetical.

Ernest Newton (1856–1922) was Lethaby's predecessor as Norman Shaw's chief clerk and one of the founder members of the Art Workers' Guild. His work spans from the year he left Shaw, 1879, to the War, and virtually all of it was in the country. He started with quite small suburban houses in Shaw's Old English style, but as his practice grew he adopted two styles, one derived from Tudor and vernacular models, the other from Georgian.

Buller's Wood at Chislehurst, Kent (1889) is an early and large example of the first manner. He surrounded a stuccoed early Victorian house with a brick building with strong stone string courses; leaded, stone mullioned windows; crow-stepped gables and tall rectangular chimneys. At Redcourt, near Haselmere, Surrey (1894) he was much more formal with round-topped sash windows set into a Georgian brick carapace. The elevations are at first glance symmetrical, and only a vestige of almost wilful Ruskinian changefulness keeps them from being totally so.

90 *Ernest Newton. Buller's Wood, Chislehurst, Kent (1889)*

91 *Newton. Redcourt, Haslemere, Surrey (1894)*

In the next decade Newton was producing completely symmetrical elevations, for instance at Luckley, Wokingham, Berkshire (1907), a charming mixture of Wrenian roof and cornice on top of low brick walls relieved by leaded lights in wooden casements. Yet Luckley retains the thin room-and-corridor Arts and Crafts plan, cunningly bent into an H shape, and the symmetry is relieved by a service wing which cranks round from the main entrance to the west.

92 *Newton. Luckley, Wokingham, Berkshire (1907)*

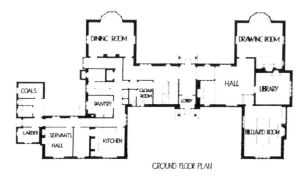

GROUND FLOOR PLAN

93 *Luckley, ground floor plan*

94 *Newton. Upton Grey Manor, Hampshire (1907)*

Newton was at his most relaxed when adding to old houses—for example Upton Grey Manor, Hampshire (1907), built for the editor of the *Studio*, where he added traditional half-timbering and tile hanging in exactly the spirit of the original building. He did the same at Oldcastle, Dallington, Sussex (1910) to produce a late (for Newton) irregular, asymmetrical complex of breathtaking horizontal sweep and simplicity; the brick ground floor is topped by a tile-hung first floor, with the tile roof cramming hard down over the eaves and sometimes swooping down to top the bricks. Again, it was an extension to an old house from which Newton adapted idioms. At Oldcastle, the servants' quarters were cranked right round a courtyard with the corridor on the inside. Newton used this device again in his most formal house—Burgh Heath, Surrey (1912) where, without an old model to develop, he created an almost Palladian front for the main rooms in totally symmetrical ashlar relieved by knapped flint wings. But the house is as usual thin, and all the offices are stuck out in a great quadrangular block at one side surrounding a glazed courtyard.

However symmetrical, however Palladian, Newton became, the plan was always paramount; Pugin's principles were never forgotten. "I emphasize the plan," he wrote "as that is really the house . . . Building must fall into some sort of style—memory, inherited forms, and ideas. But this must be accepted, not sought. Pass all through the mill of your mind and don't use forms unmeaningly, like the buttons on the back of a coat."[11]

BEDFORD & KITSON

The firm of Bedford and Kitson was as influential in creating the new suburbs of Leeds as Bidlake in Birmingham or Wood in Manchester. Muthesius commented that "their exteriors are more or less traditional in design, but inside they experiment in more independent ways, though without becoming fantastic ... and give an impression of quiet refinement."[12] They were free eclectics, drawing on both local and southern models and were early into the game of reintroducing classical idioms.

96 *William Bidlake. Woodgate, Four Oaks, Birmingham (1902 or before)*

95 *Bedford & Kitson. Red House, Chapel Allerton, Leeds (before 1904)*

Francis W. Bedford (1866–1904) was articled in Leeds and was an assistant to Ernest George & Peto before returning there. After his early death Sydney Kitson (1871–1937) gradually devoted himself to scholarship and collecting. He retired young.

WILLIAM BIDLAKE

"There is probably no architect in Birmingham who has influenced and guided the younger men of his profession to the same extent as Mr W. B. Bidlake," reported the *Studio* in 1902.[13] By then, Bidlake (1862–1938) had been teaching at Birmingham's architecture school for ten years after training in Bodley's office and being Pugin Scholar in 1885.

He set a tone of simplicity and restraint in the great suburban expansion of Birmingham round the turn of the century. His models were vernacular but he avoided "the suburban villa with samples of every manner of building—brick, half-timber, tile hanging and roughcast".[14] His houses had strong shapes, usually restricted to a combination of two main materials:

brick and stone; roughcast and brick; tile hanging and half-timbering. His St. Agatha's church at Sparkbrook has this same restraint in the use of materials but is relieved by bands of joyous carving.

REGINALD BLOMFIELD

Reginald Blomfield (1856–1942), though he became the arch-protagonist of classicism in the early years of this century (chapter 12), was much involved in the Arts and Crafts movement. He was one of the young men who gravitated to the Lethaby/Prior circle in the '80s and he was involved, with Lethaby, in Kenton & Co, the short-lived Arts and Crafts furniture firm (Chapter 11). For all his love of classical architecture he was prepared to compromise in the country. Even as late as 1909, long after he had started to preach the virtues of the Beaux Arts, he designed Wyphurst near Cranleigh, Surrey, a very complicated mixture of an existing house with a large new wing, all in diapered brickwork and half-timbering. It is a symmetrical Victorian Tudor building struggling to emerge from a vernacular complex of gables and hung tiles.

DETMAR BLOW

Detmar Blow (1867–1939) met Ruskin as a young man and was introduced to the Morris circle. He was Pugin Scholar of the Institute in 1892. In the late '90s

97 *Detmar Blow. Happisburgh Manor, Cromer, Norfolk (1900)*

he was Gimson's site clerk on the wonderfully rustic Stoneywell cottage (Chapter 11). In 1900 he built Happisburgh Manor on the sea-front near Cromer in Norfolk, a butterfly plan which geometrically out-Priors Prior's nearby (and slightly later) butterfly house at Holt by making the house angled on all four sides like an X with a stretched centre. Incidentally, Blow claimed that the inspiration for Happisburgh did not come from Prior's Exmouth Barn but "originated with my friend Mr Ernest Gimson who sent the little butterfly device on a postcard".[15]

He was as faithful to local materials as Prior but used them in a more conventional local fashion—thick flint walls are patterned and quoined in brick and capped by a thick thatched roof.

Blow's work during the next decade moved from a free interpretation of local idioms towards classicism of various kinds. By the '20s he had an extremely successful practice which built throughout the Empire—for instance Government House in Salisbury, Rhodesia. He was surveyor to the Grosvenor Estate for seventeen years, encouraging creeping neo-Georgianism over Mayfair. He died as the Lord of the Manor of Painswick, Gloucestershire.

W. H. BRIERLEY

Walter Henry Brierley (1862–1926) was articled to his father in York and his mature practice was conducted there. He ranged from country houses which freely interpreted local idiom through neo-classical banks to Gothic churches and to racecourse buildings. His obituary in the *Builder* aptly summarizes the influence of Arts and Crafts thinking on a successful provincial practitioner: "He was a master of detail,

and upheld the principle that no single item, however small, in the composition of a building was outside the scope of the architect's most scrupulous care and consideration. He insisted on the employment of the very best materials and workmanship that the means placed at his disposal allowed. He had a great admiration of the craftsmanship of the past, and skilfully

98 *W. H. Brierley. Bishopsbarns, Yorkshire, from south-east*

employed and adapted old methods . . . directing and interesting the workmen, and encouraging them to revive forgotten details of their craft, in order to secure that harmony between the design and execution of it on which the successful portrayal of his ideas so much depended."[16]

WALTER CAVE

Walter Frederick Cave (1863–1939) was an archetypal hearty Edwardian. The son of a baronet, he was articled to Sir Arthur Blomfield (Reginald's uncle). He built many robust country houses, usually in local materials. Muthesius likened him to Voysey and thought that "the external appearance of his houses is almost more successful than Voysey's; his

99 *Walter Cave. Dixcote, Streatham*

surfaces have a broader sweep and the whole is more expressive.''[17] His furniture was highly regarded.

His practice became very large and he had much urban work as well as the country houses for which he was best known.

GUY DAWBER

A King's Lynn man, Edward Guy Dawber (1862–1938) attended the Royal Academy Schools. He served his articles in Lynn and became an assistant to Ernest George & Peto, by whom he was sent, during a fit of bad sight in 1887 to be site clerk for building Batsford Park, Gloucestershire.[18]

100 *Guy Dawber. Caldicote Manor, Moreton in Marsh, Gloucestershire*

One of the first Arts and Craftsmen to discover the Cotswolds, he started his own practice two or three years later at Bourton-on-the-Hill, from where he walked miles to his first jobs—all informed by the vernacular building of the district and built on long, thin Arts and Crafts plans.

He went to London in 1891 but retained his Gloucestershire connection and became one of the most successful country house architects in England, well into the '20s, often adapting local idioms as well as the classical forms he increasingly preferred.

He was president of the RIBA in 1925–7 and founded the Council for the Preservation of Rural England.

W. A. FORSYTH

William Adam Forsyth (?–1951) was a distinguished preservationist and a devoted custodian of notable buildings like Salisbury Cathedral and St. George's Chapel, Windsor. His original work was often for

public schools ranging from Eton to Oundle where he usually offered heavy handed stripped variants of the Cotswold style. As a young man, he was inventive in garden design, and his work was illustrated by Mawson and Muthesius.

P. MORLEY HORDER

Percy Morley Horder (1870–1944) was trained in George Devey's office. He designed many large country houses and was a darling of the *Studio*. Some of his houses have characteristics in common with the work of Voysey—another product of the Devey office. But though Horder's buildings often have sweeping roofs, low eaves and rows of casement windows, houses like Spyways, Hartfield, Sussex, are more

101 *P. Morley Horder. Spyways, Hartfield, Sussex*

lush and jumbled that Voysey's and they are usually executed in local materials rather than Voysey's ubiquitous roughcast.

Horder's practice was varied and included much work for universities.

GERALD HORSLEY

The youngest of Norman Shaw's young men who founded the Art Workers' Guild, Gerald Callcott Horsley, the son of a painter, was born in 1862 and died early, in 1917. After being with Shaw, he worked for Sedding for a year before travelling to Italy and France in 1886 and to Sicily 1887–1888 (under RIBA studentships). He was a fine draughtsman and illustrated, among other books, Prior's *History of Gothic Art in England*. His own architectural work (1889 to his death) varied from romantic Old English country houses to Queen Anne buildings in town. As Arthur Keen, a fellow pupil in Shaw's office, remembered: "His regard for his master amounted almost to veneration and it led him, perhaps, into following the actual forms of Norman Shaw's work in preference to breaking new ground for himself, but he invested all that he touched with his own sense of beauty and fitness."[19]

His delicate individual touch is clear in his design for a country house (published in the *Builder*, LXVI, February 3, 1894) where sweeping hips and gables top walls of diapered brickwork, hung tiles and stone mullioned windows with leaded lights all relieved by large relief panels of Pre-Raphaelite pastoral scenes—few designs are closer to Morris's image of the Hammersmith Guest House.

The St. Paul's School for Girls, Hammersmith, (1904–1907), his chief London work, is Queen Anne at its most relaxed—ample, generous and much encrusted with the reliefs that his country clients could not afford.

102 *Gerald Horsley. Design for a country house (1894)*

ROBERT LORIMER

"Scotland will not achieve what England has already achieved—a completely national style of house-building based on the old vernacular architecture—until it follows the lead given by Lorimer."[20] Muthesius was as usual right. Robert Lorimer (1864–1929) was the father of a school of Scottish vernacular building much less original than Mackintosh's work but more faithful to traditional seventeenth- and eighteenth-century models.

Laverockdale, on the Pentlands near Edinburgh, is typical of Lorimer's large country houses. It is like a large border tower complete with crow-stepped gables and steep slated roofs, and small sash windows pocking the massive walls of local rubble. It has long thin Arts and Crafts wings.

103 *Robert Lorimer. Laverockdale near Edinburgh (before 1904)*

GEOFFREY LUCAS

Essentially a suburban architect, Thomas Geoffrey Lucas (1872–1947) built up a successful pre-War domestic and ecclesiastical practice north of London, where he built in Hampstead Garden Suburb, Ponders End and Broxbourne. In this period, he largely followed Gothic and vernacular forms. After the War, he went into partnership with the very successful H. V. Lanchester and was involved in designs for mighty classical civic buildings such as the University of Leeds. He left Lanchester for obscurity because, as the latter said, "the extent of our activities did not offer T. G. Lucas the scope he desired for giving an intensive study to specific undertakings."[21]

104 *Geoffrey Lucas. Housing (now Lucas Close), Hampstead Garden Suburb, north London*

MERVYN MACARTNEY

The least Ruskinian of Norman Shaw's young men who founded the Art Workers' Guild was Mervyn Edmund Macartney (1853–1932). The son of a Northern Irish doctor, he entered Shaw's office a year before Lethaby, with whom he was to be associated in Kenton & Co.

He started in practice in 1882 with a design for an Old English country house, Kent Hatch, and this vein persisted well into the 1900s with soft, gentle houses like Rosebank, Silchester Common, Hampshire. But he became a strong protagonist of conventional neo-Georgian, rarely achieving Newton's inventiveness in the style.

105 *Mervyn Macartney. Rosebank, Silchester Common, Hampshire (c. 1905)*

His *annus mirabilis* was 1906 when he beat Blomfield to the post of Architect to St. Paul's Cathedral and became editor of the *Architectural Review* in succession to a board which included Blomfield. The *Practical Exemplar of Architecture*, a series which showed "correct" eighteenth-century detailing, was published in the *Review* between 1906 and 1913 and become one of the most influential forces in the movement towards classicism.

CHARLES RENNIE MACKINTOSH

"The real driving force of the Scottish movement is Charles Rennie Mackintosh". According to Muthesius, the essence of the art of the Glasgow group "in fact rests in an underlying emotional and poetical quality. It seeks a highly charged . . . atmosphere of a mystical symbolic kind. One cannot imagine a greater contrast in this respect than that between the London architects working in the new forms, the most sedulous of whom is Voysey, and the Scottish architects round Mackintosh."[22]

Yet, according to F. H. Newbury, under whom Mackintosh studied at the Glasgow School of Art, Voysey was the young Mackintosh's chief inspiration.* Voysey himself disliked the work of the Glasgow artists and called them the "spook school", but elements of his work are clear in Mackintosh's country houses.

106 *Charles Rennie Mackintosh. Windyhill (1899–1901)*

107 *Mackintosh. Hill House, Helensburgh, Dunbartonshire (1902)*

The life of Mackintosh (1868–1928) has been so excellently told[23] that the career of the Glasgow policeman's son, who rose to such heroic European stature that he was dragged by students through the

---

* There is certainly a continuity in decorative elements like the long tapering verticals capped by wafer thin finials that stretches from Mackmurdo through Voysey to Mackintosh.

streets of Vienna in a flower covered carriage, does not need to be covered here.

His architectural genius flowered for only ten years from 1896 to about 1906, when it faded under the combined influence of work and whisky. During this period he built two outstanding country houses: Windyhill, Kilmalcolm, Renfrewshire (1899–1901) and Hill House, Helensburgh, Dunbartonshire (1902). Both derived much from Scottish eighteenth-century models and had slate roofs, white harlinged walls, drum stair towers and sash windows. Both had long thin Arts and Crafts plans. And both incorporated Voyseyish details—tall chimney stacks with sloping sides, strips of dormer windows (Windyhill only) and polygonal, projecting bay windows with leaded lights.

Yet the result was more changeful than anything Voysey ever wished to achieve after he had started to build. Hill House, particularly, achieved a stark vertical grandeur that is wholly Scottish yet quite original. The rooms were good but not especially remarkable for their period except that they were made magical by Mackintosh's incomparable furniture and ornament.

It was the sort of furniture and decoration that Mackintosh, his wife Margaret Macdonald and her sister Frances exhibited at the 1896 Arts and Crafts Exhibition Society show (the only time they entered). They were met with English incomprehension. The *Studio* commented that "no doubt in Glasgow there is a Rosetta stone, which makes clear the tangled meanings of these designs . . . One thing however is clear, that in their own way, unmoved by ridicule, or misconception, the Glasgow students have thought out a very fascinating scheme to puzzle, surprise and please."[24]

C. E. MALLOWS

A Bedford architect, Charles Edward Mallows (1864–1915) was deeply interested in garden design as well as building. He illustrated *Gardens for Small Country Houses* by Gertrude Jekyll and Lawrence Weaver and worked with Thomas Mawson on *The Art and Craft of Garden Making*. In partnership with various architects at different times, principally G. Grocock, Mallows executed numerous new country buildings as well as alterations and extensions to existing country houses all over the south of England. His work, as draftsman and architect, was always delicate and sensitive with deep respect for local tradition.

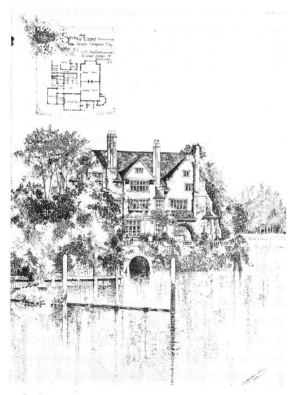

108 *Charles Edward Mallows. Design for a country house near Severn Upton (1888)*

ARNOLD MITCHELL

Arnold Mitchell (1863–1944) was trained under Sir Ernest George. He was a darling of the *Studio* in the first decade of this century, showing large country houses in England, Wales and Scotland, mostly with symmetrical elements, though he preferred variations on the typical Arts and Crafts plan. He moved from free interpretations of Tudor and vernacular motifs to almost proper Wren.

His practice became very large; he put up the main stations for the (British financed) Argentinian railways as well as buildings in Germany, Austria, Belgium and at the Asswan Dam. And he designed Lotts playbricks.

When he retired to Lyme Regis in the '20s, Mitchell returned to his first love and built himself one of the last, most beautiful and original small Arts and Crafts houses. A tall, thin five storey building in local limestone rubble, with a flat top, it is dominated by a hooded bay window with neat, stone dressed mullions and leaded lights. A big ornamental sundial enriches the lower part of the oriel which has a broad,

109 *Arnold Mitchell. Design for a house at Harrow (c. 1902)*

shallow hipped slate hat tying it to the rest of the the fenestration.

It is the house of a grown-up who has never forgotten childhood; a sea shore tower studded with superb examples of the local fossil ammonites.

NIVEN AND WIGGLESWORTH

Herbert H. Wigglesworth (1866–1949) trained under Ernest George and Peto and went into partnership with the Scot, David Barkley Niven (1864–1942), an Aston Webb man. The firm produced elegant and changeful house designs in the '90s, many of which were presented in Niven's beautiful perspectives in the *Studio*. After the turn of the century, the practice acquired a good deal of City work which was mostly neo-Georgian—for instance Hambro's Bank, Bishopsgate (1925). The partnership was dissolved in 1927.

111 *Niven and Wigglesworth. Design for a country house at Wrotham, Kent (c. 1902)*

ALFRED POWELL

G. F. Watts, the painter, described Alfred Powell's Long Copse at Ewhurst as the most beautiful house in Surrey. It was a combination of an existing thatched

110 *Mitchell's own house, Lyme Regis, Dorset (1920s)*

112 *Alfred Powell. Long Copse, Ewhurst, Surrey (1897)*

cottage and a new wing covered in stone slates. The iron casement windows with leaded lights were divided by simple stone mullions. The plan was similar to Gimson's Stoneyhurst cottage (p. 149), a series of rooms linked in line which crank round a curved staircase. The austerity was relieved by a *sgraffito* picture of peacocks in light red and white in the veranda.

Powell was both architect and contractor, and "the craftsmen (save the plumbers—an entertaining exception) were University men who worked with him".[25] Powell did little architecture but he was active in the Society for the Protection of Ancient Buildings, producing pamphlets explaining how country buildings should be restored and repaired.

EDWARD TURNER POWELL

Edward Turner Powell (1859–?) was a moderately successful country house architect. Much of his work was in Surrey and Sussex, though he had some foreign clients. He had a lush Old English touch. Fond of local materials, he used clapboarding, patterned hung tiles and brick in the home counties. He was inventive with gables.

113 *Edward Turner Powell. West Court, Limpsfield Surrey (before 1909)*

A. N. PRENTICE

Alfred Noble Prentice (1866–1941) was a Scot, articled in Glasgow, after which he worked for Colcutt. He built up a prosperous practice which included interior decoration for some of the large early twentieth-century steamships. Though an early advocate of classicism (he published *Renaissance*

114 *Alfred Noble Prentice. Design for stables at Cavenham Hall, Suffolk (before 1904)*

Architecture and Ornament in Spain in 1893), he was happy to adopt vernacular models in the country—for instance in his unexecuted design for a house at Willersey, Gloucestershire (1908) which has all the local characteristics.

C. H. B. QUENNELL

Muthesius described Charles Henry Bourne Quennell (1872–1935) as one of the architects "for the most part concerned with interior decoration and furniture design" and the "master of pen-and-ink drawing."[26] As a young man he worked at a joiner's shop. Like Baillie Scott, he designed standardized Arts and Crafts furniture (particularly inglenooks and fire places) for J. P. White of Bedford, but he had quite a large architectural practice as well, mostly devoted to small country and suburban houses based on vernacular and Georgian models.

Quennell is most widely known for his *History of Everyday Things in England* (1918) in which, with his wife Marjorie, he gave an endlessly entertaining story for children of the development of English design, ranging over everything from architecture to jewellery from the Norman Conquest to 1799 (it was supplemented by later volumes taking the story back to the Stone Age and up to the '30s). The book's exposition of the interaction of everyday life, symbolism and design must have delighted Lethaby.

After the War, Quennell became a devotee of industrialization and designed work in Essex for Crittals, the steel window manufacturers.

SMITH & BREWER

The practice of Smith & Brewer is best known for the Passmore Edwards Settlement in Bloomsbury (chap-

115 *Smith & Brewer. Fives Court, Pinner, Middlesex*

ter 10) but Arnold Dunbar Smith (1866–1933) and Cecil Brewer (1871–1918) built some distinguished country houses. For example, Fives Court, near Pinner, Middlesex was a roughcast, deep-roofed version of Voysey without his pronounced horizontality; Acremead, Crockham Hill, Kent, was a rubble house with fine cut stone dressings and many gables, some banded. Both had long thin plans.

HALSEY RICARDO

The son of a Bristol banker, Halsey Ricardo (1854–1928) was rich enough to take only the commissions he really wanted; he worked entirely by himself at home. After Rugby, he was articled in Chelmsford and worked for Basil Champneys, after which he fell under Philip Webb's spell. He started on his own in 1881 and went into partnership with William de Morgan, the Arts and Crafts potter, between 1888 and 1898. He was devoted to glazed tiles (p. 122).

Ricardo alternated between classical and vernacular idioms. In the country, he tended towards many-gabled houses in brick, stone or stucco with wooden casement windows. His radical ideas on town building, where he was mostly classical, are described in chapter 10.

116 *Halsey Ricardo. House for William Chance (1898)*

ROBERT WEIR SCHULTZ

After training in Scotland under Rowand Anderson (whose office provided Lorimer with his first steps in architecture), Robert Weir Schultz (1860–1951) moved south to join Norman Shaw in early 1884. There he befriended Lethaby and his circle: the founders of the Art Workers' Guild, Gimson and the Barnsley brothers. In 1886, he moved to Ernest George & Peto, where he overlapped with Dawber and Baker. Evening study at the R. A. schools won him a scholarship which he used for study in Italy. In 1889 he was in Greece studying Byzantine architecture with Sidney Barnsley. A common interest in Byzantine architecture was probably the point of contact between Schultz and the third Marquess of Bute,[27] perhaps the most fantastic builder of Victorian times, who had commissioned some of Burges's best work. Bute became Schultz's patron, giving him work in rural Scotland, where, in the early '90s, the architect adopted local traditional building techniques—though when necessary (for instance when adding to the Adams' Dumfries House) he was not averse to adopting a more classical approach.

117 *Robert Weir Schultz. St. Anne's Hospital, Canford Cliffs, Bournemouth, Dorset (1909–1912)*

A strong taste for symmetry permeated Schultz's mature work but it was usually leavened with an affection for local vernacular motifs and, where necessary, a freedom in planning which would have upset strict classicists. His largest—and perhaps best—building was St. Anne's Hospital, Canford

Cliffs, Bournemouth (1909–1912), almost perfectly symmetrical with two lines of room-and-corridor cranked to get the best views from the top of the cliffs; the two banks are linked by chains of rooms to form courtyards. The building was certainly institutional but with its bending, changeful, light-filled corridors and its careful maximization of sun and view for patients, it demonstrated what freedom the Arts and Crafts movement could bring to large buildings when it was given the chance. The exterior is (like some other Schultz buildings) in an austere Queen Anne with big Dutch gables topping bays, all executed in simple, straightforward brickwork with stone dressings.

Schultz built the Khartoum Cathedral between 1906–1928, carefully executed on the principles laid down in Lethaby's *Cosmos* and with techniques suitable for local builders, many of which were based on Byzantine models.

Schultz changed his name by adding another Weir to R. W. S. Weir during the anti-German hysteria of 1914. His practice declined during the War and afterwards it gradually faded away. On retirement in 1939 he went into nominal partnership with his more successful friend Troup (p. 112). He had always refused to accept full-blown classicism, and, like those of his contemporaries who stuck by their early beliefs, he paid dearly for his devotion to Arts and Crafts freedom.

LEONARD STOKES

Leonard Stokes (1858–1925) was one of the most successful Arts and Crafts architects. He started in practice in 1883 after working for Street, Collcutt and Bodley. He was irascible and swore much, despite which he did a lot of work for Roman Catholic institutes. His most notable country work was All Saints Convent, London Colney, Hertfordshire, a free interpretation of late Tudor models in brick, strongly gridded in stone. There is a fine sculpted frieze over the main door in the tower.

His country houses usually followed the Arts and Crafts plan. He obtained many telephone exchanges (see chapter 10) and, in towns, felt the need to adopt free classical forms which were increasingly carried into his country work. Muthesius commented that "in his non classicizing houses at least, he also treats the few details entirely as he pleases, in a free and witty manner that is attractive in its mixture of forcefulness and charm."[28]

118 *Leonard Stokes. All Saints Convent, London Colney, Hertfordshire (1899–1903)*

CHARLES HARRISON TOWNSEND

Though the most interesting work of Charles Harrison Townsend (1851–1928) was in London and is discussed in the next chapter, he was a successful and original designer in the country too. Articled in Liverpool, he moved to London about 1880 and had set up on his own by the end of the decade.[29]

In his larger country houses, he favoured the Arts and Crafts plan but his elevations—as for instance at Blatchfield, Blackheath near Guildford (probably about 1894) are more changeful than most, with many variations of plane and materials; it is Shaw and Nesfield's Old English style stretched out in a long line. Some of his later large houses, like the design for Cliff Towers, Salcombe, Devon, retained the long plan and the variety of materials but are more unified.

Muthesius thought that if he had had more opportunities to build houses, he would have been the most important of the post-Shaw domestic architects.[30] In fact, his practice withered in the first decade of this century because he refused to bow to neo-classicism.

119 *Townsend. Blatchfield, Blackheath, near Guildford, Surrey* (c. 1894)

120 *Townsend. St. Mary the Virgin, Great Warley, Essex* (1902–1904)

121 *Townsend. Cliff Towers, Salcombe, Devon* (design c. 1898)

Before defeat set in, Townsend designed a triumph of the Arts and Crafts spirit. St. Mary the Virgin, at Great Warley, near Brentwood, Essex (begun 1902) could at first glance be taken for a typical Essex country church with low, ample proportions, apsed end and buttressed roughcast walls pierced by simple, undecorated stone window surrounds; tiled roofs sweep down into broad eaves, and, at the west end, they are crowned by a little stubby square shingled bell tower and spire. All is quite in the local tradition, done with a simplicity and humility that would have delighted Pugin and Morris. The external unconventionalities are in the west front (which faces away from the road) with its big rose window floating over slits set in plain ashlar (the latter theme being a hallmark of Townsend's town work—see chapter 10.)

The inside is big, welcoming and simple, like Prior's early churches. Only a small change of level separates nave from chancel, and at first the small chapel that emerges on the south side cannot be seen. The space focuses on the figure of Christ in the centre of the silvered apse onto which the force of light from the rose window shines.

As the eye becomes accustomed to the comparative gloom of the interior, great richness gradually unfolds: angels and flowers are everywhere. Most of the ornament is by William Reynolds-Stephens (1852–1943), Townsend's collaborator. The simple boarded roof is supported on wide ribs decorated with white York roses on silver stems and foliage. The ribs terminate in panels of white lilies on a silver ground.*

Everywhere, the church is a mixture of plain setting and pearl ornament—squares of mother of pearl in Townsend's walnut panelling and in the mother of pearl flowers which, with glowing ruby glass pomegranites, decorate the building's glory—its rood screen. The flowers and fruits are set amongst the glittering and green foliage of six stiff brass Arts and Crafts trees. From the crown of each tree emerges an angel—a subject which, judging by its frequent occurence in the rest of the church, was a favourite of Reynold-Stephens at the time.

All the church's ornament, however luxurious, is stiff, heraldic and symmetrical. Like the surrounding

---

* When the church was first built the effect must have seemed even more strange and exotic for the silver is achieved in aluminium, a metal that had been in commercial production in Britain only since 1896. The lily panels are cast; the silvering of the ribs is done in aluminium leaf.

garden of rest with its straight axial gravel paths, cyprus avenue and pleached lime groves, the ornament expresses the Englishness, the Arts and Crafts nature, of a building that has too often been claimed to be a triumph of the Art Nouveau. Townsend and Reynolds-Stephens could not compromise with the advancing wave of neo-classicism nor could they embrace the *risqué* "squirm" of continental Art Nouveau.

At Great Warley, the Arts and Crafts movement achieved the integration of ecclesiatical art that Sedding's Holy Trinity had sketched on a much larger scale ten years before. But, by 1906, when Reynolds-Stephens had completed the decorations, few clients wanted such a humble yet gorgeous building. Taste was beginning to turn to the more obviously prestigious results of one form or another of neo-classicism.

F. W. TROUP

"This dour, uncompromising Scot, who clucks like a hen and roars like a lion yet seldom seems to have anything to say"[31] was Ashbee's picture of Francis William Troup (1859–1941).* He was an Aberdeenshire man, apprenticed to a Glasgow firm before he went to London, setting up on his own in 1890.

Troup was a close friend of Henry Wilson. His early work was heavy with Gothic; for instance the walls of the heavily gabled Sandhouse (now Kingwood), Sandhills, Surrey (before 1903) are so strongly diapered that it is difficult to see the overall

* Mrs Levson, Troup's niece, tells me that the roaring and clucking was her uncle's party trick.

massing. And his little village hall at Wooton Fitzpaine, Dorset (1906) has splendid simple timber arches and a remarkably complicated angular chimney. He was very fond of lead, "the English metal", and got excellent leadwork—in drainpipes everywhere and, at Wooton, in frilly little friezes over the door canopy. Even as early as Sandhills, the plan is symmetrical and there are classical columns supporting the entrance porch. His hall for the Art Workers' Guild (1913) in Queen Square is in inventive, free neo-Georgian style.

Troup became immensely respectable: supervising architect for rebuilding the Bank of England, and consulting architect to official bodies like the Home Office and Metropolitan Police.

THACKERAY TURNER

Hugh Thackeray Turner (1850–1937) followed Morris as the secretary of the Society for the Protection of Ancient Buildings, a post he occupied from shortly after SPAB's foundation in 1876 for twenty-nine years. In that capacity he helped save many notable buildings from excessive "restoration". His practice (with Eustace Balfour—a brother of A. J.) was partly urban; they were architects to the Grosvenor Estate in Mayfair which involved much neo-Georgian work. Of his extensive country house practice, his own Westbrook, overlooking Godalming in Surrey was, according to Troup,[32] the most notable. "Here . . . is shown Turner's intimate knowledge of the building crafts and his desire to make and his success in making every part of the structure not merely equal to its task, but to look sufficient for its work."

122 *Francis William Troup. Sandhouse, Sandhills, Surrey (1902)*

123 *Hugh Thackeray Turner. Westbrook, Godalming (1900–03)*

GEORGE WALTON

A Glaswegian, George Walton (1867–1933) was mainly an interior and fabric designer. He trained at the same school as Mackintosh, with whom he had affinities. But he studied in the evenings, for he was a bank clerk until middle life. Muthesius called him "the artist who has understood the interior as a work of art best".[33] He moved to London in 1897 and had an international practice. He designed at least one complete house, the Leys at Elstree, Hertfordshire, a show case of his art.

RANDALL WELLS

Randall Wells (1877–1942) was a model Arts and Crafts architect. He worked as site clerk for Prior at Holt and Roker and did the same for Lethaby at Brockhampton. His little church at Kempley, built for Lord Beauchamp in 1904, is near Brockhampton and, in it, Wells took the principles of Pugin and Ruskin further than Lethaby ever did.

124 *Randall Wells. Kempley Church, Hereford and Worcester (1904)*

The great roof of Forest of Dean stone (local stone roofing had fallen into disuse) is carried on mighty oak trusses cut from trees from the Beauchamp estate and used green. The eaves are about shoulder height and the walls of reddish local sandstone. There is no decoration in the stonework, apart from a few mouldings round the openings to throw off water and a relief sculpted into the tower over the door by the architect. The tracery of the great window at the end of the nave is even more simple than Prior's at Roker. It is a regular diagonal grid of stone.

Inside, there is a feast of Arts and Crafts work. The simple pews, prayer desk and altar were designed by Wells. Ernest Barnsley made the lectern and the main

125 *Kempley Church. The rood principal is original but the figures are modern*

candelabra were designed by Ernest Gimson. All these pieces are fine, but the glory of the church is its rood screen—an elaborate ornamented truss.

The *Architectural Review* reported that "the edges of the Rood principal were ornamented by the carpenters with draw-knife and chisel in the traditional village manner. The pattern was gouged and cut into the oak by the architect, assisted by his brother, Mr. Linley Wells, so that it could be easily repainted by the village painter. After gouging the whole principal was given a thin coat of ivory black, the pattern was then grounded in with broken white and the colours were filled in on top. The colours used were Chinese vermilion, ruby madder, golden ochre, chrome yellow, chrome green, permanent blue and indigo."[34] Figures on the beam were carved by the only ships' figurehead carver left in London but were removed by a priggish Bishop of Gloucester. Their modern replacements are crude without being vigorous.

Wells was not prolific. He designed a few cottages

and a country house or two. He ran off with Lady Noble, the wife of one of his clients, and married her in 1917. The two set up a late Arts and Crafts guild, the St. Veronica's Workshop. During and after the War, Wells designed large reinforced concrete buildings for London sites, using the expertise he had acquired with Prior. None was built. He did manage to put up a bank at Teddington and a church at Halton near Leeds. Most of his buildings incorporated concrete and everything he did was individualistic.[35]

HENRY WILSON

Henry Wilson (1864–1934) studied under John Oldrid Scott and Belcher and became John Dando Sedding's chief assistant, inheriting the practice after Sedding's death in 1891. Most of his architectural work was ecclesiastical (he finished Sedding's Holy

126 *Henry Wilson. Tower, St. Clement's, Bournemouth, Dorset (1895)*

Trinity Church, Chelsea in 1900, p. 54) and added the splendid tower to St. Clement's in the Bournemouth suburbs (1895). His domestic work was rare; his main job was for the library and chapel of Welbeck Abbey (1890–96) for the Duke of Portland.

His career was very varied. He was the first editor of the *Architectural Review* (1896–1901), which he made an Arts and Crafts magazine. Increasingly, from the early 1900s, he concentrated on metalwork, church plate, enamelwork and jewellery (he was the first designer to introduce small electric batteries into jewellery). He designed the immense sculpted bronze monument to Bishop Elphinstone in King's College, Aberdeen and the bronze doors of the Cathedral of St. John the Divine, New York. Perhaps his greatest work was the gorgeous Byzantine interior of St. Bartholomew's, Brighton.

Wilson was associated with Lethaby in the Liverpool Cathedral competition design (p. 64) and taught with him at the Royal College of Art. Refusing to compromise with neo-Georgianism, he retired to France in 1922.

EDGAR WOOD AND HENRY SELLERS

The leading Mancunian Arts and Crafts architects were Edgar Wood (1860–1935) and J. Henry Sellers (1861–1954). Both were born near Manchester and trained in local offices. Wood started his own practice in about 1885, and his work spread over south Lancashire and west Yorkshire—mostly country buildings with a great feeling for locality. Inside, they were sensitive too. Muthesius said of Wood's rooms that they "do not merely interest or stimulate, they transport one into an agreeable, warm atmosphere to which one is glad to submit. Every room has its extremely attractive fire place in the form of an ingle-nook, in which a sculptured overmantle is the *pièce de résistance.*"[36]

After he was joined by Sellers in the early 1900s, Wood's work became more formal and axial and his rooms less cosy. And it was probably under Sellers's influence that Wood took the radical step of introducing flat roofs to some of his later houses. The first of these, Upmeads at Stafford (1908), was described by Lawrence Weaver in *Small Country Houses of Today* as "fortress like. It not only lacks anything approaching *prettiness*, which is all to the good, but presents an air of austerity, which shows the designer's devotion to extreme simplicity and restraint."[37] In fact the effect now seems comical, as if the whole top hamper

127 *Wood and Sellers. Upmeads, Stafford (1908)*

of a rather austere brick-and-stone-trim Arts and Crafts house had been raggedly sliced off with a celestial razor, for to make the skyline less than boringly horizontal, Wood had to introduce uneasy little jumps in his perimeter walls.

Wood had moved the concrete first floor, so loved by Prior, up to the roof and justified the innovation to Weaver by explaining that, with a flat roof, it was much easier to cover a complicated plan shape than with conventional roofs. In fact, Wood's plans of this period are simple assemblies of rectangles, very easy to roof under pitches. At Upmeads, the roof was a simple slab of concrete with neither insulation nor weatherproofing. Only with hindsight can we pity the owners who must have had to face vast maintenance and heating bills.

The entrance elevation of Upmeads is symmetrical but the others retain Ruskinian changefulness. Wood was spared the necessity of adopting neo-Georgian, to which, in an eccentric manner, he was tending, by coming into a legacy in 1910 which allowed him to devote the latter part of his life to painting.

1 Muthesius, Hermann *Das englische Haus*, published as *The English House*, Crosby Lockwood Staples, 1979, p. 239

2 Redesdale, Lord *Memories*, Hutchinson, London 1915, p. 710

3 Ryder, Vera *The Little Victims Play*, Robert Hale, London 1974 pp. 18–19

4 Benson, E. F. *Queen Lucia*, London 1920, republished Heinemann, London 1970, p. 20

5 Warren, H. Langford "Recent domestic architecture in England" *Architectural Review*, Boston, Vol. XI, 1904, p. 5

6 *Ibid.*, p. 12

7 Medici-Mall, Katharina *Das Landhaus Waldbühl*, Gesellschaft für Schweizerische Kunstgeschichte, Bern 1979, p. 85

8 Henry James in conversation with Ford Madox Hueffer. Ford, Ford Madox *Ford Madox Ford*, Vol. V, The Bodley Head, p. 416

9 Woolf, Virginia *Roger Fry, a Biography*, Hogarth, London 1940, pp. 163–164

10 Mitchison, Naomi *All Change Here: a Girlhood and Marriage*, Bodley Head, London 1975, p. 14

11 Newton, William Godfrey *The Work of Ernest Newton RA*, The Architectural Press, London 1925, p. 16

12 Muthesius *op. cit*, p. 58

13 *Studio*, Vol. XXV, 1902 p. 245

14 *Ibid.*

15 Weaver, Lawrence *Small Country Houses of Today*, Second Series, Country Life, London 1919, p. 24

16 *Builder*, Vol. CXXXI, 1926, p. 365

17 Muthesius *op. cit.*, pp. 43–44

18 Reilly, C. H. *Representative British Architects of the Present Day*, Batsford, London 1931, p 86

19 Keen, Arthur *RIBA Journal*, Vol. XXIV, 1917, p. 221

20 Muthesius *op. cit.*, p. 62

21 *RIBA Journal*, Vol. LV, p. 39

22 Muthesius *op. cit.*, p. 51

23 Principally in Howarth, Thomas *Charles Rennie Mackintosh and the Modern Movement*, Routledge and Kegan Paul, London 1952 and Macleod, Robert *Charles Rennie Mackintosh*, Hamlyn, Feltham 1963

24 *Studio*, Vol. IX, 1897, p. 204

25 Weaver, Lawrence *Small Country Houses*, First Series, Country Life, London n.d., p. 122

26 Muthesius, *op. cit.*, p. 46

27 The best published study on Schultz so far is by Ottewill, David in *Architectural History*, Vol. XXII, 1979, pp. 88–115. This account is based on that essay

28 Muthesius, *op. cit.*, p. 45

29 A detailed account of Townsend is given in Service, Alastair *Edwardian Architecture and its Origins*, The Architectural Press, London 1975, pp. 162–182

30 Muthesius *op. cit.*, p. 41

31 Ashbee, C. R. *Memoirs*, typescript in Victoria and Albert Museum library, Vol. VII, p. 332

32 *RIBA Journal*, Vol. XLV, 1938, p. 258

33 Muthesius *op. cit.*, p. 53

34 *Architectural Review*, Vol. XVI, 1904, pp. 184–185

35 The best published description of Wells's work is Pevsner, Nikolaus and Enid Radcliffe, "Randall Wells" *Architectural Review*, Vol. CXXXVI, 1964, pp. 366–368

36 Muthesius *op. cit.*, p. 47

37 Weaver *Small Country Houses*, First Series *op. cit.*, p. 187

10 The Lost City

Just where Regent Street curves into Portland Place, the curiously named Riding House Street snakes away eastward in the direction of Bloomsbury. On a corner, about halfway along this tall narrow thoroughfare are the offices of T. J. Boulting & Sons, Sanitary and Hot Water Engineers, whose name is emblazoned high on both faces with elegant elongated Edwardian capitals in gold on big green mosaic panels.

Apart from these, the building is almost severe. Above the ground floor, plain brick walls are relieved by bays of windows (originally all with leaded lights) in very simple square-section stone frames and mullions. The bays rise to a varied series of dormers, silhouetted against a slate mansard roof with great square chimney stacks against the sky behind.

The ground floor is equally simple but more changeful with some of the bays carried down to pavement level, others corbelling out to ease pedestrian traffic round the corner and provide an entrance (now hideously disfigured). The plain brick panels terminate over large, mullioned display windows.

If you ignore the colourful mosaic panels, the building (designed in 1903 by H. Fuller Clark) is the corner of a Tudorish Arts and Crafts country house set down in the middle of London. Boulting & Sons is a fragment of the lost Arts and Crafts city.

This rich and wonderful city is lost for several reasons. First of all, the attitude of the Arts and Crafts movement to cities was ambivalent. Stemming from at least as far back as *News from Nowhere*, there was a distrust of urbanism fuelled by revulsion from the squalor of nineteenth-century cities, many of which had exploded unplanned from tiny villages during the industrial revolution. Arts and Crafts architects built mainly in the countryside, partly because their work was of a kind that attracted country clients, partly because they wanted to anyway.

It is no coincidence that the main Arts and Crafts contribution to planning—the Garden City movement—was at least partly intended to destroy cities as they then were: to create new independent communities* so that pressures on existing conurbations could be reduced and they could be remodelled on healthier lines.

But the remodelling of existing cities was never fully explored by the movement. Arts and Crafts theorists spent little time on discussing what should be done, and the ideas that were propounded were so gentle that they could (mistakenly) be interpreted as a lack of determination to reform urban life. Lethaby, for instance, lecturing to the Arts and Crafts Society in 1896, suggested that "we should begin on the humblest scale by sweeping streets better, washing and whitewashing the houses, and taking care that such railings and lamp-posts as are required are good lamp-posts and railings, the work of the best artists available."[1]

Lethaby repudiated the fashionable "idea of grandifying London at a *coup*, or to any extent formalising it" by striking great avenues between important buildings. But he was prepared to recommend one major scheme—cutting a grand pedestrian avenue between Waterloo Bridge and the British Museum—which he regarded as the apex of the triangle of central London, the other two angles of which were found at Westminster Abbey and St. Paul's. This one project would, he thought, allow "all future improvements . . . [to] fall into place, without any large and violent change in the direction of the streets."[2] This half mile of avenue, and a green belt round the city, were the only grand proposals Lethaby produced for planning great cities.

Again and again, he returned to his theme that

---

* See chapter 13.

128 *H. Fuller Clark. Boulting & Sons, Riding House Street, London (designed 1903)*

urban improvement should start humbly and gradually develop, with increasing civic consciousness, into a movement for improving every aspect of a citizen's life. "A town", he said, "is a work of art according to its quality as a dwelling-place for men. Its art is its service and stimulus to life."[3]*

Lethaby's call for gradual but deep and thorough city reform was echoed by the other Arts and Crafts theoretician, C. R. Ashbee, who urged that improvement should take place "little by little and from within ... Let us have a wise body of ordinances, a park or lung here, the gradual development of a Zone-system first in this, then in that city; let us have green belts round all our cities."[4]

The buildings in which this programme of improvement would take form would, according to Lethaby, not be "betrayed by the mysterious word Architecture away from reality into a realm of pretence about styles and orders and proportions and periods and conception and composition."[5]

Those Arts and Crafts architects who *did* work in cities found that their buildings, country bred and free of orders, were not in great demand. Most of the major competitions of the '90s were judged by men like the great formalist Waterhouse and Shaw (then a firm classicist), so free, changeful designs were rarely chosen for public buildings. Increasingly, formal styles were preferred (see chapter 12). One result was that those urban Arts and Crafts buildings that did get built were, like Boulting & Sons, quite small, so they are literally lost amongst their surroundings and are rarely noticed.

The formal tendency was reinforced because, stemming from as far back as Pugin, one of the ideals that had inspired the movement was the notion that a new building should fit in with its surroundings. In the country and in small country towns, this idea was relatively easy to achieve, for existing vernacular forms and materials could be adapted. But in cities, the model was not vernacular Gothic but (in the South at least) vernacular Georgian. So most Arts and

Crafts architects were torn between Ruskinian savageness and changefulness (which, when thoroughly followed, led to buildings of great originality) and an attempt to achieve fidelity to place, which led to neo-Georgian architecture.

Neo-Georgian emerged from the more genteel wing of the Arts and Crafts movement, and it was a style with which most Arts and Crafts architects at least toyed, apart from those completely dedicated to the Gothic spirit such as Lethaby, Prior, Voysey, Townsend and Mackintosh.

The irony is that as society threw up more and more functions, forms were adopted that were instrinsically inflexible. Although many architects used Georgian forms with some freedom, particularly initially, there was an underlying tendency to order. Many of the rules of Georgian, and hence of neo-Georgian, building are strict—for instance there must be a gradation of window size from medium windows on the entrance floor to very large ones on the first floor to smaller and smaller windows as attic is piled upon attic. The lighting and size of rooms is determined by the rules of elevation. Pugin and Ruskin had demanded the precise opposite. "Queen Anne" had shown a way of adapting classical forms to new needs—Norman Shaw's own house is a particularly good example of how this could be done (p. 40)—but such freedom was increasingly forgotten in the pursuit of Rule and propriety.

The career of a successful turn of the century architect of no fixed principle is exemplified by Herbert Baker (1862–1946). Baker was one of the most successful architects of his generation—only Lutyens outstripped him in the Establishment acclaim. His training was in the office of Ernest George where he overlapped with Dawber and Schultz. He was chief draftsman when Lutyens made his brief appearance as apprentice.

Baker emigrated to South Africa in the early '90s, and met Cecil Rhodes, under whose patronage he gained much official work. By the time he was forty, Baker had already built three cathedrals, Government House and the Union Buildings in Pretoria. He worked in many styles, notably a heavy stripped classicism enlivened by ornament executed by local craftsmen.

His other styles included, for domestic work, references to vernacular building—for instance in South Africa, he adapted colonial Dutch motifs. In 1903 Ashbee was greatly taken with "Baker's own house ... springing like a jewel castle from out of the

* In his rejection of immense city reorganization, fashionable in the wake of the boulevards of Paris and Vienna's Ringstrasse, Lethaby was being true to the spirit of London, that vast and varied agglomeration of distinct villages. Only Nash, ninety years before, and by the turn of the century very much out of fashion, had tried to impose a great Baroque organization on Britain's capital. Lethaby's avenue was in intention a bow to Nash's grand design.

Lethaby was not always consistent; though he normally preached gentle change, on at least one occasion he urged that "except for a hundred or two of buildings, London needs to be rebuilt from end to end" (in *Architecture* (1911) p. 245).

rock ... it is one of the most exquisite pieces of architecture I have ever seen.'"*

Baker's Government House, Pretoria was tinged with Boer vernacular, just as his Delhi Secretariats (which flank Lutyens's Viceregal Lodge) have reminders of Mogul ornament.

He returned to England before the War to carry on a large and varied practice. His big buildings were usually neo-classical—or nearly so—in plan but he never quite forgot the lessons of Pugin and sometimes attempted to fit the bulk of his huge commissions quietly into context; for instance his Church House (1937–1940). This Westminster Abbey complex with its squared flints and patterned brick was intended to harmonize with the disparate architecture of the area and to evoke the original building of 1758. Ruskinian savageness was remembered too. Even Baker's highly classical South Africa House (1935) in Trafalgar Square has a profusion of sculptured detail—particularly animal heads;—a last echo of the belief in free craftsmanship.

One compelling reason why designing to Rule became increasingly so popular was explained by H. S. Goodhart-Rendel, a doyen of ordered architec-

* Ashbee, C. R. Memoirs, Typescript in the Victoria and Albert Museum Library, Vol II, p. 195.

129 *Herbert Baker. Church House, Westminster, west front (1937–1940)*

ture between the wars: the free style was simply uneconomic. "If", he said, "we wished now to build in [an] informal and unhurried manner, we should find its cost prohibitive, not to the employer but to the architect. Just as in building itself, our methods have changed owing to the enormously increased cost of labour in relation to that of materials, so in ... practice we now must save all we can of the principal's time and that of his draughtsmen if any profit at all is to be got out of the six per cent fee." Yet even the arch reactionary Goodhart-Rendel was prepared to admit that, "In its results, however, the old method was better than is any of the same kind achieved by other means. The man of the future may prefer that his house should be no more visibly peculiar to himself than his suit of clothes or the body of his motor-car, but at present to most men home-building still means, as it meant in Victorian times, a competition in self expression between themselves and their architects.'"[6]

In the '20s and '30s neo-Georgian was stretched and stretched to cover acres of offices and flats until, in the impoverished days after the Second War, the thin, taught crust was cracked off, revealing the concrete bones behind—which, in an uneasy marriage with neo-classic modernist sinews introduced from the continent, produced some of the crudest commercial architecture ever seen.

It is unfair to judge a style in its decadence and decay. Neo-Georgian started as a kindly, gentle response to the cities in which Arts and Crafts architects found themselves working. In architects' terms it had a fine pedigree, going back to "Queen Anne" and to Webb's Georgian days, and from it came some of the minor masterpieces of Arts and Craftsmen, particularly when they transplanted the style to the country.

But their greatest city successes emerged when they tried to use the full panoply of Puginian and Ruskinian theory in the urban context. From the relatively few masterpieces that were so produced, we can catch a glimpse of what the lost Arts and Crafts city would have been like if the confident British ethos had not begun to change dramatically during the economic pressures of the first decade of the twentieth century.

The easiest transition from the country to the city was in house design. John Dando Sedding's All Saints Vicarage, Harwell Street, Plymouth (1880) is a country vicarage brought to town. It is a Butterfield parsonage seen through Old English spectacles, with complicated gables and patterned tile hanging, but its tall polygonal bays stretching up from basement to a tiled hat over the first floor foreshadows much later urban Arts and Crafts work.

Eleven years later, Voysey designed his only two really urban houses, a gentle intrusion into Hans Road, a curving little street in Knightsbridge just behind Harrods. At first sight, 14 and 16 Hans Road are symmetrical, with a pair of polygonal, close mullioned bay windows. Voysey's favourite simple square-section stone mullions and leaded lights are set in brickwork which matches the rest of the terrace. The first design was indeed perfectly symmetrical, but on closer examination of what was built, subtle asymmetries emerge: there are only three oriel windows above the doors instead of the four symmetry would have required. And the bay of number 16 terminates at the bottom with a row of little windows, revealing a complicated series of floor levels within, while the bay of number 14 shows a much more regular disposition of floors; even though the room heights were lower than most of the rest of the houses in the terrace except number 12, designed by Mackmurdo in 1894, after Voysey and his client had quar-

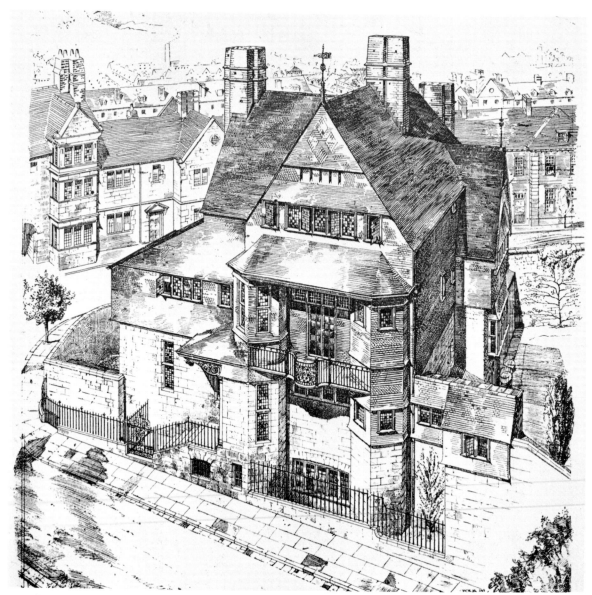

130 *J. D. Sedding. All Saints Vicarage, Plymouth, Devon (1880)*

131 *C. F. A. Voysey. Houses, Hans Road, London (1891). The house under scaffolding is by Mackmurdo (1894)*

132 *Halsey Ricardo. 8 Addison Road, London (1905–1907)*

relled. This house picks up Voysey's floor heights, his oriel and his brick but in its details shows Mackmurdo's strong renaissance affections. Mackmurdo's most free London house was 25 Cadogan Gardens, Chelsea, which has three tall oriel bays, complete with leaded lights which top a complicated ground floor fenestration and are capped by a wide, carved, curving early Shavian cornice. The side elevation repeats the oriel motif but is flat. It is a design of great elegance and wit. See p. 51.

An equally elegant but much more dramatic Arts and Crafts town house was Halsey Ricardo's number 8 Addison Road, Kensington (1905–7). The building goes much further towards classicism than conventional neo-Georgian; it has pilasters and capitals, arches, roundels and elaborate cornices. Its prime attraction is the glazed turquoise and green brickwork. Ricardo was a partner of William De Morgan, the great Arts and Crafts potter, between 1888 and 1898. And, as a disciple of Butterfield, he was a great believer in glazed material and colour for city building: "In the country and those favoured cities where houses have gardens, where creepers hang in rich festoons . . . the local building materials will probably supply us with colour enough to set off and harmonize with the palette set by Nature. But in the street, where all the colour there is of man's own making, it should be full and strong."[7] Ricardo's belief that colour could enable the British architect to "dispense with much of the architectural frippery felt to be requisite to prevent the surface of ungraduated plain

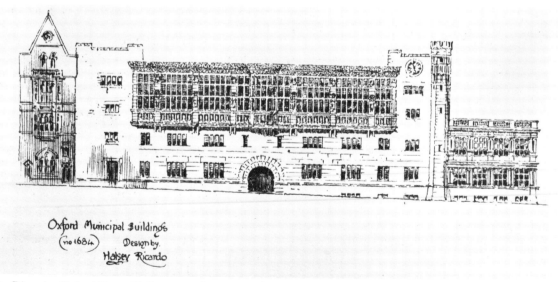

133 *Ricardo. Oxford Town Hall competition entry (1892)*

134 *Charles Holden. A market hall, Soane medallion design (1896)*

tint appearing too bald''⁰ was sadly not shared by many of his contemporaries: the streets of the lost city shine only in the imagination.

The Addison Road house is so large that, in any other town but London, it could be a great public building. When they did design for smaller cities, Arts and Craftsmen were more true to type. For instance, in 1892 Ricardo himself had produced a design for the Oxford Town Hall competition which involved a great bank of Jacobean glass in simple stone mullions between asymmetrical stone stair towers—a very early and elegant design for a glazed office block which, because of the size and mass of the stone mullions and transoms might have avoided the problems of modern glass-and-metal offices—overheating in summer and chill bite in winter.

Charles Holden's Soane medallion competition design for a provincial market hall, published in the first issue of the *Architectural Review* 1896, was a much more humble affair. It was basically a buttressed and pitched medieval market hall covering an open undercroft (with curiously classical arches) and enlivened by an asymmetrical front door and tower.

The austerity of the design was set against rich bands of Arts and Crafts relief that linked the hall and tower together.

In practice, Holden (1875–1960) was rarely able to use such expensive decoration. By the time he could, in the British Medical Association building in the Strand (1907) where Epstein was commissioned to do the relief sculptures, Holden was becoming classical. But before he evolved the stripped heavily Muscovite style which balances him uneasily between Modern Movement and classicism in the '20s and '30s, Holden was a most free and inventive Arts and Crafts architect. His Belgrave Hospital for Children at the Oval (designed when he was chief assistant to Percy Adams in 1900) is a Grimm but Webbian monument of the lost city, and his Bristol Central Reference Library (1905–1906) is a most ingenious symmetrical Jacobean series of stone planes and broad mullioned, flat, polygonal bays which is said by some to have had a good deal to do with the origins of Mackintosh's

135 *Holden. Belgrave Hospital for Children, Oval, London (1900)*

136 *Holden. Bristol Central Reference Library (1905–1906)*

137 *Smith & Brewer. Passmore Edwards Settlement (now Mary Ward House) (1895)*

celebrated masterpiece, the west wing of the Glasgow School of Art.

Quieter than the Bristol library and built ten years previously was the Passmore Edwards Settlement in Tavistock Place, Bloomsbury (now Mary Ward House). Designed by Smith & Brewer in 1895, it was a new type of building, part hostel, part community centre. As the *Studio* reported, it was intended to bring together "persons of kindred tastes and interests, more especially those engaged in social and educational work in a given neighbourhood to form a home in which the conveniences of family life shall be combined with individual seclusion and liberty."[9] Morris's Hammersmith Guest House had taken real shape.

The worthy inhabitants lived in a rather spartan atmosphere enriched by Arts and Crafts elegance. The main rooms were basically undecorated except by the odd semi-classical moulding and a few fine pots; the furniture, when not designed by the architects, was modelled on simple country styles; the fireplaces were designed by Lethaby, Voysey, New-

ton, Troup and Dawber with grates by the architects based on the chastest eighteenth-century models. Where any special work was needed—as for instance in the dining hall fireplace designed in "Lethaby brick"—the work was "carried out by the ordinary manufacturers from instructions and sketches supplied by the architects", which was welcomed by the *Studio* because "it is only by bringing modern design to bear directly upon ordinary production that any aesthetic growth can be effected in the commercial world; and thereby upon the public taste."[10]

The public was initially wary of the outside of the building. The front elevation is extremely simple: projecting wings at each end frame the blank brick wall of the hall, which has very deep projecting eaves over a deep plain white-rendered cornice. The white rendering is picked up again in the upper storey of the towers which are themselves completely symmetrical, with the stair windows forming opposing diagon-

138 *W. R. Lethaby. Eagle Insurance Office, Colmore Row, Birmingham (1899–1902)*

als at each end of the composition. The design is saved from total symmetry by the entrance porch which grows smoothly out of the curves of the balustrading to form a massive stone block projecting forward to the pavement, penetrated by a broad welcoming arched opening. The stone eggs on top of the porch derive from Lethaby's *Cosmos*, in which eggs are identified as symbols of creation.

Lethaby's only urban building, the Eagle Insurance office in Colmore Row, Birmingham (1899–1900) is also topped by mystic ornament: an eagle surrounded by circles and wavy lines—symbols of the sun and clouds. But below this deep cornice, the building is extraordinarily spare. The top three storeys have five simple bays of full-height sash windows divided by a grid of mullions and transoms moulded only enough to ensure that water would be thrown off so the stone would not stain. This top hamper sits on a storey and a half which is completely different but equally simple. An ashlar wall is dominated by the big window of the main office, stone gridded in almost Tudor proportions, flanked symmetrically by doors for public and staff with ample flattish arches. Behind is a completely asymmetrical plan, which, amongst other ingenuities, gives the director's office a great glass tent of a ceiling.

It is unlikely that Lethaby would have fully approved of the overtly classical detailing of Leonard Stokes's telephone exchanges, yet stripped of their swags and their heavy bracketed cornices, the best of Stokes's many exchanges have all Lethaby's simplicity and freshness. The Southampton exchange (1900), for example, was simply five bays of simple windows between massive plain brick pilasters. In Stoke's masterpiece, Gerrard Street, London (1904), four wide bays of leaded windows sat on top of massive semi-circular arches. The basic material was brick, tied together with Stokes's favourite bands of stone. Now destroyed, the building showed how successfully, given the chance, Arts and Crafts architects could cope with the large single function buildings which have been the hallmark of this century's clients' requirements.

The classical twiddles on the Gerrard Street telephone exchange were not the only way in which Arts and Crafts architects attempted to achieve richness. Henry Wilson won the competition for the public ibrary at Ladbroke Grove, Kensington in 1890, while he was still working for Sedding. Big, stone mullioned windows and a wide, shallow arched entrance were to have been set within thin projecting brick towers, thinly reeded and increasingly elaborated by relief sculpture until their crowning cupolas were united with the walls in an intricate, sinuous, swooping band of intertwined figures and foliage, all crowned with the high pitch of a roof topped by a complicated spire. Sadly, much of the decoration had to be abandoned for lack of money, but enough survived of the original design to give a notion of what might have been, even if the result looks a bit like a well decorated Board School.

A much smaller example of decorated urban Arts

139 *Stokes. Gerrard Street Telephone Exchange, London (1904, now destroyed)*

140 *Henry Wilson. Ladbroke Grove Library, London (designed 1890)*

141 *H. Fuller Clark. The Black Friar, north of Black-friars Bridge, London (1905)*

and Crafts work is the Black Friar pub (1905) in Queen Victoria Street, London, where H. Fuller Clark (the architect of Boulting & Sons) redesigned the ground floor of a mid-Victorian office block. Here, the architect's intentions were really carried out in full. Rarely can such a quantity of arts and crafts have been compressed into such a small space. The result is extraordinarily jolly. The design is basically very simple—only two sides of the thin wedge shaped site can be seen; they are faced in smooth granite with big windows divided into leaded squares by stone mullions and transoms topped with a deep fascia announcing the name of the pub in Clark's favourite green and gold mosaic.

Onto this monastically chaste undercoat, no opportunity of imposing friars has been missed. The composition is dominated by a three dimensional gigantic black friar beaming from the apex of the triangle towards Blackfriars Bridge; the door surrounds and the brackets which support the cornice are carved with grotesque friars in every stage of inebriation; the panels above the doors are of coloured mosaic showing sober friars preparing liquor, and at eye level

142 *C. H. Townsend. Bishopsgate Institute, London (1892)*

between the windows are delicate bronze reliefs of kindly friars pointing the way to the different bars.

The interior is more restrained with simple chunky Arts and Crafts furniture, a great coppery inglenook and some lively narrative bronze friezes (friars again) designed by Henry Poole. Anyone who believes that the Arts and Crafts movement was excessively solemn should take a drink at the Black Friar.

The man who brought decorated Arts and Crafts buildings to town in a big way was Townsend. The first of his three major London buildings was the Bishopsgate Institute designed in 1892, two years after Wilson's library scheme with which, as Alastair Service has pointed out,[11] it shares many features; it has shallow projecting towers, capped with cupolas, enclosing a large area of glass and the whole is topped with a steeply pitched roof. But (perhaps because he

143 *Townsend. Whitechapel Art Gallery, London (designed 1901)*

144 *Townsend. Horniman Museum, Forest Hill, London (designed 1896)*

was required by his clients to keep the inside utterly simple) Townsend did find the money to decorate the outside in bands of relief in his favourite motif: trees with short, slender trunks and large overlapping leaves, which in this building are laced together by sinuous branches.

Townsend's next major design was for a very similar long site with a narrow street frontage—the Whitechapel Art Gallery, a proposal for which he exhibited at the Academy in 1896. It was like an expanded version of the Bishopsgate elevation with two ampler towers symmetrically flanking a great arched doorway. Over this was a row of wide windows with semi-circular heads, topped by a deep pictorial frieze.

The final design (completed in 1901) had to be squashed to fit onto a much a narrower site than was originally intended. The entrance arch was pushed out of centre to allow a less obtrusive exit doorway to be accommodated by its side. So the whole of the ground floor became asymmetrical and the original symmetry only gradually reasserts itself as the building rises through a band of plain rectangular leaded windows on the first floor to two projecting towers enriched by Townsend's leafy trees on the second. They flank a large rectangular area of dirty grey rendering (the rest of the elevation is in buff terra cotta like the Bishopsgate Institute). The rectangle was intended to hold the elevation's crowning glory, a mosaic frieze by Walter Crane depicting "the sphere and message of art". Cash ran out so it was never constructed, and the panel itself has been penetrated by mean little windows to light the caretaker's room—the inadequate lighting of which caused the *Architectural Review* to make one of its few criticisms of the ingenious planning of the building.[12]

Townsend's third major London building was the Horniman Free Museum at Forest Hill in south London, where he did manage to get a big mosaic put up. Unlike the other two buildings which were constructed for charities, the museum was built for a rich philanthropic tea merchant, F. J. Horniman, who commissioned Townsend to design a special gallery for his anthropological collections in 1896 after being driven to distraction by allowing the public to visit them in his own house.

Again the site was long and thin, but this time it sloped up hill from the road. So Townsend arranged the entrance at the top of a flight of cranked stairs which carried you up under the mosaic panel (by Robert Anning Bell). This covered the thin end of the

145 *Horniman Museum, the tower*

146 *Edgar Wood. Lindley tower, near Huddersfield, Yorkshire (1902)*

gallery and was surmounted by a row of leaf-capped pilasters under the curve which fronted the long glazed barrel vault.

At the top of the steps, you faced one of Townsend's mighty arched doorways in the side of the tower which dominates the elevation. Inside, you emerged on to the balcony of the south gallery through which you moved to the north (uphill) gallery before going downstairs to the lower part of the south gallery and out again at the front of the tower. It was (before being mauled by the present proprietors) one of Townsend's most ingenious plans.

The tower is still extraordinary. It starts off as a square plan with rounded corners and gradually tapers until the radius of each corner turns into a little circular turret surrounding a round tower. On the way up, it passes large clocks (philanthropic gesture by Horniman to the non-watch-wearing poor), a drift of leafy trees and a massive circular cornice.

When first built, the design must have seemed to many grotesquely unusual for the *Studio* felt impelled to produce a spirited defence: "the architecture, whether liked or disliked, is not in the least degree an imitation, an echo of some old master's merit. It stands there at Forest Hill as a new series of frank and fearless thoughts expressed and co-ordinated in *stone.*"[13]

147 *Wood. George and Dragon Inn, Castleton, Derbyshire (1898)*

If the citizens of Forest Hill were disturbed by Townsend's tower, those of Huddersfield must have felt just as worried when, in 1902, Edgar Wood's clock tower at nearby Lindley was unveiled from its scaffolding. Wood's tower is as strange as Townsend's but its idiom is completely different: a four-square plan has a diagonal buttress at each corner so the effect is sharp and slightly reeded and not at all rounded apart from the drum stair for the clock winder. The buttresses rise past gargoyles to provide sharp pinnacles round the octagonal metal warlock's hat which gracefully terminates the tower.

Were it not for this roof, the tower would resemble that of an Arts and Crafts church—Gothic but straightened out and simplified. Wood's earlier designs for town buildings, for instance his George and Dragon Inn, Castleton, Derbyshire of 1898, were almost excessively medievalist. But, during the first years of this century Wood became less historically inclined.

His First Church of Christ Scientist at Victoria Park, Manchester (1903–1908) is in a sort of stripped Gothic with a great Townsendish arched door under a crucifix shaped window, set into the tall, thin, white rendered gable. From this, two stone semi-Gothic wings project diagonally *à la* Prior and the composition is completed (and made more Hansel-and-Gretelish) by a squat, conically capped, round stone tower nestling against the right hand side of the gable. The building shows the freedom that Arts and Crafts architects might have achieved in ecclesiastical architecture if they had not usually worked for the Established church.

A similar kind of freedom was shown in Wood's Wesleyan School, Long Street, Middleton (1899–1902), a composition in which the white walls, leaded lights and interlocking gables owe something to Voysey; but its use of tall, thin motifs under the gables was new, as was the higgledy-piggledy arrangement of a school round a courtyard. The adjoining chapel is restrained Arts and Crafts Gothic.

Composition became more formal after Sellers (who was a devoted flat roof man) joined the practice. Under its roof planes, the Durnford Street School, Middleton (1908–10) is a curious amalgam of board school architecture with wide, high windows let into a background of brick from which stone-clad bays, many mullioned and finely detailed, Tudorishly project from a semi-industrial backdrop.

Two hundred miles further north, Mackintosh had already experienced the difficulties of trying to give

148 *Wood. First Church of Christ Scientist, Victoria Park, Manchester (1903–1908)*

149 *Wood. Wesleyan School and Chapel, Long Street, Middleton, near Manchester (1899–1902). The school buildings are through the arch*

life to stereotyped school design. His Scotland Street school in Glasgow (1903–1906) had to be designed on a conventional board school plan, but, in elevation, it was enlivened with small paned windows (rather than the ubiquitous sheet glass). And it had two conically capped semi-circular stair towers in the Scottish tradition—but they were not really what they seemed to be, for instead of containing a winding staircase, each drum enclosed a perfectly conventional pair of straight flights terminating at landings which came out only as far as the main walls, leaving a great vertiginious semi-circular chute of space soaring from top to bottom of the building. Sadly, the local school board denied Mackinstosh his small paned windows (except on the drums) because they were more expensive than sheet glass.

150 *Wood and Sellers. Durnford Street School, Middleton (1908–1910)*

151 *C. R. Mackintosh. Scotland Street School, Glasgow (1903–1906)*

152 *Scotland Street School, interior of stairwell*

Mackintosh's Glasgow School of Art is one of the great works of Arts and Crafts genius of the turn of the century. It was built in two stages, 1896–1899 and 1907–1909, and is, in effect, three or four buildings. The first, on the north side, is a big windowed, big paned row of studios, much like a board school, but relieved by Art Nouveauish wrought-iron brackets supporting the mullions. The centre of this regular and conventional elevation is penetrated by an asymmetrical ashlar entrance bay of great originality. The roofline breaks and a small tower suddenly appears over an irregular set of windows in a series of ashlar planes dominated by a Smith-and-Brewer shallow arch over the entrance.

The east elevation is quite different, a great plane relieved by a tall, flat, polygonal bay and a curious curved and ornately coved hood over the windows of the lower school. The south side is an amalgam of the original studio windows and the projecting "hen-run", a long glazed gallery, added after the original building was completed.

The masterpiece of this wonderfully changeful building is the west elevation (1907–1909) which towers above one of Britain's most steeply sloping streets. The double-height library of the art college rises behind three soaring bays full of leaded lights starting stark out of the ashlar. The full-height bays are carried on in a sub-rhythm of careful leaded projections until one turns the corner and meets the relative sobriety of the north front again.

The west elevation of the Glasgow School of Art has an even more inventive but less controlled precedent in England; the Euston Road fire station by the London County Council architect's department (1901–1902).

By the late '90s the LCC department was responsible for designing housing and some public buildings including fire stations. Most of its fine pre-war work was coloured by Arts and Crafts motifs—in housing schemes, for instance, it is easy to see the influence of Webb and of Smith and Brewer's Mary Ward Settlement; in the fire stations there are elements of Webb again, and of Voysey.

The influence of Arts and Crafts was not limited to copying details. Some of the younger members of the department were in direct contact with Lethaby, Webb and Morris through the Society for the Protection of Ancient Buildings. The influence of Arts and Crafts socialism must have been strong for, at the time, only pronounced idealism could have made a up of such powerful talents work virtually

153 *Mackintosh. Glasgow School of Art, east elevation (1896–1899)*

154 *Glasgow School of Art, west elevation (1907–09)*

155 *L.C.C. architect's department. Euston Road Fire Station, London (1901–1902)*

anonymously for a public office. The architects in charge, Thomas Blashill (up to 1899) and W. E. Riley (until 1920) deserve praise for setting up the system which allowed individual talent to flower but less for allowing credit for individual works to be obscured to the general public.

The chief designer of the Euston Road fire station, the department's masterpiece was Charles Canning Winmill. He was faced with a difficult problem: that of combining a complicated barrack block with offices

and large halls for the fire engines—a large and varied bulk which all had to be crammed onto a small site in central London.

The solution showed how details adapted from vernacular buildings and combined under the principle of Ruskinian changefulness could produce an architecture sufficiently flexible to cope with the most complicated set of urban requirements, while retaining dignity and domestic character.

The building is of brick over a stone ground floor which is occasionally enlivened with semi-classical details. Above this level, it relies entirely on Gothic domestic precedents: the brick is relieved by bands of stone and a regular series of leaded casement windows. Against these planes of brick is a quite irregular rhythm of bays, both square and three-sided, which gradually builds up to a collar topped by wide eaves and (to turn the corner), little gables with circular windows like the one Ashbee had used a couple of years before in Cheyne Walk (p. 145).

As at Boulting & Sons, if a few details were stripped off the Euston Road fire station, it could be the corner of a (very large) Arts and Crafts country house. It shows that, at its best, Arts and Crafts architecture knew no differentiation between public and private buildings and none between provision for the rich or the poor. The lost city of the Arts and Crafts movement would have been less grand than the Edwardian cities that really were built. But it would have been a city with a human face; gentle, witty, occasionally dramatic, kind to its surroundings and responsive to the needs of its citizens.

1 Lethaby, W. R. "Of beautiful cities" in *Art and Life and the Building and Decoration of Cities*, lectures at the fifth Arts and Crafts exhibition 1896, Rivington Percival, London 1897, pp. 103–104
2 *Ibid.*, p. 108
3 Lethaby, W. R. "Towns to live in" first published in the *Hibbert Journal*, 1918, republished in *Form in Civilisation* 1957, p. 19
4 Ashbee, C. R. *Where the Great City Stands* Essex House Press London 1917, p. 67
5 Lethaby, W. R. "Towns to live in", *op. cit.*, p. 25
6 Goodhart-Rendel, H. S. "The work of Beresford Pite and Halsey Ricardo", *RIBA Journal*, Vol. XLIII, 1935, p. 118
7 Ricardo, Halsey R. "The architect's use of colour", *RIBA Journal* Vol. III, 1896, p. 366
8 *Ibid.*, p. 367
9 Morris, G. L. and Wood, Esther "The architecture of the Passmore Edwards settlement", *Studio*, Vol. XVI, 1899, p. 11
10 *Ibid.*, p. 17
11 Service, Alastair *Edwardian Architecture and its Origins*, Architectural Press, London 1975, p. 169
12 "The Whitechapel Art Gallery" *Architectural Review*, Vol. IX, 1901, p. 130
13 "The Horniman Free Museum", *Studio*, Vol. XXIV, 1902, p. 198

Henry Poole. Sign at the Black Friar

11 The Attempt on the Summit

By far the most original thinker of the later Arts and Crafts movement emerged in the darkest heart of the Victorian city—London's East End. Charles Robert Ashbee (1863–1942) did more than any other Arts and Crafts architect to try to turn Morris's ideals into practice.

As a young man, a Wellingtonian just down from King's Cambridge, Ashbee was articled to G. F. Bodley, friend of Webb and one of the first patrons of the Morris firm. While Bodley's apprentice he lived at Toynbee Hall, a pioneer university settlement in the East End set up to enable young graduates to pass on something of their education to the poor. Ashbee's social conscience seems to have wakened early. In a semi-autobiographical novel he recalled, "One of the most dreadful recollections of an otherwise happy childhood [he was the son of a prosperous merchant*] was when I heard in the London streets a chant—a slow marching chant—it was always the same, and went tramp, tramp, tramp tramp, tramp:

'We've got no work to do-oo

We've got no work to do-oo'.

When you looked you saw some thirty or forty men; they may have been agricultural labourers . . . they were well built, kindly, humble, haggard, willing to do as they were bid. It was a dreadful sight."[1]

At Toynbee Hall he started a Ruskin class in 1886 which originally consisted of three pupils. Inspired by Ruskin's *Fors Clavigera*, Ashbee expanded his activities to start a school which taught, in conjunc-tion with Ruskinian theory, painting, modelling, plaster casting and "the study of heraldic forms."[2] To be truly Ruskinian, he had to associate the school with a practical workshop: "the men in this workshop should be the teachers in the school, and . . . the pupils of the School should be drafted into the work-shop."[3] The school was formally opened by the Minister of Education in 1888. The workshop was established at the same time. It became the founda-tion of the Guild of Handicraft, the most interesting of all the Arts and Crafts guilds.

Morris, by then a fierce revolutionary, was highly sceptical of the venture. Ashbee mentioned in his diary that when he went to see the Great Man he was told that "It is useless and that I am about to do a thing with no basis to do it on . . . I could not exchange a single argument with him till I granted his whole position as a Socialist and then said, 'Look, I am going to forge a weapon for you:—and thus I too work with you for the overthrow of Society.' To which he replied, 'the weapon is too small to be of any value.'"[4]

From the first, Ashbee realized that what he was starting must be "a workman's movement; that it shall be one for the nobility and advance of English Art and Handicraft; that it shall be developed not on the basis of mastership in the ordinary sense, but co-operatively as an industrial* partnership and that the arts and crafts, united in the Guild, shall be the children of the mother art of architecture."[5]

The Guild's original three members started by selling woodwork, metalwork (Ashbee was a distin-

---

* His childhood may have been happy but his early manhood was not. His father was in the Hamburg trade, married one of the daughters of the great merchant house with which he dealt and prospered exceedingly. He was also the notorious Victorian por-nographile "Pisianus Fraxi". The marriage broke up (which explains why Ashbee's first house was for his mother), and Ashbee himself was disinherited by his father.

* Ashbee's use of the word industrial is contradictory and confus-ing. Here from the context, he intended to mean no more than "systematically economic", a use common in Arts and Crafts cir-cles of the '90s (see for instance *Studio*, Vol. XVIII, 1900, p. 120). But sometimes he used the word in its modern sense of machine dominated.

guished designer of silverware and jewellery) and decorative painting, but its scope quickly grew to cover all the arts and crafts. Increasing affluence allowed the Guild and School to move in 1891 to Essex House in the Mile End Road, an early eighteenth-century house which the Guild adapted and extended into classrooms, workshops and club-rooms. In 1898, Ashbee opened a shop in Brook Street and set up the Essex House Press.

By the end of the decade, the venture was an established success, and it appeared to be living up to its principles. The *Studio* reported of the 1899 Arts and Crafts Exhibition Society show that "the work to which the name of Mr. C. R. Ashbee is attached ought to be regarded less as his individual work than as that of the Guild of Handicraft in its collective capacity. For between the productions of Essex House and those issuing from elsewhere there is broadly this difference, that whereas many contemporary artists cause their designs to be carried out by artisans working under them and implicitly obeying their orders, Mr. Ashbee, as head of the Guild founded by him, seeks rather to elicit the potential talent of the work-shop; his responsibility being comprised in general supervision, sometimes merely in advice or sugges-tion, as distinct from absolute dictation; and in so acting he claims, indeed, to be fulfilling in its most literal sense the original purpose for which the Arts and Crafts Society was called into existence."[6]

Quite early in his career, the practical problems of running the Guild convinced Ashbee of the impor-tance of coming to terms with machine production. As a "constructive" rather than revolutionary social-ist, Ashbee did not follow Morris in advocating the violent destruction of Victorian capitalism and its machinery.

In 1894 he explained that "the industrial organiza-tion of the mine, the mill and the dockyard must always remain quite a different thing from that of the builder's yard, the cabinet maker's, jeweller's or blacksmith's shop, or any form of production in which the hand and its individuality may prevail over the machine, but I believe that object lessons from the reconstruction of the latter may be drawn for the use of the former."[7]

Fourteen years later he was more explicit. "What I seek to show is that this Arts and Crafts movement, which began with the earnestness of the Pre-Raphaelite painters, the prophetic enthusiasm of Ruskin and the titanic energy of Morris, is not what the public has thought it to be, or is seeking to make

it: a nursery for luxuries, a hothouse for the produc-tion of mere trivialities and useless things for the rich. It is a movement for the stamping out of such things by sound production on the one hand and the in-evitable regulation of machine production and cheap labour on the other . . . To the men of this movement, who are seeking to compass the destruction of the commercial system, to discredit it, undermine it, overthrow it, their mission is just as serious and just as sacred as was that of their great grandfathers who first helped raise it into being . . . They want to put into the place of the old order that is passing away, some-thing finer, nobler, saner; they want to determine the limitations of the factory system, to regulate machin-ery, to get back to realities in labour and human life."[8]

He was never opposed to using machinery in craft-work itself: "thus a timber plank [the Guild held] could be sawn by a circular saw but it should not be subsequently carved by machinery": the client should not "be put off with the machine-made article on the score of cheapness, neatness or trade finish."[9]

If machinery was really to be regulated, if crafts-manship was to be an example to the factory system, craftwork would have to be able to compete on more equal terms with the machine so that its products were not just expensive luxuries for the rich but could be freely chosen by everyone. So the economic basis of craftsmanship had to be reorganized.

The Guild's co-operative workshop was one way of doing this. But it was not enough, and, in 1902 when the Essex House lease expired, Ashbee took the revolutionary step of leading the Guild (150 men, women and children from the East End accompanied him after a democratic vote) to Chipping Campden, a "little forgotten Cotswold town of the Age of the Arts and Crafts where industrialism had never touched, where there was an old silk mill and empty cottages ready to hand, left almost as when the Arts and Crafts ended in the eighteenth century."[10]

The motives were many, not least to establish the poetic relationship between people, craftsmanship and the land described in *News from Nowhere*. It later became clear that one advantage was that living off the land could provide a subsidy for craftwork. As smallholders, the workers could produce much of their own food which, coupled with the cheaper rents of country property, was supposed to allow them to charge less for their craft objects and so to allow these to compete with machine products.

At first, the project prospered. About half the craftsmen and their families took to cultivation seri-

156 *Charles Robert Ashbee. Magpie and Stump, Cheyne Walk, Chelsea, London (1894, now destroyed)*
The house is nearest the camera, with the still existing nos. 38 and 39 behind

ously; new cottages were built and old ones improved; a school of higher education was founded on the lines of Essex House; all kinds of recreation were started: a drama society, a swimming club with its own bathing lake, and the town band was revitalized. Yet the Cockneys were never really accepted by the country folk, gentry and peasants alike. In 1905 trade began to fall off and by the end of 1907 the position was so desperate that the Guild had to be wound up as a limited company.

Ashbee attributed the failure partly to the decreasing purchasing power of the Guild's established clients and to the growing fashion for buying antiques instead of new made objects. But some of the difficulties were inherent in working in the country: it was difficult to keep in proper touch with clients in London from the heart of Gloucestershire; the Guild was at the mercy of the railway companies which appear to have been just as inefficient and rapacious as British Rail is now; and isolation in the countryside meant that guildsmen could not exploit a wider labour market as they had been able to in London. In the bad times at Essex House, craftsmen had simply found work elsewhere, to return when the Guild was in better straits.

After the crash, some craftsmen had to leave Chipping Campden altogether and, though the Guild was reconstituted with the help of the American socialist millionaire Joseph Fels (it paid him four and a half per cent on his investment), neither the Guild nor Ashbee seems to have fully recovered self-confidence. The Guild staggered on until 1919 when, as a late casualty of the War, it was finally disbanded, though several craftsmen stayed on in Campden until their deaths.

In fact, the realities of Guildwork may have been rather different from the idyllic pastoral painted by Ashbee. Alec Miller, who joined the Campden group, wrote to Ashbee afterwards that "the Guild was never a real Guild . . . since I knew it in 1902. Most of the Guildsmen . . . regarded the Guild as a nuisance . . . The higher ideals of Craftsmanship also, as I soon saw, were not in the craftsmen—but were in you—and, if you as director said that beaten and hammered silver work was better than spun work they accepted it . . . The Guild never produced things co-operatively since I knew it—it produced things working under your direction."[11] Miller thought that in the successful years at Campden, the Guild was too big to allow any real co-operation.

Ashbee continued to believe that "the Standard of work and the Standard of life are one; that beauty of work and goodness are for craftsmen best expressed in the making of things that are serviceable; that this implies the acceptance by the Community of Standard . . . and that the Socialistic State or the State at which we are aiming is not possible without the recognition of Standard."[12] If agriculture would not suffice to sustain the Arts and Crafts to fight on equal terms with machine production, other means must be found. Ashbee, the life long educationist, saw the answer in the schools of art and design.

In "Should we stop teaching art" published in 1911, he proposed reconstituting these in association with workshops on the lines of the Guild and School of Handicraft. But there was to be an essential difference. The state would put up an interest free capital fund (of quite modest size) which would provide, free, all the materials needed by the craftsmen and pay up to half their labour costs. In return, a craftsman would accept at least one apprentice from the school. Once the system was working properly, the state could withdraw, for the profits from the sale of craftwork could be used to re-endow the fund and sponsor more and more craftworkers.

Ashbee's attitude to machinery changed. He continued to believe that, though it was immoral to produce certain types of metal work, furniture or clothing by machine, "it is just as immoral to keep men making mechanical things by hand—chains, for instance, in which the links have to be exact—when the machine would do the work better."[13] The Standard should be still set by craftwork, yet here too machines had an increased part to play—but machines of a particular sort. "The whole tendency of what is known in America as 'fine machine tool production' is in the direction of personal skill, and the use by the individual of the tool, and the power behind it under his direct control. All mechanism that helps individuality may also help the Arts."[14]

Ashbee's understanding of machinery was far more profound than that of many of his contemporaries. In a sense, his insistence that "there is a way of distinguishing between the good and the bad in machine production" so that "it becomes much more difficult to be revolutionary"[15] brings Morris into the twentieth century. But perhaps Ashbee's qualified acceptance would have been less emphatic had he realized then how long it would take for machines which aid individuality to become readily available and how often, once they did, forms of contract would ensure that workpeople remained enslaved to what he called

Mechanism. Certainly in his lifetime, Ashbee saw little progress. Governments were so uninterested in Standard that they preferred to pay people to remain unemployed rather than to experiment with Ashbee's system for subsidizing the crafts.

Ashbee had practised as an architect from the early '90s and in building, as in everything else, he firmly adhered to Guild principles. "The first duty of the architect", he believed, "is to interpret his client's wishes, and the first duty of a builder is honesty." And he despised "the relationship in which modern industrial development has placed the architect and the builder towards one another, setting the former to check the latter."[16]

"Architecture, the 'Mother Art' which should be guardian and helper of all Arts and Crafts, has, through the agency of industrial machinery and the contract system become in large measure the instrument of their destruction—an evil mother, destroying her little ones."[17] So Ashbee often did away with the general contractor and worked direct as builder and architect with Guildsmen "a group of conscientious workmen, say a joiner or two, a few masons, and a couple of blacksmiths, all of whom were intimate with me, knew my ways and worked in my spirit."[18]*

The first fruits of this collaboration were Ashbee's mother's house and his own offices, the Magpie and Stump in Cheyne Walk, Chelsea. Completed in 1894 it was† a tall, thin London house with a big three-storey oriel, all quietly clad in soft red brick with stone dressings, not unlike Voysey's Hans Road. Inside, the house was simple but relieved by touches of rich craftsmanship. The chimney breast in the hall, for instance, ran without a mantel-shelf from floor to frieze covered in copper squares, many of which said the *Studio* were "enriched by the results of various experiments in enamels. Thus spots of gorgeous crimsons, purples and greens, inserted apparently by chance among the plain copper squares, give a jewelled effect to the whole."[19] Roger Fry (a friend from Cambridge days) painted the mural over the drawing-room fireplace, and the curtains and piano cover were embroidered by Ashbee's mother. The *Studio* was particularly keen on the light fittings. "Mr.

* Alan Crawford tells me that, under what Ashbee called the Guild system of building, Guild workmen did the wood and metal work while bricklayers and mason were employed for the duration of each job.

† The building has been scandalously demolished within the last ten years to make way for an elephantine monument to greed and mediocrity.

157 *Magpie and Stump, hall fireplace*

158 *Magpie and Stump, light fitting*

159 *Ashbee. 38 and 39 Cheyne Walk (1899)*

Ashbee has avoided the attempt to imitate gaseliers ... Recognizing that a wire and not a tube was the essential factor, he has shown you the structure of the fittings boldly ... In the drawing-room the corona is further enriched by pendulous balls of jewel like enamel which catch the light and sparkle in spots of superb colour purely as ornament"[20]—a perfect summary of Ashbee's attitude, ready to welcome new technology and express it directly, yet always insistent on impressing the stamp of craftsmanship.

The much less gorgeous craftsmanship of the exterior is the hallmark of Ashbee's architecture. Almost every building he designed was carefully, almost humbly, designed to fit in with its surroundings—yet all show individuality. His work was divided between town houses in Chelsea, country cottages and loving restorations, (for instance of Turner's and Carlyle's houses in Chelsea and of his own first house in Campden, the Woolstapler's Hall).

Ashbee built several other houses in Cheyne Walk, but only two, numbers 38 and 39 (1899), remain. They originally formed a very free group, dominated by the white-rendered asymmetrical gable that fronted number 39's studio. The gable was pierced by a circular window, a motif occasionally taken up by other Arts and Crafts architects. Simple but decorative ironwork protected those areas with a design of verticals imposed on large semi-circles, all topped with gold finials. Even more free was his design (1897) for Danvers Tower, an unexecuted group of studio flats which was to have been built on the corner of Cheyne Walk and Danvers Street. Here, a great

160 *Ashbee and Charles Holden. Danvers Tower, design for Cheyne Walk (1897)*

white tower, divided asymmetrically by a vertical strip of windows and finished with a shallow metal hat, was to have terminated a lower block in brick and stone with pronounced horizontals and irregular strips of window, topped by a great green pitched roof. Many of the motifs are similar to Voysey's but they are used with a freedom at which Voysey never aimed.*

The early Cheyne Walk designs have materials and, to some extent, window proportions in common with the undistinguished Georgian artisans' dwellings they replaced. But, even when they were grouped as at the Magpie and Stump, each was consciously individual—nearly always asymmetrical, they had odd, completely un-Georgian emphases, like 39's gable or the lozenge-shaped windows of numbers 72 and 73 (1897). Ashbee was trying to create a new, picturesque, changeful Chelsea in place of Georgian regularity and uniformity.

Ashbee was gradually infected with the growing fashion for classical building and he acquired a humbler attitude to the Georgian nature of Cheyne Walk. He designed a block of flats which was to have terminated against Cheyne Walk in two identical five-storey, nearly neo-Georgian blocks connected by a colonnade. It was never built and nor was Ashbee's

In his *Memoirs*, Ashbee said "the drawings and much of the invention were by Charles Holden, then working in my office".[21]

most interesting big design of this period, Shrewsbury Court, a complex of student dwellings which
was to have fronted Cheyne Walk with the mighty
machicolated tower of the men's hostel joining a big
arched entrance gate; it was an elevation as inventive
as many of Mackintosh's. But in the courts beyond
the gate were two large hostels for women and mar-

ried students designed in strictest symmetrical stripped classic.

This affection for classical architecture is very
rarely seen in Ashbee's country work. On new, open

161 *Ashbee. 72 and 73 Cheyne Walk (1897, now destroyed)*

162 *Ashbee. Shrewsbury Court, design for Cheyne Walk (c. 1911)*

163 *Ashbee. Little Coppice, Iver Heath, Buckinghamshire (1905)*

sites he tended to use white roughcast or brick for the same reason as Voysey—economy. And on occasion he would use Voysey-like buttresses, for instance in Little Coppice at Iver Heath, Buckinghamshire (1905), where he adopted a remarkably economical square plan with white-rendered ground floor walls irregularly pierced with windows. The upper floor is in a pyramidal roof covered with a grey-green slate which, he thought, "certainly looks well against the dark wall of pines at the side of the garden."[22]

Most of his country work was in and around Chipping Campden, much of which he rebuilt and restored for Guild members after 1902. Izod's Cottage (now, regrettably called Shreelaine) in the High Street is typical. Partly built from materials found in the two dilapidated cottages on the site, it has stone mullions and iron casements, stone walls coursed so that the largest blocks are at the bottom and a dormered roof on which the stone slates are "laid in gradation—the larger and heavier at the eaves, the smaller near the ridge. The beauty of old masonry and roofing lies in observing details of this kind."[23] Now, it is almost impossible to distinguish between Ashbee's buildings and those hundreds of years older.

His most ambitious amalgam of old and new work was Norman Chapel at Broad Campden, done for the Ceylonese philosopher Coomarswamy, a house eventually occupied by Ashbee himself. He found an eleventh-century church, converted into a house in the fourteenth century, all derelict. (The Cotswolds were very different before they were invaded by rich midlands businessmen and aristocrats escaping from the Irish troubles after the First War.) Ashbee scrupulously preserved the old work "while adapting it to modern needs" and brought his new "into harmony with it without in any way working to a period or falsifying history—the old work is old and the new new."[24] Today it stands, a higgledy mixture of building bound together by materials unchanged over nine hundred years and a community of craftsmanship down the centuries. In its savageness and changefulness, its truth to tradition and to contemporary need, it is one of the greatest achievements of that side of Arts and Crafts building which tried tenderly and humbly to fulfill Pugin's plea for local English architecture.

When Ashbee started to settle his band of craftsmen in north Gloucestershire, a similar group was already celebrating its ninth birthday on the southern edge of the county. Ashbee visited it just before the War and commented, "the future of the arts must be

164 *Ashbee. Norman Chapel, Broad Campden, Gloucestershire (1906)*

in groups and schools and this little Sapperton group stands for something live and fine . . . I've not discovered yet which of these three men, Ernest or Sidney Barnsley or Gimson, has the inspiration. All work in the same mood. Perhaps they inspire each other, that is as it should be."[25]

Ernest Gimson (1864–1919) was the son of a wealthy Leicester engineer and had met Morris in his parents' house. Morris advised him to go to London to train as an architect under J. D. Sedding (whose office was then next door to the Morris shop in Bond Street). There, in 1886, he met Ernest Barnsley (1861–1926), the son of a successful Birmingham builder, and through Barnsley's brother Sidney (1863–1926), who was in Shaw's office, he was gradually introduced to the inner Arts and Crafts circle.

In 1890, Gimson and Sidney Barnsley set up a furniture firm in partnership with Lethaby, Macartney, Blomfield and a Colonel Mallet. Kenton & Co. flourished for a couple of years until it had to be wound up for lack of capital.[26] The architects acted as designers for Kenton & Co. and did not make the furniture themselves but this was not enough for Gimson, who apprenticed himself to a firm of plasterers and to an old fashioned furniture maker near Ledbury who produced high-backed chairs turned on a pole lathe.

His plasterwork was put to immediate use by Lethaby who employed him to design and execute the elaborate ceilings in the main rooms at Avon Tyrell, where Lethaby recalled that in the summer of 1872, "he lodged for months in a cottage close by, and after my visits to the 'works' in the morning we played cricket with the children in the afternoon."[27]

The attractions of country life were too strong to be resisted and, in 1893, Gimson and Sidney Barnsley moved to Ewen in South Gloucestershire and persuaded Ernest, who was practising as an architect in Birmingham, to join them. A year later they moved to nearby Pinbury Park and in 1902 they transferred to Sapperton. Throughout this period, all three were involved in furniture production in a workshop which they ran jointly, Gimson mainly as a designer, though Sidney Barnsley made all his own furniture himself. Gimson believed in handwork though, like Ashbee, he was prepared to allow machines like circular saws. And, like Ashbee, he was prepared to let machine production look after itself. "He desired commercial-

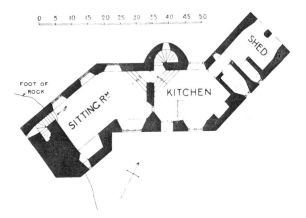

ism might leave handiwork and the arts alone and make use of its own wits and its own machinery. Let machinery be honest, he said, and make its own machine-buildings and its own machine furniture; let it make its chairs and tables of stamped aluminium if it likes: why not?"[28] But Gimson lacked Ashbee's understanding that machine production would inevitably win unless society could be radically changed.

Gimson's architecture was mostly designed in the '90s. There are two houses in Leicester done for members of his family in a free Georgian style, one with a most ingenious compact plan. Near Leicester, on the edge of Charnwood forest which rises hummocky, dark and mysterious in the middle of one of England's most pastoral counties, Gimson built three summer houses for the same clients. Henry Wilson commented in the *Architectural Review*, when Gimson showed photographs at the 1899 Arts and Crafts show, "The buildings look as solid and lasting as the pyramids, and though they are built with almost stern rudeness, yet they look gracious and homelike."[29] Stoneywell Cottage, the best of the three, was built for Gimson's brother Sidney. It cranks up and round the curve of one of the heathery Charnwood hummocks and grows out of the rock more like a series of

165 *Ernest Gimson. Stoneywell Cottage near Leicester (1898). The cottage was re-roofed in slate and partly redesigned after a fire*

166 *Stoneywell Cottage, plan*

167 *Gimson. Living room, Leasowes, Sapperton*

168 *Gimson. Bedales School library (1920)*

169 *Gimson. Bedales School library interior*

imposed strata than a building. Great flat stones project from the masonry both outside and in (where they are used as shelves). It was roofed in dark thatch* which rose to a ridge capped with straw, giving the back of the building the impression of a crested and amiable dragon worming its way round the hill. Inside, the bare rock was exposed in the sitting room, and partitions were made of halved tree trunks with plaster and lath between. "The actual building was done by Mr. Detmar Blow . . . captaining a little band of masons and gaining that practical knowledge of the crafts which has since stood him in good stead."[30]

The cottage is Arts and Crafts architecture at its most earthy—if nature made buildings, they would surely look something like Stoneywell. Gimson built

* There was a fire in 1938, after which the roof was replaced with slates by another Gimson. Most of the internal timber remains and the walls were unaffected—though some of the windows were enlarged.

little else: a few buildings at Kelmscott as a memorial to William Morris, his own house at Sapperton and a cottage near Budleigh Salterton made out of local thatch and cobb (rammed earth). He only once caught the naturalism of Stoneywell again, in his last job, the library of Bedales School, finished by Sidney Barnsley after Gimson's early death. Outside, the building is conventionally neo-Tudor, brick with leaded casements. Inside, the roof is supported on great rough-sawn timbers which branch tree-like at gallery level into curved supports for the roof forming a covered grove of beautiful stateliness and simplicity.

Like Gimson, Ernest Barnsley often worked as an architect. He did work for SPAB, his own house at Sapperton which, like Norman Chapel, was a beautifully harmonious extension of an existing building, and he produced one of the largest and last Arts and Crafts country houses, Rodmarton Manor, Gloucestershire, on which the client, the Hon. Claude Biddulph, spent £5,000 a year between 1909

170 *Ernest Barnsley. Upper Dorvil house, Sapperton, Gloucestershire (1902). Original cottage in centre*

171 *Sidney Barnsley. Beechanger, Sapperton (1902). The lean-to and the right-hand gable are additions*

172 *Ernest Barnsley. Rodmarton Manor, Gloucestershire (started 1909, completed by Norman Jewson 1929)*

and Barnsley's death in 1926, interrupted only by the War. At first sight the house, warm, mullioned and many-gabled, seems vast. It *is* big, but the Arts and Crafts plan, one-room-and-a-corridor deep, which wanders over the site, makes it seem much larger than it really is.

It is built in strictest Cotswold tradition with virtually no new motifs. All the timber was found locally and all the stone quarried on the estate. And it was built by hand—even the circular saw was eschewed and the wood was sawn in a pit. It is one of the most determined applications of Ruskinian precepts. Ashbee, who visited the works in October 1914, said that "I've seen no modern work to equal it . . . And when I ask why, I find the answer in the system, the method rather than the man. It is a house built on the basis not of contract but of confidence . . . The English Arts and Crafts Movement at its best is here."[31] Rodmarton is magnificent* but it is a dead end; a medieval house created in a medieval way in one of the last pockets of feudalism in England. Barnsley was lucky to have a rich client prepared to take his time. By 1914 time was critical.

On his visit to Sapperton, Ashbee recalled that

* It also shows the worst side of the Arts and Crafts dislike of machinery. While Gimson and the Barnsleys were leading an idyllic life combining creative work and close contact with the countryside, two men, a father and son, spent a large portion of their lives in the backbreaking repetitive labour of sawing planks by hand. The task would have been much more easily and less demeaningly done with a circular saw, as architects like Ashbee and Voysey realized.

173 *Rodmarton Manor, a garden court*

"Gimson took me over his workshops and his house. He glowed happily at having a kindred spirit to confide in [and said] 'It's a frightful problem to keep things going: how to keep the men employed, how to keep your standard up' . . . In the middle of our talk Gimson suddenly seized the iron fire clippers. 'There,' he said, 'can any smith of yours make a piece like that? . . . It's the most difficult double joint you can forge.' I thought of Bill Thornton and Charley Downer also at work in their Cotswold valley. 'It's all a matter of time' [I replied]. 'Ah yes', he said, 'time. That's it. Time. Let's forget these d-d economics and get to constructive facts again.'"[32]

Ashbee, less well insulated by a handsome private income than Gimson and the Barnsleys, and much more socially idealistic, was never one to forget the d-d economics. He was becoming more optimistic in the first half of 1914. The Campden community seemed to be a real Guild; there was plenty to do and the partnership of craft and agriculture was apparently working. Yet it was a false dawn; "The war and its aftermath was to reveal what we did not then know, how limited and precarious was the patronage"[33]—there was no time left.

1 Ashbee, C. R. *Trivialities of Tom, being reflections on a Victorian boyhood*, unpublished manuscript in Victoria and Albert Museum, 1940–41, p. 7

2 Ashbee, C. R. *Transactions of the Guild and School of Handicraft*, Vol. I, 1890, p. 19

3 *Ibid*

4 Ashbee, C. R. *Memoirs*, typescript in Victoria and Albert Museum library, Vol. I, p. 45

5 *Transactions, op. cit.*, p. 22

6 *Studio*, Vol. XVIII, 1900, p. 118

7 Ashbee, C. R. *A few Chapters in Workshop Reconstruction and Citizenship*, Essex House, London 1894, p. 10

8 Ashbee, C. R. *Craftsmanship in Competitive Industry*, Essex House, Campden, Gloucestershire 1908, p. 9

9 *Ibid.*, p. 18

10 *Ibid.*, p. 42

11 Letter from Alec Miller to Ashbee, 1911, quoted in *Memoirs*, Vol. III, p. 190

12 *Craftsmanship, op. cit.*, p. 224

13 Ashbee, C. R. *Should we stop teaching art* Batsford, London 1911, p. 13

14 *Ibid.*, p. 98

15 *Ibid.*, p. 115

16 Ashbee, C. R. *A Book of Cottages and Little Houses*, Batsford, London 1906, p. 97

17 Ashbee, C. R. *Craftsmanship, op. cit.*, p. 125

18 *Ibid.*, p. 142

19 *Studio*, Vol. V, 1895, p. 72

20 *Ibid.*, p. 74

21 Ashbee, C. R. *Memoirs*, Vol. I, p. 111

22 Ashbee, C. R. "On the Bromleigh Estate at Iver Heath", *Studio*, Vol. XXXVI, 1905, p. 50

23 Ashbee, C. R. *A Book of Cottages, op. cit.*, p. 9

24 Ashbee, C. R. "The Norman Chapel buildings at Broad Campden", *Studio*, Vol. XLI, 1907, p. 290

25 Ashbee, C. R. *Memoirs, op. cit.*, Vol III, p. 366

26 The history of Kenton & Co. is summarized in Lethaby's contribution to *Ernest Gimson, His Life and Work*, Stratford, Oxford and London 1924, p. 6 and in Blomfield's *Memoirs of an Architect*, Macmillan, London 1932, p. 76–78.

27 Lethaby, W. R. *Ernest Gimson, op. cit.*, p. 7

28 Powell, Alfred H. *Ernest Gimson, op. cit.*, p. 14

29 Wilson, H. "The Arts and Crafts Society's Exhibition", *Architectural Review*, Vol. VI, 1899, p. 214

30 Weaver, Lawrence *Small Country Houses of Today*, second series, 1919, p. 16

31 Quoted by Clive Aslet in *Country Life*, Vol. CLXIV, 1978, p. 1181

32 Ashbee, C. R. *Memoirs, op. cit.*, Vol. IV, p. 71

33 *Ibid.*, Vol. III, pp. 367–368

12 The Descent

The War virtually killed Arts and Crafts architecture. Ashbee very rarely practised as architect afterwards—though he did sterling service as civil advisor to the Palestine government between 1917 and 1923, repairing Jerusalem's walls according to SPAB principles.

A few anachronistic clients clung to the free style after the War, but Arts and Crafts architecture had been dying for a decade before 1914. Without a radical change in society, it was impossible for the movement to have any more permanent basis than the production of luxuries for the upper middle class. When upper middle class taste began to change, the architect and designer had to change too. As the social ideals of Morris and Ruskin lost their force in the imagination of the time, the Gothic spirit withered, and architects turned increasingly to classical styles for inspiration. The few Arts and Crafts men who stuck to Gothic principles were increasingly left out.

After 1906, for instance, Voysey got few architectural commissions, and those he did get were not large; he began to use overtly Gothic detailing which must have made him increasingly less popular. Lethaby built nothing after 1902. Prior gradually faded out as an architect. The lesser followers of Pugin, Ruskin and Morris: people like Troup, Dawber, Blow and Ricardo, gradually changed their style to classic symmetry and severity in the decade around the War, though almost all of them returned to less formal designs occasionally.

The change in style was related to a change in the status of England. In the two middle quarters of the nineteenth century, Britain had been the workshop of the world, achieving her economic pre-eminence by unparalleled commercial exploitation of the machin- against which Ruskin and Morris had railed so ely. But from the 1870s, Britain's success became ndoing; the civilized nations began to erect tarif

walls against British goods, and by 1900 the Continent, the US and even the white colonies such as Australia and Canada were protected by high import levies. Real incomes in Britain, which had grown throughout the last decade of the nineteenth century, virtually stagnated between 1900 and 1914.

The prosperous middle classes on whom the Arts and Crafts movement had relied so much had the butter taken off their bread—particularly after the Liberal government of 1906 increasingly introduced reforms to alleviate the lot of working people, a process that culminated in Lloyd George's notorious 1909 budget which raised death duties, income tax from one shilling to a grievous one shilling and twopence and introduced super-tax and (abortively) Land Value duties. If you were wealthy and middle class, the years after 1906 were not a good time to build. But even if you felt secure enough to do so, your attitude to what was proper in building was likely to be very different from that of the previous generation.

To ensure a balance of trade and to finance reforms at home, Britain was increasingly forced to exploit colonies in Asia and Africa and semi-colonies like China. With the colonization of Africa a new element had entered British imperialism; economic necessity forced Britain to promote forms of serfdom and near slavery. Instead of being left to the doubtful mercies of the market, natives were exploited by government. For instance, all the land in Kenya was declared forfeit in 1898, forcing natives into overcrowded reserves on inferior soil whence they were obliged to toil on farms owned by Europeans by a punitive system of taxation. In South Africa, the last war of Victoria's reign was fought to obtain control of the Johannesburg gold fields; when Britain won, mass immigration from India was encouraged to provide indentured labour to work the mines.

This was the dark side of an Empire on which Britain was ever more dependent. London was rebuilt as an imperial capital in the first decade of the century and Ruskin would not have been surprised to find that the great schemes—for example Admiralty Arch, built by Aston Webb between 1906 and 1911—were all erected in the high classical style which he had so scathingly decried as the architecture of slavery.*

Throughout middle class life, from the boy scout movement to the Stock Exchange, there was new emphasis on order and leadership, on things established, old looking and tested. Antique collecting became the rage to the detriment of working craftsmen. In architecture, the main spokesman of the new mood was Reginald Blomfield. Though a member of the Art Workers' Guild and the Arts and Crafts Exhibition Society from their earliest years, friend of

Lethaby and Gimson, Blomfield had long been a classicist and published several books calling for increased formality in building. His *Short History of Renaissance Architecture in England* (1897) paralleled Prior's book on English Gothic, and in the 1900 edition Blomfield made his position clear. Commenting on the late nineteenth century he urged that because "the co-operative art of the Middle Ages was no longer possible, some-one must take the lead. A strong individual intelligence was needed to restore order in this chaos of eclecticism."[1]

Made professor of architecture at the Royal Academy in 1906, Blomfield was in a strong position to proselytize. He hoped "against hope to divert students from the fashion for the picturesque and abundance of ornament prevalent at the time to a loftier conception of architecture as the art of *ordonnance*."[2] In his lectures, he stressed that the student "need not concern himself with dogmatic theories of the relation of art and morality in studying architecture"[3]: it was the perennial conservative plea that art has nothing to do with politics and that it should implicitly support the *status quo*. His ideal was a return to eighteenth-century traditions of craftsmanship in which the workman could be guaranteed to turn out work by

* Classicism was not limited to London. It permeated the whole empire. Herbert Baker was sent by the great imperialist Cecil Rhodes, to "visit the old countries of the Mediterranean to get inspiration for any 'thoughts' he might 'undertake'." Rhodes's "thoughts" included war memorials and a great Greek temple half way up a mountain. (Baker, Herbert *Architecture and Personalities*, Country Life, London 1944, p. 35.)

174 *R. Norman Shaw. Bryanston, Dorset (1889–1894)*

rote without any troublesome individuality creeping in. "When an architect can depend on his men, he is spared the necessity of spending half his time in explaining to builders details which ought to be matters of common knowledge, he has leisure to devote his energy to his real business of thinking out the central conception of his design."[4]

In 1906, classical architecture was no recent introduction. From about 1890 on, Shaw was almost entirely a classicist, creating buildings of great formality like Bryanston (1889–1894) and the Lower Regent Street Quadrant (finished by Blomfield after many vicissitudes). By 1902, Shaw believed that "we have now no proper traditional architecture, for it died away imperceptibly at the beginning of the last century... From the date of the Exhibition of 1851 until recently we were all intensely Gothic—and intensely wrong. We were trying to revive a style which was quite unsuited to the present day. Since 1880, however, we have been gradually awakening to this fact. After spending millions of pounds we came to the conclusion that it had been to no purpose. The Gothic revival, for all practical purposes, is dead, and the tendency of late years has been to return to the English Renaissance. I was trained on the older Gothic lines, I am personally devoted to it, admire it in the abstract, and think it superb; but it is totally unsuited to modern requirements. When it came to building, especially in places like the City, we found it would not answer."[5]

Another early user of classical forms was John Belcher (1841–1913), who had sat in the chair at the meeting which founded the Art Workers' Guild. He produced the Institute of Chartered Accountants building between 1889 and 1893. With its mansard roof, free use of tuscan columns and heavy rustication, it was immensely influential. Less influential was the way in which, in proper Art Workers' Guild fashion, it incorporated an intricate frieze of figure sculpture above the windows of the piano nobile (by Hamo Thornycroft, another AWG man) and delicate female figures above the ground floor columns. Inside, Belcher and his assistant Beresford Pite gave the newly respectable accounting profession an appropriately grand setting with a council chamber lined with vast murals and topped by a staggeringly tall drum and dome. The building was the work of an older generation of Guildsmen than Prior and Lethaby but it was one which demonstrated all their love of working together and incorporating painting and sculpture into architecture. That it lacked any

175 *John Belcher. Institute of Chartered Accountants, London (1889–1893)*

allegiance to the principles of Ruskin and Morris, so revered by the younger men, showed the contradictory nature of the Guild.

In the next two decades, free neo-baroque became a major style for new civic architecture throughout Britain, with many grandiose buildings to its credit—Deptford Town Hall (1902–1904) by Lanchester and Rickards for instance, and their Central Hall, Westminster (1905).

Other classical idioms emerged. There was a Wrenaissance following Bryanston in which Wren became a model for country houses and less grand town buildings. Early in this century, a much more severe and correct classical style emerged—based on the French renaissance (the style was not unrelated to the monarch's continental predilections). One of the

first examples was the Ritz Hotel in Piccadilly by
Mewès and Davis (completed 1906). It made a tremendous impression. Charles Reilly, professor of
architecture at Liverpool from 1904, recalled that
when the Mewès and Davis work first appeared,
"they seemed to set a new, and for an Englishman, an
almost impossible standard of elegance".[6] The schools
had joined the profession in support of classicism.

Yet against this background, two Arts and Crafts
architects, Lutyens and Baillie-Scott, continued to
get work and even increase their practices. Each
coped with the new climate in his own way.

Edwin Landseer Lutyens (1869–1944) was the
eleventh of fourteen children of an army captain who
retired from the service to train under Landseer and
became a moderately successful sporting painter.
Because of illness and the relative poverty of his
parents, Ned (as Edwin not surprisingly preferred to
be known) was educated at home, and was virtually
self-taught, in the Surrey countryside, until at sixteen
he was sent to what became the Royal College of Art
to study architecture. At about this time, he met
Norman Shaw and "after a little conversation the PRA
of the future was telling Norman Shaw RA of his
experiments in the type of building suited to agricultural enterprise; just mud-encased on wooden piles,
roofed with heather, resistant to wind and weather,
warm in winter, cool in summer, conforming with the
surroundings . . . with what he called 'my fixed principles'—this made Shaw smile—and those were that
anything put up by man should harmonize with what
Nature, who had been there first, should dictate.
Materials should be drawn from those obtainable in
the area and foreign elements strictly eliminated.
'Very interesting, my boy, but not always feasible',
interrupted the great man. 'All right for cowsheds,
but human beings demand something a little more in
keeping with the age in which we live, and if you had
my experience you would find that the newly-rich,
who are after all the patrons of today, demand
replicas of something they have seen in other countries they have visited.'"[7]

Shaw, the early Shaw of Old English, was
Lutyens's model when he set up on his own at twenty
after a couple of years at school and another two in the
office of Ernest George & Peto. Lutyens's early
houses are rather clumsy, heavy with brick, half-
timber and great tile roofs. He found Webb's work in
the early '90s and became an immediate disciple. He
recalled, of his first sight of Webb's Joldwynds:
"'That's good . . ., I wonder who the young man is.'

176 *Edwin Landseer Lutyens. Munstead Wood
(1896), for Gertrude Jekyll*

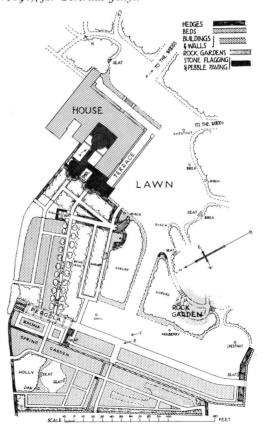

177 *Gertrude Jekyll. Garden plan for Munstead Wood*

The freshness and originality which Webb maintained in all his work, I, in my ignorance, attributed to youth."[8]

Another strong influence on the young Lutyens was Gertrude Jekyll. Munstead Wood, which Lutyens built for Jekyll in 1896, was made with all the thoroughness and attention to tradition that Webb would have wished. Miss Jekyll recounted that "the architect has a thorough knowledge of the local ways of using the sandstone that grows in our hills, and that for many centuries has been the building materials of the district, and of all the lesser incidental methods of adapting means to ends that mark the well-defined way of building of the country, so that what he builds seems to grow naturally out of the ground . . . I hold as a convincing canon in architecture that every building should look like what it is.'"[9] The tiled roof comes right down to the top of the doors and is relieved by large gables containing the first floor rooms; windows are strips of oak-framed casements with leaded lights—a Voyseyish composition, but Munstead Wood is Voysey made particular: virtually every detail is derived from a Surrey precedent.

It was the first of a succession of lovely Surrey houses in which, while being faithful to vernacular motifs, Lutyens began to show his powers of invention. Deanery Garden, Sonning, built in 1899 for Edward Hudson, managing editor of *Country Life* (to which Miss Jekyll contributed gardening articles) is a fine example. Lutyens took the room-and-a-corridor plan and cranked it round three sides of a courtyard (he was one of the first Arts and Crafts architects to bend the plan in this way and often used three- and four-sided courtyards later). But, even more inventive, he rammed the south-eastern corridor straight through from back to front of the house, making a partly open, partly covered route for the family from entrance to garden with stairs, sitting room and hall (a big drawing room in country house tradition) opening straight off it. This convenient, economical, yet grand plan was given walls of small local bricks, roofs of sandy tiles (to attract lichen) and a great double-height square bay in the hall made of oak with pegged joints and leaded lights.

At Deanery Garden the main (south-west) front would have been virtually symmetrical about the hall

178 *Lutyens. Deanery Garden, Sonning, Berkshire (1899)*

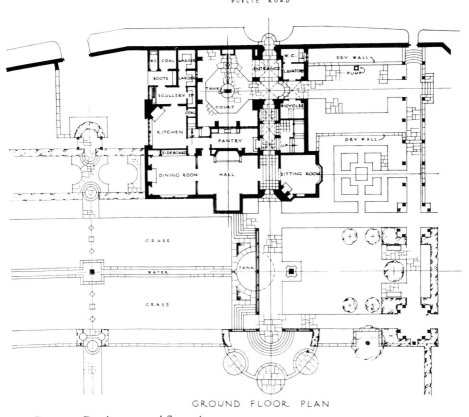

179 *Deanery Garden, ground floor plan*

180 *Lutyens. Homewood (1899)*

bay if it had not been breached by the arch opening of
the corridor which was balanced by a large Webbian
chimney (much bigger than it need have been to serve
three small fireplaces). The changefulness soon disappeared. In the same year Lutyens completed
Homewood. The house owes much to Webb's middle
period, with boarded gables similar to Webb's at
Jolwynds (p. 35), and symmetrical elevations. And
for the first time Lutyens introduced overtly classical
detailing on the outside: the timber gables are, curiously, supported on walls enriched with rusticated
classical pilasters. As Roderick Gradidge has pointed
out in his perceptive analysis,[10] it is significant that
this first emergence of the orders* was in an Arts and
Crafts house executed for a vicerene of India—
Lutyens's mother-in-law, the wife of Lord Lytton,
one of the odder viceroys.

Symmetry became increasingly important to
Lutyens. His finest work of the early 1900s is in
vernacular style, set to symmetrical plans: for
instance Marsh Court near Stockbridge in Hampshire (1901), and his variant on Prior's butterfly plan,
Papillon Court near Market Harborough (1903—
now demolished).

The introduction of symmetry was not without
problems. As A. S. G. Butler explained in the
Lutyens Memorial,† "the deliberate disorder culti-
vated by romantic-minded architects of his youth did
not appeal to him . . . He preferred increasingly to
avoid a rambling plan, to constrain the wings of a
house into a balanced form and even to fold them
back neatly within a rectangle, roofing the house as he
could. For it is difficult to accomplish exact symmetry
in a domestic building and, at the same time, house
the inmates quite as they should be . . . It postulates
nearly always some sacrifice of convenience by the
owner."[11] How Pugin would have agreed.

But, Butler emphasized, symmetry "does provide
the only channel through which an architect may
touch the highest performance. For if, through all the
intricacies of modern requirements and the techni-
calities of up-to-date building, he can produce a work
which can be enjoyed in detail when explored both
inside and out, and, at the same time, can be appreci-
ated in one delightful glance from any direction or
distance, he is supreme."

* Classical detailing was to be seen in Lutyens's *interiors* at least as
early as Fulbrook (1897).

† A large three volume work full of detailed drawings and photographs. No other British architect has ever been so quickly and
magnificently memorialized.

Inside Papillon was a round baisin court, hugged
between two of the diagonal wings, in which the roof
of the cloister was supported by impeccable Tuscan
columns and pilasters. Next year, Lutyens came out
with the full blown neo-classical elevation of the
Country Life building in Covent Garden, totally
symmetrical and formal with a high tiled roof, rusticated ground floor and stone dressings to the brick
upper floors, all in a lively Wrenian fashion.

Lutyens was becoming a convinced classicist. In
1903, he wrote to Herbert Baker, "in architecture
Palladio is the game. It is so big. Few appreciate it
now and it requires considerable training to value and
realize it. The way Wren handled it was marvellous
. . . It means hard thought all through. If it is
laboured it fails . . . it is a big game, a high game."[12]

In 1906, Lutyens completed Heathcote, a villa in
the suburbs of Ilkley in which for the first time he
embraced the full panoply of Roman Doric, not just a
few columns or pilasters but metopes, guttae, tryg-
lyphs—the lot. The plan is fiercely symmetrical with
the sitting room balancing the dining room across a
country house hall on the main front. Lutyens knew
he had been daring. A few years later, he wrote to
Baker, "I have been scolded for not being Yorkshire
in Yorkshire. The other view—have a window for
this, a door for that etc.—a pot-pourri of ornithologi-
cal details. The result is futile, absolutely unconvin-
cing. My house stands there plumb. I don't think it
could have been built anywhere else! Would Wren
(had he gone to Australia) have burnt his knowledge
and experience to produce a lame marsupial style,
though it reflect the character of her aborigines? He
would surely have done his best. . . In modern work
—unlike the old—the thinking machine is separated
from the labour machine so that the modern architect
cannot have the same absolution as we give the old
men when the thought and labour was the same
individual. . . The thought and design should, in that
they are specialized, become superthought—and, in
that we specialize—must be in advance and distinctly
beyond the conceptions of the architect's fellow
men."[13] It was the architecture of authority, of an
Empire which stretched from Ilkley to India.

As a viceregal son-in-law and author of some of the
most distinguished classical buildings in England,
Lutyens was an obvious choice for his greatest work
—the viceroy's house in Delhi; a commission he
gained in 1912, though the vast building was not
completed until 1930. In its overpowering symmetry
and blend of classical and Indian detailing, its endless

181 *Lutyens. Papillon Court, near Market Harborough, Leicestershire (1903, now destroyed)*

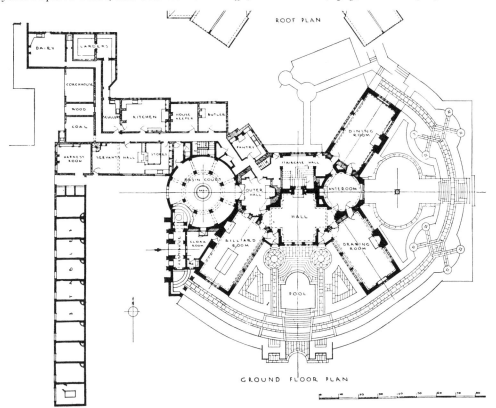

182 *Papillon, plan*

183 *Lutyens. Heathcote, Ilkley, Yorkshire (completed 1906)*

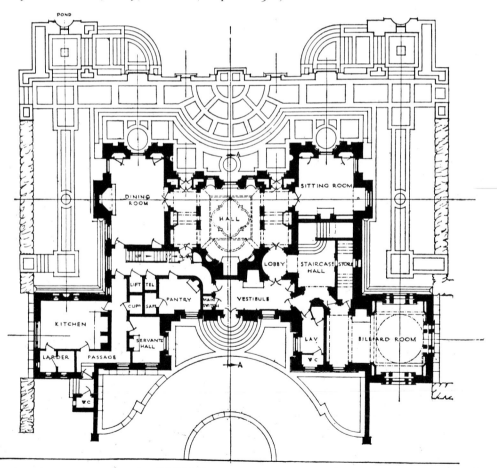

GROUND FLOOR PLAN

184 *Heathcote, ground floor plan*

corridors and jokey incidents, the palace summarizes the worst—and the best—of the last decades of Empire.

The job ensured Lutyens's continuing popularity amongst the upper and upper middle classes. In the '20s and '30s Lutyens rarely returned to the full blown classicism of Heathcote but preferred a more gentle neo-Georgian, used inventively in many country houses and spread lamentably thinly over Park Lane. But he never wholly forgot his Arts and Crafts origins: many of the later country houses, though almost always symmetrical, are informed by local vernacular.

And, in India, he was brought back to a closer relationship with craftsmen. He advocated making the Delhi works "a training centre of craftsmanship, a kind of technical university, not only for carvers and painters but engineers and plumbers; and not merely for the immediate needs but as the missing counterpoint to the immense material and intellectual benefits brought to India by the English. For he felt strongly that whilst the raj had suppressed abominable practices, given India the finest engineering in the world, medicine and sanitation and virtually abolished famine, it had destroyed the Indian arts though not more than we have done in England".[14] The British, said Lutyens, had taught the Indians

"all our evil bureaucratic tricks and little else." His proposals had no more success than Ashbee's a decade before. They were turned down out of hand by bureaucracy.

Mackay Hugh Baillie Scott (1865–1945) would have applauded Lutyens's idea for a school of craftsmanship for, throughout his long life as a practising architect, he never abandoned the pursuit of craftsmanly architecture or the teachings of Ruskin and Morris.

Scott was born near Ramsgate, the son of a minor

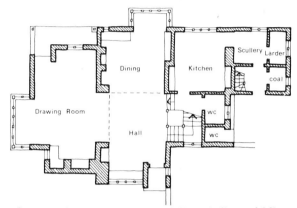

185 *Red House, plan. Dotted lines indicate folding screens*

186 *Mackay Hugh Baillie Scott. Oakleigh, Douglas, Isle of Man (1892–1893)*

but wealthy Scottish aristocrat. He was originally
trained at Cirencester agricultural college with a view
to running the family's sheep stations in Australia.
But, though he passed all the examinations in 1885,
he decided on no very clear grounds* to become an
architect, and in 1886 he was articled to Major
Charles Davis, the city architect of Bath who was
responsible for the podgy Empire Hotel which, until
the desecrations of the last twenty years, was one of
the few cancers on Bath's Georgian fabric.

After this inauspicious beginning, Scott left Bath
and settled in the Isle of Man in 1889—again an
apparent whim. John Betjeman, as a young *Architectural Review* editor, was told by Scott that, "I went to
the Isle of Man for a holiday. I was so seasick I
couldn't face the journey back so I set up in practice
there."[16]

His first buildings were mostly heavily half-
timbered variants of the Old English style, owing
little to their surroundings and much more to the

---

* For lack of personal papers, Scott's personality and private history remain shadowy, despite the attentions of James D. Kornwolf
who has written down everything there is to know about Scott and a
great deal more.[15]

VIEW FROM N.E.

187, 188 *Baillie Scott. Ideal house, published in the
"Studio" 1894*

early Shaw and to Ernest George. Inside, they were
not so conventional. In his own house, the Red House
in Douglas (1892–3), Scott invented a new way of
planning in which the living room/hall was separated
from the drawing and dining rooms by folding
screens so that all three could be thrown together into
one large irregular space or separated into individual
rooms. Living halls modelled in miniature on those of
country houses and folding screens allowing inter-
connected spaces were to be Scott's passions, despite
their multitudinous disadvantages for families with
children.

In 1894, Scott wrote an article in the *Studio* in
which he described the virtues of a hypothetical
house* in which a high hall flanked by drawing and
dining rooms, all separated by folding screens, were
stretched in Arts and Crafts fashion along a corridor
where "to get some idea of its general effect I must
transport you to some old Cheshire farm house,
somewhere in the country where people have not yet
grown to be ashamed of plain bricks and whitewash."[17] The hall itself had an inglenook over which
Scott placed a small gallery in much the way that
Shaw slung his study over the dining room inglenook
in his own house (p. 40)—but with much less practical purpose; the gallery was intended to house musi-
cians who would entertain the family taking its ease
round the fire, or strike up for a dance when the three
main rooms would be thrown into one by folding back
the screens. The idea of a late nineteenth-century
mini Medici living in suburban splendour complete
with a court band now seems preposterous, but it was
sufficiently attractive and credible at the time to earn
Scott many commissions.

The finest manifestation of Scott's inglenook and
gallery is at Blackwell, a large country house near
Bowness in Westmorland (1898–1899) where he
adopted a Voysey-like purity outside; white harling
and strips of stone-mullioned windows sat under a
slate roof with Scottish gables. The half-timbering
was brought inside, where it ran rather Teutonic riot
round the hall which contained a giant inglenook
supporting a half-timbered gallery. The drawing
room—a space which Scott thought ought to be
"dainty"—was all white and delicate. Slender columns were topped by hemispherical foliated basket

---

* Just as Voysey got his first commission after publishing hypothetical work in the *British Architect*, Scott's earliest commissions
from England and the Continent followed his articles on ideal
houses in the *Studio*.

189 *Baillie Scott. Blackwell, Westmorland (1898–1899) The Hall*

190 *Blackwell, drawing room*

191 *Baillie Scott. White Lodge, Wantage, Oxfordshire
(1898–1899)*

capitals supporting a thin shelf which ran round the
whole room.

The design had all the fine-drawn Mackmurdoish
elegance of Mackintosh at Hill House three years
later. As Muthesius remarked, "In Baillie Scott's
work each room is an individual creation, the elements of which do not just happen to be available but
spring from the over-all idea. Baillie Scott is the first
to have realized the interior as an autonomous work
of art."[18]

In the same years, Scott was building the White
Lodge at Wantage in Oxfordshire for the chaplain of
St. Mary's Convent. Externally the house could easily
be mistaken for a Voysey until you notice the absence
of strong horizontal string courses and the slightly
elongated proportions of the mullioned windows—it
is a Voysey house yawning. Inside there was yet
another decorative approach in the first floor drawing
room, which had a white semi-circular vault under
which were elaborate and unclerical paintings of colourful peacocks and flowers.

This richness is an echo of Scott's work for the
Grand Duke of Hesse at Darmstadt. In 1897, Scott
and Ashbee were separately commissioned by Grand
Duke Ernst Ludwig to design interiors for the palace.
Scott did the white-panelled dining and drawing

192 *Baillie Scott. Dining room for Grand Duke of
Hesse, Darmstadt (1897)*

rooms which were made rich with embossed leather friezes of Voysey-like birds and flowers executed by Ashbee's Guild of Handicraft. In the drawings, published in *Building News*, the furniture looks over-carved and lumpen. Yet, in fact, most of the forms were simple. Perfectly flat surfaces bore painted or inlaid floral ornament which like other Arts and Crafts work, however luxuriant, avoided the sinuous intertwinings of Art Nouveau in favour of heraldic stiffness.

Darmstadt was the foundation of a flourishing continental practice for Scott which, though commissions never again reached the magnificence of the Grand Ducal palace, included the interiors of a tree house for the Crown Princess of Romania (a Hesse offspring) and several large aristocratic mansions in and around Germany.

At home, life was more humdrum. To be near J. P. White's Pyghtle works for which he designed furniture, Scott moved in 1901 from the Isle of Man to Bedford, one of England's least romantic country towns, where he adapted a large cottage and worked in rural ease. His Voyseyish style continued well into the decade, and Scott was not afraid to confess his admiration of the older architect. "If one were asked to sum up in a few words the scope and purposes of Mr. Voysey's work," he wrote in 1908, "one might say that it consists mainly in the application of severely sane, practical and rational ideas to home making."[19]

One of Scott's largest white buildings was Waterlow Court, an Associated Home for ladies, in Hampstead Garden Suburb. It is a courtyard surrounded by flats. Here, as *The British Architect* enthused,

193 *Baillie Scott. Landhaus Waldbühl, Switzerland (1907–13)*

194 *Baillie Scott. Waterlow Court, Hampstead Garden Suburb (1909)*

195 *Baillie Scott. The Cloisters, Regents Park, London (1912–1913, destroyed)*

"Mr. Baillie Scott has shown that our old type of almshouse design, built in quadrangular form, may be dealt with in a sensible modern spirit so as to make economical and artistic housing a possibility. A lady may live here with a companion in charming rooms at a cost as low as four and threepence per week."[20] The quadrangle is all whitewashed brick (one of his favourite aphorisms was "when in doubt whitewash"[21]). Big round arches form the cloister above which strips of Voyseyish windows nestle under the eaves of the steep, red-tiled roof. Outside, the block is less severe with a half-timbered first floor on top of dusky reddish purple brick.

By the time Waterlow Court was built in 1909, Scott had moved away from Voyseyish austerity. At Bill House, Selsey on Sea (1906–7) he relieved the white roughcast with jolly chequered patterns of local brick and stone. The Cloisters, Regents Park (1912–13—now demolished) was one of his largest houses, all diapered brickwork enclosing a great half-timbered hall and sumptuously panelled living rooms. It was built for Sir Boverton Redwood, a petrol magnate, and it was so consciously anachronistic that even Lawrence Weaver, one of the most faithful publicists of Arts and Crafts architecture, had a few qualms: "Redwood", he wrote, "can shut his door, entrenched in the Middle Ages tempered by bath taps (h and c) and electric light . . . As to whether the Cloisters represents *him* and his contribution to civilization as well as it represents Mr. Baillie Scott's devotion to the spirit of medieval craftsmanship is one of those difficult questions which it would be impertinent to explore."[22]

Only a year after the Cloisters was finished, Baillie Scott designed his first neo-Georgian house: he had stood out against the new fashion as long as he could. The house was an ordinary little red brick box with a plan contorted to allow the windows to be arranged in regular rows. It was the antithesis of everything Scott had stood for up to that time. He had increasingly adopted symmetry throughout the previous decade, but the planning had been linear and free and all his forms had been derived from local models.

Neo-Georgian was to be one of the several styles between which Scott alternated in the '20s and '30s. He continued to preach against machine production and regularity, developing his theme that "instead of the callous, brutal methods of the modern factory, art makes the workshop into a school, where materials may be 'educated' in the literal sense. And the chief aim of this education is not to force the material into the strait waistcoat of preconceived forms, but so to deal with it that, having first sympathetically discovered its character, that character may be expressed properly subordinated to the fulfillment of practical functions."[23]

But Scott, though he seems to have had no financial compulsion to go on working (he owned, amongst other property, the Kensington Palace Hotel) continued to attract clients, and he had to fall in with their taste, which in many cases was for neo-Georgian discipline. Occasionally, as in his house at Mudeford Green, Hampshire (1924), he achieved a clumsy originality by changefully disposing Georgian elements in a style similar to Queen Anne. But usually, his houses were small, well built, well mannered brick boxes. The Tudor derived style continued and there were other idioms too—a flat-topped, white-walled bungalow in Hong Kong and flat-roofed, castle-like houses in Cornwall.

Whatever the style, contemporaries still respected his craftsmanship. In 1925 John Clarke wrote, "His plain brick wall is a joy. There is the same difference between it and the average brick wall that there is between a Persian rug and an Axminster carpet. It brings us back again to the old question that has been discussed and debated so often. Can we with our modern machine-made materials and machine-like labour hope to produce as satisfying work as was produced before machinery came to curse or bless us? Mr. Baillie Scott says 'No'. His answer is: 'A study of old building one finds in . . . villages, suggests that it is not only better than any modern building, but has some essential difference. . . This difference largely consists in the character of the workmanship which, like handwriting, conveys personality instead of being a lifeless mechanical formula.'"[24]

So Scott retained his beliefs, however much his clients demanded neo-Georgian and the bye-laws required him to use fire-resistant fake half-timbering rather than the real thing. Yet his talent had been eaten away. Even his best architecture rarely achieved the originality of Voysey, Prior, Lethaby, Ashbee or Lutyens; after the War, he became a pasticheur of whose work the chief characteristic was, according to Clarke, ". . . charm. There is no other word that describes it so well. It is all charming, whether it be Tudor or Georgian. It is pookish, unexpected. It has the same quality that appears in Barrie's plays; a quality that is at the moment held lightly."[25]

It still is. Scott's later houses were a part of Barrie's Never-Never Land, owned by middle-aged

196 *Baillie Scott. House at Mudeford Green, Hampshire (1924)*

Wendies—a sugary upper-middle class realization of the Nowhere to which Morris's hero had been transported.

Arts and Crafts architecture had descended to scene painting. Yet Scott should not be judged too harshly. He did his best but the times were against him. As A. L. N. Russel wrote towards the end of Scott's long career, surely few architects "have built so much all over England and done so little violence to its amenities"[26]—not a bad epitaph for the big, quiet, unassuming man who loved the country and lived in it all his life.

1 Blomfield, R. *A Short History of Renaissance Architecture in England*, George Bell, London 1900, p. 296
2 Blomfield, R. *Memoirs of an Architect*, MacMillan, London 1932, p. 113
3 Blomfield, R. *The Mistress Art*, Edward Arnold, London 1908, p. 10
4 *Ibid.*, p. 85
5 Lethaby, W. R. *Philip Webb and His Work*, Oxford 1935, p. 76
6 Macleod, Robert *Style and Society*, RIBA, London 1971, p. 101
7 Stuart-Wortley, Violet *Grow Old Along With Me* (1952), quoted in Saint *Norman Shaw*, *op. cit.*, p. 311

8 Hussey, Christopher *The Life of Sir Edwin Lutyens*, Country Life, London 1950, p. 26
9 Jekyll, Gertrude *House and Garden*
10 Gradidge, Roderick "Edwin Lutyens" in *Seven Victorian Architects*, Thames & Hudson, London 1976, p. 127
11 Butler, A. S. G. *The Architecture of Sir Edwin Lutyens*, Vol. 1, Country Life, London 1950, p. 30
12 *Ibid.*, p. 34
13 *Ibid.*, p. 33
14 Hussey *Life*, *op. cit.*, p. 347
15 Kornwolf, James D. *M. H. Baillie Scott and the Arts and Crafts Movement*, Johns Hopkins, Baltimore and London 1972
16 Betjeman, John *Journal of the Manx Museum*, Vol. VII, 1968, p. 78
17 Scott, M. H. Baillie "An ideal suburban house", *Studio*, Vol. IV, 1894, p. 127
18 Muthesius, H. *op. cit.*, p. 51
19 Scott, M. H. Baillie "On the characteristics of Mr. C. F. A. Voysey's architecture", *Studio*, Vol. XLII, 1908, p. 19
20 *The British Architect*, Vol. LXXII, 1909, p. 19
21 Kornwolf *op. cit.*, *passim*
22 Weaver, Lawrence *Small Country Houses of Today*, Second series, Country Life, London 1919, p. 94
23 Scott, M. H. Baillie "Ideals in Building, False and True" from *The Arts Connected with Building*, Batsford, London 1909, p. 142
24 Clarke, John D. "The work of Baillie Scott and Beresford" *Architects' Journal*, Vol. LXI, 1925, p. 60
25 *Ibid.*
26 Russel, A. L. N. *RIBA Journal*, Vol. XL, 1933, p. 636

13 Quietly Home

"There is a boom coming for Garden Cities", Lutyens wrote to Herbert Baker in 1909. "I am in the train for Tavistock to lay out a building estate for the Duke of Bedford. I have an estate to lay out at Romford* . . . and then there is the Central Square at Hampstead."[1] Most Arts and Crafts architects were trying to catch similar trains.

The Garden City movement had begun to take shape six years earlier at Letchworth under the guidance of Barry Parker (1867–1947) and Raymond Unwin (1863–1940). Parker and Unwin were half cousins, both born near Sheffield, though Unwin was brought up in Oxford. Their relationship was made closer when Unwin married Parker's sister Ethel in 1893 and, three years later, the two teetotal socialists went into partnership as architects and planners.

Late in life Mrs. Parker remembered, "As I see the partnership, Unwin had all the zeal of a social reformer with a gift for speaking and writing and was inspired by Morris, Carpenter and the early days of the Labour Movement. Parker was primarily an artist. Texture, light, shade, vistas, form and beauty were his chief concern. He wanted the home to be a setting for a life of aesthetic worth.

"I always felt the Parker, Unwin partnership was an ideal one; each had a deep affection for the other and admiration for each other's gifts—so profoundly different and yet complementary."[2]

Unwin had attended Ruskin's lectures in Oxford and he was a friend of Edward Carpenter,† probably through whom he met William Morris. Unwin became a socialist and an enthusiastic contributor to Morris's *Commonweal*. His first job was as apprentice engineer for the Stavely Coal and Iron Company, for which he worked on miners' housing.

Parker was articled in 1889 to G. Faulkner Armitage, who, besides having a drawing office, owned a workshop and smithy—an excellent training ground for a young Arts and Crafts architect. When Parker first set up on his own at Buxton in 1895, he, like Voysey fourteen years before, earned most of his living from designs for textiles, wallpaper and furniture rather than architecture.

The first big commission gained by the Parker and Unwin partnership was at New Earswick near York, where in 1901 the chocolate magnate Joseph Rowntree had bought an estate on which to house his workers. It was to be a philanthropic model village, in the tradition of Port Sunlight and Bournville, created by Rowntree's fellow Quaker cocoa kings, the Cadburys.* The roots of the tradition ran deep—one strand went at least as far back as Saltaire, near Bradford, the model village built for his workers by Sir Titus Salt in the mid-nineteenth century; another strand touched the bosky tastefulness of Bedford Park.

At New Earswick, Parker and Unwin started a series of experiments in layout which were to continue throughout their association (which formally ended in 1914). The aim was to reduce the amount of expensive road needed to give access to all houses on a site while giving every house its pleasant view. They were particularly vehement about the horror of the

---

* In the event neither of these jobs came to much.

† Edward Carpenter (1844–1929) was ordained but broke from the church to spend his life working with the poor. He set up as a market gardener at Millthorpe in Derbyshire near Sheffield and became an influential figure in the socialist circles of the '80s and '90s. He also made sandals on the Indian pattern: they were so popular that they became the hallmark of a whole class of English intellectuals. He shared with his friend Ashbee an enthusiasm for homogenic love (Platonic homosexuality).

* The master plan for Port Sunlight, Lord Leverhulme's model village for soapworkers, was implemented by Thomas Mawson, the Arts and Crafts landscape architect, on the formal lines of an Arts and Crafts garden. Its cottagy rows of houses were to be built in a blend of Old English and Voysey.

197 *Parker & Unwin. New Earswick, near York (from 1901)*

back yards created by the parallel rows of bye-law housing, the standard for working people. In a 1902 Fabian tract Unwin wrote, "It does not seem to be realized hundreds of thousands of working women spend the bulk of their lives with nothing better to look on than the ghastly prospect offered by these back yards, the squalid ugliness of which is unrelieved by a scrap of fresh green to speak of spring, or a fading leaf to tell of autumn."[3] Sunlight was vital too. "It must be looked upon as an absolute *essential*, second only to air-space."[4]

Parker and Unwin solved the problem of view and sunlight by abolishing the old cottage parlour and making a living room which ran from front to back of the house. This allowed the cottages to be laid out in terraces and yet attract sunlight no matter how they were turned. The planners were convinced that, when building cheap houses for the working classes, "however desirable a parlour may be, it cannot be said to be necessary to health or family life."[5]

The through living room was developed in "Cottages near a town"[6] shown by the partners at the 1903

Northern Art Workers' Guild exhibition in Manchester.* They illustrated plans for semi-detached cottages, with long living rooms, enhanced by a bay at one end and incorporating a snug inglenook round the range. They were to be laid out in a chequered pattern so that streets fronts alternated between pairs of cottages and pairs of gardens; the streets were parallel but the effect—houses set amongst greenery—was intended to be the antithesis of the corridor-like bye-law layout.

In October of the same year, Parker and Unwin were asked to compete with a combination of Lethaby and Ricardo, and with two local architects for the post of planners for the first garden city at Letchworth. The Northeners won and so became the chief interpreters of the new movement.

The idea of garden cities had originated in *Tomorrow: A Peaceful Path to Real Reform*, published in 1898 by Ebenezer Howard, in which the solution to late Victorian urban problems was suggested to be a series of new towns. They would counteract the pull

---

* The scheme was originally designed for a real site at Starbeck near Harrogate in 1902. A prototype pair was built.

of the cities by offering all the amenities of urban life as well as the pleasures of living in a balanced, semi-rural community. Each garden city was to be defined in size and surrounded by a belt of agricultural land sufficient to feed the predetermined maximum population.

Howard's vision of houses set in gardens in the countryside was very similar to that of *News from Nowhere*, but it was firmly tied to the practicalities of the late nineteenth century. For instance, in *Tomorrow*'s successor, *Garden Cities of Tomorrow* (1902), a ring of garden cities was to surround each great metropolis, connected to it radially and to each other in a circle by fast railways. In *News*, the railway, like all other machines Morris hated, had become obsolete.

At Letchworth 3,826 acres were purchased by a joint stock company set up by Howard's disciples and, in January 1904, Parker and Unwin started work. They took 1,300 acres for the town,[7] leaving the rest as the agricultural belt. Their design bore more than passing resemblance to Howard's diagrams of the ideal garden city, in which central public buildings were surrounded by a park, and then rings of houses and gardens, all girdled by a railway and factories on the edge of the agricultural belt. But, as Mervyn Macartney recorded in the *Architectural Review*, when Letchworth began to take shape, "The present plan . . . is much more rational. The centre of the town will be taken up by the municipal buildings upon which a number of straight roads converge like the spokes of a cycle upon the hub, and round the centre will be conveniently grouped such buildings as

198 *Parker & Unwin. Letchworth (design 1903) from the west. Formal avenues focus on town centre (top right)*

the public hall, institute, museum, school, post office, and so forth. This part of the town all lies south of the G.N.R. which runs right through the middle of the estate, and half a mile or so eastwards come the factories. By this arrangement the factories not only gain direct access to the main line through their goods station and sidings, but also are so placed that their smoke, smell and noise will be carried away from the town by the prevailing wind."[8]

Typical of the south of the town are streets edged with broad belts of grass planted with flowering trees; then there are footpaths, the hedges of the front gardens and the houses well set back, usually in semi-detached blocks or short terraces; behind them are ample back gardens. The avenue was common in the affluent suburbs of large manufacturing towns like Leeds and Birmingham in the '90s but through Parker and Unwin planning, its amenities became accessible to relatively poor people.

To the north of the railway, the layout is more economical, lacking so many tree-lined roads but still with sizeable front and back gardens. This was the area in which a cheap cottage competition was held in 1905; several Arts and Crafts architects entered, including Smith and Brewer, Troup, Baillie Scott and Randall Wells.

The layout of the more formal part, south of the railway, is remarkably like an Arts and Crafts garden. While virtually all the houses (by Parker and Unwin and other architects) are based on irregular vernacular models, the streets show the love of vista, axes and order that Prior had so strenuously advocated in garden making. It is a gentle irony that the layout now focuses on a grand symmetrical design of tall poplars which outline the plan of the formal municipal buildings that were never constructed for lack of funds.

Unwin shared Prior's horror of landscape gardening, believing that "any attempt to copy nature must be futile, for the conditions of natural growth are so complex as to be quite beyond the power of the gardener to understand or reproduce." Yet formalism could go too far, for "the formalist needs to remember that his design is subordinate to the site, that the undulation of the ground and the presence of natural features of beauty worth preserving will frequently require some departure from the regularity of his treatment."[9]

Planning, like gardening, should take a middle way between formal and naturalistic. Unwin was sceptical of attempts to recapture the picturesque interest of old irregular village streets which grew up over a long period of time. In any case, he believed that "the relationships of feudalism have gone, and democracy has yet to evolve some definite relationships of its own, which when they come will doubtless be as picturesque as the old forms."[10]

A degree of order in the main features of a town plan would make it easier to understand but excessive symmetry, for instance, could result in inconvenience and over rigid imposition of formal rules could lead to the destruction of natural features such as trees and hedgerows which would help to relate buildings to the countryside.

Raymond Unwin got another chance to test his planning theories when, in 1905, he was made planner of the Hampstead Garden Suburb. The idea of the suburb originated with Mrs. Barnett, a lifelong worker in the East End slums who was instrumental in setting up the Whitechapel Art Gallery, later given its permanent home by Townsend (p. 129). An extension of the underground railway made possible redevelopment on the northern approaches to Hampstead Heath, which until then had been countryside. Mrs. Barnett was determined to preserve at least part of the country as open land and, beyond that, to create an area where working men, at the expense of a twopenny tube fare, could enjoy a life of freedom among gardens and tree lined streets.

Mrs. Barnett secured her piece of countryside, a long thin strip running north from the Heath, and Parker and Unwin were required to work out development in the long thin tongues of land surrounding it and on the hill which terminated the extension to the north. The first plan was full of informal curved roads snaking round the top of the hill on which Mrs. Barnett was determined to build an Anglican church as the community's focus. In the long western tongue of development land next to the Heath extension, the planners proposed a small area of the chequered housing they had exhibited at the 1903 Northern Art Workers' Guild exhibition.

The final plan (1912) was more formal, with a fan of avenues stretching east from Lutyens's central square and its two churches, Anglican and free. On the westward slope, development was more irregular along gently curving streets. To the north, across Lyttleton Road, was an area of semi-detached houses for workers' families on long cul-de-sacs (for which a special Act of Parliament had to be passed to overcome the bye-law insistence on through streets). In the troublesome western strip against the Heath, the planners elaborated cul-de-sac plans by placing

199 *Hampstead Garden Suburb centre, from the west*

courtyards at the end of each. (Baillie Scott's Waterlow Court was the most complete of these.) The aims, as usual, were to allow maximum use of the site for minimum road length and to provide all dwellings with sunlight and garden views, both front and back.

Other than in this strip, the Suburb (carefully so called because it did not possess all the urban amenities of a Garden City) was laid out according to Unwin's rule that there should be no more than twelve houses to the acre. The rule was based on sound economic principle, elaborated in Unwin's pamphlet "Nothing gained by overcrowding", in which he showed that, except where land was unusually expensive, such developments "cause the cost of roads to outweigh the saving in cost of land which results from there being more than twelve houses to the acre."[11]

This low density was later to produce some of Britain's dullest housing estates from the drawing boards of local authorities and speculative builders in the inter-war years. But the Garden Suburb as seen from the long north slope of Hampstead Heath is a complete Arts and Crafts village, rising sharp out of the green (though not quite as crisply as Unwin, who advocated a great town wall which was only partly built, would have liked). It is tight-knit, yet leafy, with tile pitch piled upon brick gable until the whole composition is crowned by the leaded spire of Lutyens's superb Gothic-cum-Georgian church —wonderfully picturesque, but scarcely the image of a new democracy for which Unwin was searching.

The style of the church is symptomatic of the suburb in which the alteration in Arts and Crafts inspiration from vernacular to Georgian is frozen at the point of transition. Parker and Unwin had learned from the experience of Letchworth that some kind of visual control was necessary over development. At

200 *Hampstead Garden Suburb, view from the Heath today dominated by Lutyens's St. Jude's Church*

Letchworth, in theory, the company was to build virtually everything, but actually lack of capital necessitated involving many other developers and their architects, resulting in a great variety of architectural expression. For all the strong planning, Letchworth is architecturally chaotic, often no better than a low key, low density suburb. At Hampstead, care was taken over eaves lines, roof pitches and textures, unifying the composition. Yet below the eaves, architects were more or less free to do what they liked, Gothic or Georgian, within a restricted palette of materials. As well as Parker and Unwin, distinguished Arts and Crafts architects such as Geoffrey Lucas, Curtis Green and A. J. Penty contributed housing.

Parker and Unwin themselves usually stuck to vernacular models. From the first, they were committed Ruskinian Goths, working from the inside out. Parker, in an 1895 lecture, urged the virtues of large living rooms in small houses, then usually stuffed with small rooms modelled in miniature on the houses of the rich. The number of rooms should, he

urged, be reduced, "keeping such rooms as we do retain, large enough to be healthy, comfortable and habitable . . . But if your big room is to be comfortable it *must* have recesses. There is great charm in a room broken up in plan, where that slight feeling of mystery is given to it which arises when you cannot see the whole room from any one point in which you are likely to sit; when there is always something *round the corner.*"[12] This is as clear a description of changefulness applied to domestic planning as the Arts and Crafts movement ever produced.

Equally clear is the echo of Morris. "The true method of making a room beautiful is to make all the necessary and useful things in it beautiful; so much is this true that it becomes almost impossible to design a really beautiful room that is to have no useful work done in it or natural life lived in it."[13]

The combination of these two principles created living rooms of subtlety and great simplicity of construction—white walls, exposed beams with rugs on simple timber or tiled floors: the "decorative properties inherent in the construction and in the details necessary to the building,"[14] which Parker, following Morris, dearly loved.

It was the vernacular cottage idiom but adopted, so

Parker and Unwin claimed, not for sentimental but for practical and artistic reasons. Even the beauty of the leaded light windows they favoured "has nothing to do with [an] old fashioned look, with romantic associations or quaintness of effect; it is simply an inherent property of all leaded glazing; due to the wonderful and never ending charm of the play of light and shade on different panes, each one catching the light slightly differently from any other, some glistening brightly, others dead and sombre, and the rest occupying every tone between the two."[15]

Furniture should, as far as possible, be built in to avoid the clutter of miscellaneous ornament and achieve the sensation of "reposefulness" which was the architects' main goal. The largest pieces of built-in furniture were the settles round the inglenooks, a device favoured by very many Arts and Crafts architects, which Parker and Unwin incorporated in virtually every house, no matter how small. These inglenooks were one variety of recess used to complicate and add variety to the basic oblong of their living rooms. Elsewhere, the architects rarely lost an opportunity to make a bay window or a niche for a piano.

No effort was spared to catch a view or a ray of sunlight by opening small lights wherever they were needed. The living-rooms and living halls are the great achievement of Parker and Unwin houses. They are as spare as Voysey's spaces yet more snug; they are as spatially inventive as Baillie Scott's without (except when compelled by economy in houses for the poor) adopting all the excesses of his open planning.

For all their spatial and constructional ingenuity, the outsides of Parker and Unwin houses are often disappointing. Part of the disappointment is caused by lack of originality, part by the hamfistedness which bedevils most young architects' work but which the cousins never entirely outgrew. Originality was consciously eschewed by Parker and Unwin. Parker was insistent that architects should "do nothing different from what we have done before, until we feel it to be better than what we have done before."[16] By the time that Parker and Unwin started to practise, a good deal *had* been done before by the Arts and Crafts architects born in the '50s. To architects of Parker and Unwin's generation, they were models of inspiration.

201 *Parker & Unwin. A living room (from "The Art of Building a Home", 1901)*

202 *Parker & Unwin. The Homestead, Chesterfield, Derbyshire (1903)*

203 *Parker & Unwin. Own houses, Letchworth Lane, Letchworth (1904)*

204 *Parker & Unwin. The Den, Croft Lane, Letchworth (1905)*

Voysey was the main early influence,* yet externally Parker and Unwin's houses rarely achieved his serenity. For instance, their Homestead at Ashgate Road near Chesterfield (1903–5) is plainly derived from Voysey's Broadleys (1898–99)—it has the same double-height curved bays, the steeply pitched hipped roof and the buttresses. But the Parker and Unwin version is like a couple of bays of Broadleys with the rest lopped off. The roof comes down only just beyond the top of the bays, instead of engulfing them in Voysey's generous warm hug, so the eaves are high, making the house stilted and vertical. The awkwardness is enhanced by the material: rough ashlar instead of Voysey's smooth harling.

A similar gawkiness is seen in the semi-detached houses the partners built for themselves in Letchworth Lane, Letchworth (1904). Here they had the courage to carry the tiled roof all the way down to the top of the ground floor bay which projects uneasily in

brick from the harling of the rest of the mass. The roof is sprigged with spiky gables, and the building terminates unhappily to the south in a tower with vestigial half-timbering on the upper floor.*

More coherence was achieved in the Den, Croft Lane, Letchworth (1905) where a complicated series of white wall planes is tied together by a cosy of thatch which swoops down to near head height over the veranda—a kind of outdoor inglenook. One of the best houses of this period was 102 Wilbury Road, Letchworth (1908), designed for Stanley Parker, Barry's brother, an artist craftsman. The white walled, stone trimmed influence of Voysey is very clear, yet the manner is used with much more confidence than Parker and Unwin had achieved before. And the result, roofs sweeping down to ground floor round a

---

* Other influences ranged from Old English and Baillie Scott in his heavier moods to, curiously, Hoffmann. There is a design for a girls' club in Manchester (*c*.1909) which is plainly derived from Hoffmann's Palais Stoclet (p. 205).

* The tower was added by Parker in 1914 to provide a sleeping balcony, a very popular feature in Letchworth. The timbering framed glazing which could be thrown open on three sides to let in the health giving night air.

high gable with staggered fenestration, is something that Voysey would never have attempted but which achieves much of his clarity and calm.

In the Hampstead Garden Suburb, Parker and Unwin amalgamated vernacular and Georgian in red brick houses which, under their steep, hipped roofs, combined strips of mullioned leaded lights from the seventeenth century with brick string courses and quoins from the eighteenth. Despite their disparate origins, these semis achieve a quiet four-square elegance which, though never reaching the heights of Arts and Crafts work, shows what an excellent second eleven the movement could field, given the opportunity.

Of the little non-domestic work produced by the partnership, the shops at the entrance to Hampstead Garden Suburb are the most dramatic example. High and Hanseatic, the buildings were intended to be a formal gate to the suburb, but, instead of choosing classical forms to make a monumental statement, Parker and Unwin stuck to their ideals and produced a group in brick topped with hipped

205 *Parker & Unwin. 102 Wilbury Road, Letchworth (1908), for Stanley Parker*

gables and a little tower. It was a monument in the Gothic spirit though the architects had to turn to Germany for inspiration.

Parker was one of the very few Arts and Crafts architects able to pursue the movement's ideals relatively free of commercial and stylistic pressures long after the War.

In 1901 Parker had dictated that "the influence of machinery on art is one of the most degrading we have to contend with, for every advance made by machinery must mean a corresponding retreat on the part of art."[17] But by 1925, he accepted that "the introduction of machines into art and craft has changed everything. The machine has come to stay and we must accept it. It is useless to hark back and demand only things made by hand. As a work of art, a thing which can be made as well by a machine as it can be made by hand is equally good made either way."[18]

If the machine was accepted, the quietness of

206 *Parker & Unwin. Houses, Hampstead Garden Suburb*

207 *Parker & Unwin. Shops at entrance to Hampstead Garden Suburb*

Parker's designs was unaffected. His clumsy gentleness continued in buildings like the Royston Cottage Hospital (1924–28) and the library and dining hall of King Alfred's School, Hampstead (1927–29).

By the time he was working on King Alfred's, Parker was a man out of his time. Most architects had accepted the rule of the Orders. A few were struggling to establish the fledgling Modern Movement, which was to subject architecture unequivocally to the rule of the Machine.

H. S. Goodhart-Rendel summed up the inter-war mood of the majority: "In the present market . . . Victorian liberty is depreciated, and the few traditions the Victorians did not sever are at a premium. We cannot understand why when Adam had perfected orderly planning the Puginists must innovate disorderly planning: why when Cockrell had brought to England the independent doctrine of the French rationalists Ruskin must force architecture to become the unquestioning handmaid of Protestant morals: why when at last secular Gothic was systemized by Waterhouse and Street it was necessary to turn from it and woo Queen Anne with bric-a-brac. We cannot understand these reactions because the memory of the actions that produced them has faded away. We have been born to freedom and find it cheap and unsatisfying; we see it against no background of broken tyranny; we see it rather as a heritage of outlawry, as the curse of the wandering Jew. We feel that we need not a Rousseau but a Mussolini."[19]

The great Arts and Crafts architects lingered on disdainful alike of neo-Georgian and the Modern Movement. Lethaby jeered at "ye olde modernist style" then appearing on the continent (p. 66). Voysey, who was hailed as a father of the Modern Movement, railed against the Movement's "vulgarly aggressive" proportions, its "mountebank eccentricity in detail and windows lying down on their sides." Baillie Scott spent much of his later years attacking the Modern Movement's pretentions in yards of woffly invective. Ashbee retired to keep a cynical eye on curious new developments from deepest Kent. When he met Voysey in the street in the late '30s, he "asked him how, as he looked so down and out, he was getting on. He, who had built more houses than any of us, shook his head ruefully and said 'Any house is good enough to start a car from'."[20]

Yet it was precisely in the houses from which most of the cheap cars were started that the Arts and Crafts tradition lingered longest. Abandoned by architects, the forms were adopted by speculative builders and local authorities. Round every sizeable town in England there is a ring of Arts and Crafts suburbs where, following planning rules drawn up by Unwin, behind laburnums and flowering cherries, the architecture of Voysey, Baillie Scott, Parker and early Lutyens lives on in endless copies of hips and gables, half-timbering and harling, mullions and leaded bay windows, with here and there an inglenook. The builders did what the architects, for all their high ideals, failed to accomplish. They brought Arts and Crafts to the people.

The image is not so very different from that seen by the man who brought news from nowhere. Cheap transport and the builders' crude copies of Arts and Crafts architecture offered a new life of individuality and freedom to multitudes who escaped from deprivation in the hearts of cities. For a movement which had started with the ideals of Ruskin and Morris, the inter-war suburb was not an entirely ignoble ending.

1 Hussey *The Life of Sir Edwyn Lutyens*, Country Life, London 1950, p. 187
2 Mrs Parker, letter to Walter Creese 25 March 1960, Parker papers
3 Unwin, Raymond "Cottage Plans and Common Sense", Fabian Tract no. 109, London 1902, p. 4
4 *Ibid.*, p. 3
5 *Ibid.*, p. 13
6 Parker, Barry and Raymond Unwin "Cottages near a town", pamphlet in the RIBA collection
7 Creese, Walter L. *The Search for Environment*, Yale 1966, p. 205
8 Macartney, Mervyn "The first garden city", *Architectural Review*, Vol. XVIII, 1905, p. 15
9 Unwin, Raymond *Town Planning in Practice*, T. Fisher Unwin, London 1909, pp. 119 and 125
10 Unwin, Raymond "Co-operation in building" in Parker and Unwin *The Art of Building a Home*, Longmans Green, London 1901, p. 95
11 Unwin, Raymond *Nothing gained by overcrowding! or how the Garden City type of development may benefit both owner and occupier*, Garden Cities and Town Planning Association, London 1912
12 Parker, Barry "The smaller middle class house", lecture "delivered before an audience of architects in 1895", printed in *The Art of Building a Home, op. cit.*, p. 3
13 *Ibid.*, pp. 17–18
14 Parker, Barry and Raymond Unwin *The Art of Building a Home, op. cit.*, Introduction, p. 11
15 Parker, Barry "The dignity of all true art" in *The Art of Building a home, op. cit.*, p. 32
16 Parker, Barry "The smaller middle class house", *op. cit.*, p. 9
17 Parker, Barry "The dignity of all true art", *op. cit.*, p. 30
18 Parker, Barry "Art in industry", lecture delivered at Balliol College, Oxford, 3 October 1925, p. 7, Parker papers
19 Goodhart-Rendell, H. S. *RIBA Journal*, Vol. XXXIII, 1926, p. 468
20 Ashbee, C. R. *Memoirs, op. cit.*, Vol. VII, p. 333

14 Transatlantic Excursion

The suburbs, not of England but in the United States, were the setting of one of the most ingenious and integrated Arts and Crafts building experiments. Gustav Stickley (1857–1942) was a Wisconsin man who moved east to train as a furniture maker and stonemason. After a visit to Europe in 1898, during which he met Voysey and Ashbee, he changed the name of his firm to Craftsman Workshops and tried to reorganize it much on the lines of Ashbee's Guild of Handicraft.

In 1901, he founded a magazine, *The Craftsman*, the first two issues of which were taken up with panegyrics on Morris and Ruskin. *The Craftsman* was partly a means of publicizing Stickley's products but it quickly expanded to cover all aspects of crafts, decorative arts, architecture and Morrisian socialism. In May 1903 was published the first "Craftsman Home" design, a two-storey rubble house, illustrated with plans and a brief description of its construction. Stickley urged subscribers to apply for information on "processes or details incident to the building, furnishing, or decoration of the 'Craftsman House'."[1] From January 1904 until the magazine's death in December 1916 Stickley published monthly details of detached residences "of which the cost should range between two and fifteen thousand dollars".

The houses were usually four-square in plan, compressed to avoid corridors in the American tradition. Living rooms often had inglenooks, and the stairs frequently ascended directly from them. It was the kind of economical planning that Parker and Unwin thought suitable for working class families, but on a rather more opulent scale.

Externally, the houses were undistinguished and derivative of a mass of origins ranging from Californian mission, New England farmhouse and log cabin to Old English, Voysey and even, here and there, the Tyrol. Stickley and his architects (a group working under Harvey Ellis) were consciously pursuing a native American architecture which necessitated variety appropriate both to a democracy in which "every man should have the right to think out the plan for his house to suit himself" and to a vast and varied countryside: "A house that is built of stone where stones are in the fields, of concrete where the soil is sandy, of brick where brick can be had reasonably, or of wood if the house is in a mountainous, wooded region, will from the beginning belong to the landscape."[2] The Puginian doctrine of fidelity to place had reached a new frontier.

For a decade, Stickley's enterprises were remarkably successful. There can have been few who built a Craftsman Home who did not wish to furnish it with the simple Webbian products of the Craftsman studios. If they could not afford the objects themselves, members of Stickley's Home Builders' Club were provided free with designs for wood, metal and leatherwork. In 1910 he founded the Craftsman Home Building Company which built houses in the New York area. An estate agents' wing was founded; advice was offered on landscaping and education. A large building was acquired near Fifth Avenue, New York to house the whole enterprise.

By 1915, Stickley claimed that in that year alone twenty million dollars-worth of homes were built on Craftsman principles from Alaska to the Fiji Islands. But in 1916, Stickley was bankrupt; he had tried to do too much at a time when big firms were producing cheaper imitations of the products of the Craftsman Workshops, which were the economic mainspring of the whole operation. Stickley had met the same fate as Ashbee: he was unable to cope with competition from big capital. Yet his curious marriage of commercial Arts and Crafts with individualistic socialism for the suburbs was the most successful of all the twentieth-century attempts to popularize true Arts and Crafts

208, 209, 210, 211 *Craftsman homes*

principles, and, if it never produced great architecture, the craftsman movement left its stamp on cities all over the American continent.

The Craftsman was never simply a vehicle for promoting Stickley's housebuilding enterprises. The work of architects considered sympathetic to the craftsman ideal was frequently featured—there was a series of articles by Parker on Parker and Unwin for instance. In a more than usually adulatory article, the magazine reported the work of Greene and Greene of Pasadena as exemplifying "the type of home that abounds today in California—a type in which practical comfort and art are skillfully wedded . . . It is a vital product of the time, place and people, with roots deep in geographical and human needs. It has a definite relation to the kind of climate and soil, the habits of the people and their ways of looking at civilization and nature. It is equally rich in historic traditions and in provision for present needs. Based on the Old Mission forms . . . modern Californian architecture has nevertheless made those traditions servants, not masters."[3]

When the brothers Charles Sumner Greene (1868–1957) and Henry Mather Greene (1870–1954) set up their Pasadena architectural practice in 1893, their first work was a medley of Old English, Spanish mission, Queen Anne and Colonial themes. By the early years of this century, their architecture began to acquire a characteristic stamp. It was a style in which complexity was built up from elements of great simplicity, an architecture of timber in which beam was piled on beam, rafter on rafter to form ordered nests of smooth sticks with great overhanging eaves and projecting balconies to provide shade from the sun. Every member and every joint is made explicit. The sources are as diverse as the Anglo-Indian bungalow and the simple peg and tenon joints of Stickley's furniture. (The brothers furnished the James A. Cuthbertson house, Pasadena, with Stickley furniture within months of the first appearance of *The Craftsman* to which they were subscribers.[4])

Ralph Adams Cram enthused in *American Country Houses of Today* (the transatlantic equivalent of Lawrence Weaver's books) that "there are things [in Greene and Greene's style] Japanese; things that are Scandinavian; things that hint at Sikkim, Bhutan and the frontiers of Tibet, and yet it all hangs together, it is beautiful, it is contemporary, and for some reason or other it seems to fit California. Structurally it is a blessing; only too often the exigencies of our assured precedents lead us into the wide and easy road of structural duplicity, but in this sort of thing there is an honesty that is sometimes almost brazen. It is a wooden style built woodenly."[5]*

* Ashbee thought "C. Sumner Greene's work beautiful; among the best there is in this country. Like Lloyd Wright, the spell of Japan is upon him, he feels the beauty and makes magic out of the horizontal line, but there is in his work more tenderness, more subtlety, more self effacement than in Wright's work. It is more refined and has more repose. Perhaps it loses in strength, perhaps it is California that speaks rather Illinois." (*Memoirs*, Vol. III, p. 106.)

212 *Greene and Greene. Gamble House, Pasadena, California (1908)*

213 *Gamble House, hall*

Greene and Greene often experimented with the thin one-room-and-a corridor plan, sometimes wrapping it round a planted courtyard in the manner of a Californian mission. But their best preserved building—the Gamble house at Westmorland Place, Pasadena, now a national historic landmark, has a much more conventional lay-out. A hall penetrates an oblong with, on one side, the living room and den and, on the other, the kitchen and dining-room.

The internal woodwork and the furniture are typical of mature Greene and Green houses: each piece of timber can be seen clearly, each is smoothed and slightly rounded with sandpaper so that the wood's ruddy resonance is beautifully expressed. The smaller items like the living room inglenook seats are pegged together with square dowels (sometimes the square pegs hide screws), and in the larger structures like the staircase the tongued ends of the treads and risers are clearly exposed in the thick horizontal planks which provide the support. Throughout, the rectilinear geometry of simple timber construction is softened by the gentle curves of Chinese architecture—for instance at the ends of corbels and in the structure which encloses the inglenook. Oriental too

are the metal straps which hold corbelled beams together; these are tightened by a pair of counterposed wedges which, when driven together locked the structure rigid.

Outside, the structural emphatic-ness is continued. The beams, rafters and purlins, all smoothed with the same meticulous care as the timbers of the interior, project to show exactly how the house is built. The house largely takes its character from the horizontal striations of the sleeping balconies of the three main bedrooms, each under a generous overhanging roof. Walls are covered with large wooden shingles which harmonize with the structural timber yet, by their plainness, emphasize the frenetic elaboration of the structure.

A Californian contemporary of the Greenes who must have been slightly sickened by the fussiness of their effects was Irving Gill (1870–1936). Like the Greenes, he was an immigrant from the east, and he finally settled at San Diego in the far south of California in 1902. There, he was much influenced by the clear white architecture of the Spanish missions. "The Missions", he wrote in *The Craftsman*, "are a part of [California's] history that should be preserved

214 *Irving Gill. Women's club, La Jolla (1913)*

and in their long, low lines, graceful arcades, tile roofs, bell towers, arched doorways and walled gardens we find a most expressive medium of retaining tradition, history and romance."[6] Virtually the only idiom the Greenes and Gill held in common was the pergola derived from mission architecture.

Gill's architecture was as simple and solid as the Greenes' was complicated and carpenterish. In his houses, Gill said in *The Craftsman*, "walls are finished flush with the casings and the line where the wall joins the floor is slightly rounded, so that it forms one continuous piece with no place for dust to enter or lodge, or crack for vermin of any kind to exist. There is no moulding for pictures, plates or chairs, no baseboards, panelling or wainscoting to catch and hold the dust."[7] The remark recalls the *Studio's* comments on Voysey's Chiswick house twenty-five years before (p. 90).

In this simplicity and in his affection for the *locus* of his architecture Gill was an Arts and Crafts architect. But in his methods, he was more a forerunner of the Modern Movement. He bought from the U.S. Army machinery for producing prefabricated barracks, and with his tilt slab system* of concrete construction he built such elegant minor masterpieces as the Women's Club La Jolla (1913), a white, flat-roofed, arcaded building, surrounded by pergolas covered in lush plants.

Gill's technical innovations and the simplicity of his style were unrecognized in Europe, where the Modern Movement emerged. On the international scene much the most influential American Arts and Crafts architect was Frank Lloyd Wright (1867–1959). Gill had worked with Wright in the Chicago office of Adler and Sullivan, where Wright served his time as trainee clerk from 1887 to 1893, when he set up on his own. His first office was in the loft of Steinway Hall, an eleven-storey office block in central Chicago, where he shared a draughting room and secretary with a group of young architects, Harold Perkins, Robert Clossen Spencer, and Myron Hunt. Other architects gradually joined the group, either actually on the premises or in spirit, all found-

ing the Prairie School—the Arts and Crafts movement's manifestation in the mid-west.[8]

That Chicago should have preceded New York and California as the birth-place of U.S. Arts and Crafts architecture seems odd at first sight. But, by the '90s, the city was more generally wealthy than the west coast, while being free of the stylistic predilections of the established east. Critic Arthur C. David noted in 1903 that the clients of the Prairie School "the well-to-do western gentlemen for whom the houses are built, do not seem to demand the use of European styles and remnants to the same extent as do the eastern owners of expensive buildings."[9]

Walter Crane, the socialist, illustrator and friend of William Morris, lectured and exhibited at the Chicago Art Institute at the turn of 1891/2. Ashbee's Guild first exhibited at the Chicago Architectural Club in 1898, and Ashbee himself gave ten lectures in the city in the winter of 1900. It was then that he formed a lifelong, though sometimes acrimonious, friendship with Wright who agreed to be the local secretary of the National Trust (the body which had sent Ashbee to America to drum up transatlantic support and funds).

Other English influences were through the *Studio*, which was published in America as the *International Studio*, and *House Beautiful*, which, published in Chicago, illustrated the work of Voysey, Baillie Scott, Townsend (and Wright) before the turn of the century. But Wright was a very much a man on his own and direct references to the work of others in his architecture are rare. He once did a neo-colonial house, once a neo-Cotswold terrace and once a full blown but very individualistic essay in Old English—the Nathan G. Moore residence at Oak Park. After such fumblings in the '90s, Wright began to evolve a style of his own about the turn of the century. Its open planning recalls Baillie Scott's experiments* and its horizontality is occasionally reminiscent of Voysey. Here and there, there is a dash of Japanese. But the Prairie houses that Wright evolved in the first decade of the century were as original, consistent and influential in America as were (in a completely different way) Voysey's in England.

The typical grand Prairie house, built in the new

---

* The system was developed during the Spanish-American war. It consisted of a gigantic table which was tilted at 15° to the horizontal onto which were laid metal strips to act as reinforcement and barrow-runs for the concrete pourers. Thickness was made up with hollow pots laid on the table. When the concrete was cured and finished, the whole wall could be pulled vertical with a small engine. Crude as it was, the system was much more sophisticated than almost everything tried by the European architects of the machine worshipping Modern Movement in the '20s and '30s.

---

* There was a tradition of open planning in America that dated back at least to the early '80s. Vincent Scully in *The Shingle Style* has shown how the English tradition of the great central living hall was developed into a continuous space embracing the functions of drawing and dining rooms. The American middle classes seem to have cherished privacy less than their British contemporaries.

215 *Frank Lloyd Wright's Old English essay, the Nathan G. Moore house, Oak Park, Illinois (1895)*

Chicago suburbs for a banker or businessman, is two, sometimes three, storeys high but the chief impression is of horizontality and lowness. (Wright, like Voysey, liked to restrict the height of his rooms, and, Voysey-like, he believed that "the horizontal line is the line of domesticity."[10]) The Robie House in Chicago (designed 1906) sums up the Prairie style at its finest and calmest. The ground floor is a long, low podium of Roman brick capped with simple concrete strips; it contains the entrance hall and billiard and playrooms. The main spaces are on the first floor: living room and dining room are one great space separated by a mighty fireplace that is more than half way to becoming that favourite Arts and Crafts totem, the inglenook. The street front is a continuous band of casement windows, the mullions of which form props for the shallow hipped roof that sur-

216 *Frank Lloyd Wright. Robie House, Chicago (1906)*

rounds the house with wide, generous eaves and sails out at each end in fantastic (for the time) cantilevers to form open porches—seemingly essential elements of the suburban American way of life. The second floor, containing the family bedrooms, has an equally sweeping hipped roof carried on mullions which sails at right angles across the thrust of the two big spaces below. The whole composition is tied together by the rectilinear vertical bulk of the chimney of the living room fireplace—symbolically and formally the pivot of the place.

Those wide eaves were characteristic of Wright's work, even in the early '90s, when he was using much steeper pitched roofs. They caused some disquiet to contemporaries. Wright's fellow Chicagoan, Robert Spencer, asked in the Boston *Architectural Review* what was the justification for "these almost unvarying broad eaves . . . It will not do to say that their use in the north gives a quaint and pleasing southern air to a building. That would be frank condemnation, surely. There are at least two points in their favour. Practically they exclude the sun from the upper rooms only during the hotter hours of summer days . . . [And] the soffits are treated in light reflecting tones, giving the second storey rooms a glow as agreeable as it is surprising to those who expect to find the rooms darkened by the eaves."[11]

Spencer's 1899 review of Wright's architecture was an extraordinary accolade for "a young man's work, a boy's work, perhaps, as he is but thirty-two",[12] which acclaimed that "it is a pleasure to see how style may be given to the cheapest structure . . . when dull or useless precedent is abandoned and materials are handled not merely with a sound knowledge of the basic laws of planning and structure, but with a keen poetic insight into the subtle sources of beauty . . . Our beautiful buildings must not be the forced fruits of an artifical civilization, but must be the natural bloom of a hardy native growth with its roots deep in the soil."[13] Pugin's philosophy had found yet another new frontier.

Wright was steeped in the theories that produced the English Arts and Crafts movement. Ruskin's *Seven Lamps* was one of the first books he owned on architecture and Morris was one of his early heroes. When working for Sullivan, he would stay in the office into the night arguing for revival of "the Gothic spirit in the Middle West".[14]

But in one key respect he departed from his English masters. He attacked Ashbee in 1900 saying: "My God . . . is Machinery, and the art of the future will be the expression of the individual artist through the thousand powers of the machine—the machine doing all those things that the individual workman cannot do. The creative artist is the man who controls all this and understands it."[15]

Wright's resolution of the Puginian paradox was brutal, and Ashbee, the (theoretical) protagonist of freedom for craftsmen, made what seems to have been the feeble riposte that the "individuality of the average had to be considered in addition to that of the 'artistic creator' himself."[16]

Wright was plainly not impressed, for a few months later he gave a speech at Hull House* on the Art and Craft of the Machine in which he sang the praises of the machine which "by its wonderful cutting, shaping, smoothing and reinterpretive capacity has made it possible so [to produce] without waste that the poor as well as the rich may enjoy today beautiful surface treatments of clear strong forms that . . . Sheraton and Chippendale only hinted at, with dire extragavance, and which the middle ages utterly ignored."[17]

Yet Wright's buildings of the early years of the century are not notably more products of machines than those of English contemporaries such as Voysey with his smooth, square-sectioned stair balusters. Even in Wright's big buildings of the period (he was one of the few Arts and Crafts architects to obtain large commissions in the first decade of the century), there was little sign of machine manufacture. True, his headquarters building for the Larkin mail order company in Buffalo† (1903, demolished 1950) had sealed, double-glazed, plate glass windows and a sophisticated (for its time) form of air conditioning. But in both the use of large areas of glass and in mechanical ventilation, he had been anticipated by Mackintosh in the north block of the Glasgow School of Art. Neither the Buffalo nor the Glasgow building was dominated by the machine aesthetic of smooth-

---

* Hull House, founded by Jane Addams, was based on the idea of Toynbee Hall in Whitechapel, the University settlement where Ashbee had lodged and taught as a young man, and which had itself been founded by Canon and Mrs. Barrett, patrons of Townsend and Parker and Unwin.

† The Larkin building was Wright's first important commission outside the mid-west. One of the co-founders of the company was Elbert Hubbard (1850–1945) who had met Morris on a trip to England and who, in the '90s, set up the Roycroft community at East Aurora, New York state. Ashbee, who visited the Roycrofters in 1900, thought their work—furniture and printing—promising but untutored and ugly.

217 *Frank Lloyd Wright. Unity Church, Oak Park (1904)*

ness and repetition. The Larkin building was clad in brick and the Glasgow one in stone—the most ancient and labour intensive building materials.*

Smoothness was one of the chief characteristics of Wright's next major non-domestic building, the Unity Church at Oak Park, Illinois (1904). It is constructed of poured concrete, the pebbles of which give the outside the texture of a great block of striated stone. Its eaves project like those of flat roofed prairie houses and are propped in the same way by the mullions of clerestorey windows. The square internal space derives much of its character from these windows with their rectilinear pattern of coloured glass, but its effect of being in a cubical bath of light could not have been achieved without the laylights between the beams of the concrete roof.

Concrete was chosen as the material for Unity Church because of its cheapness ($35,000 was the price limit). Structurally the concept was not innovative, and concrete was used in the cheapest possible way—then, as now, a sort of mud was poured by unskilled labour into wooden boxes, themselves prepared with the simplest carpentry and later thrown away. So the contribution to design of the individual labourer was reduced to the absolute minimum—in complete contrast to the way of handling concrete envisaged by Lethaby and his team in their virtually contemporary Liverpool Cathedral competition design (p. 64). If that had been built, elaborate craftsmanship would have been needed to construct the scheme's complicated curves and tapers. The Liverpool design was turned down on the grounds not of the expense of its handwork, but of style. At Oak Park the building process could not at the time be carried out by machine, but Wright was determined to make it as machine-like as possible.† Perhaps it was the vague neo-classicism of the result that made it acceptable to a proper middle class congregation.

Wright's productive career spanned a prodigious period—from the 1890s to the late 1950s. After about 1910, he received few commissions for some twenty-five years but in the late '30s his practice picked up again and, after the second world war, he was venerated as the greatest living American architect and enjoyed a correspondingly large practice and large ideas—one of his last projects was for a mile high skyscraper. But he never quite forgot his Arts and Crafts origins and preached truth-to-materials and relevance to place to the last.

In the lean years of the early '30s, Wright set up the Taliesin Fellowship, a community based on craft teaching and agriculture that rather resembled Ashbee's Campden Guild (except that most members had to pay Wright for the privilege of belonging to the Fellowship). And, at the same time, he began to evolve proposals for Broadacre City, a low density interweaving of town and country with "*little* farms, *little* homes for industry, *little* factories, *little* schools, a *little* university going to people most by way of their interest in the ground".[18] It was a (never realized) translation of *News From Nowhere* into the language of middle America: a city in which "quality is in all, for all, alike".

However wayward he may have been in his later years, in the first decade of the century Wright's influence on architects of the mid-west was clear. His open plans and sweeping roofs with great eaves supported by the mullions of a band of windows became trademarks of the Prairie School. Even Wright's old master Sullivan adopted the idioms in his later domestic work when his practice was declining.

The people most directly influenced by Wright were the assistants at his Oak Park Studio. His office was as fertile a breeding ground of talent as Shaw's had been twenty years before. Of all Wright's assistants of those years, Walter Burley Griffin (1876–1937) developed the most individual approach. He was Wright's chief draughtsman until they parted after a quarrel in 1905 when Griffin set up on his own to produce a series of houses often distinguished by wide overhanging gables and strong vertical elements, more overtly Japanese than Wright's work. In 1911 Griffin married Marion Mahoney (1871–1962) an assistant who designed many of Wright's renderings and some of his furnishings. In 1912, he won the competition for planning Australia's federal capital, Canberra, with a design that had all the formal qualities of an Arts and Crafts garden. Griffin left America before the Prairie School's decline had become serious, but in the next ten years it quietly faded just as the movement in Britain had done a few years earlier. The reasons were much the same; an increasing affection for classical and other historical styles in a client class ever more concerned with order and obvious respectability.

---

* But the building's furniture which Wright specially designed *was* innovatory. It was made of standardized steel components.

† It is only fair to point out that this was exactly Voysey's approach. He achieved similarly simple effects by coating crude brick walls with render—a type of construction that requires no initiative on the part of workmen.

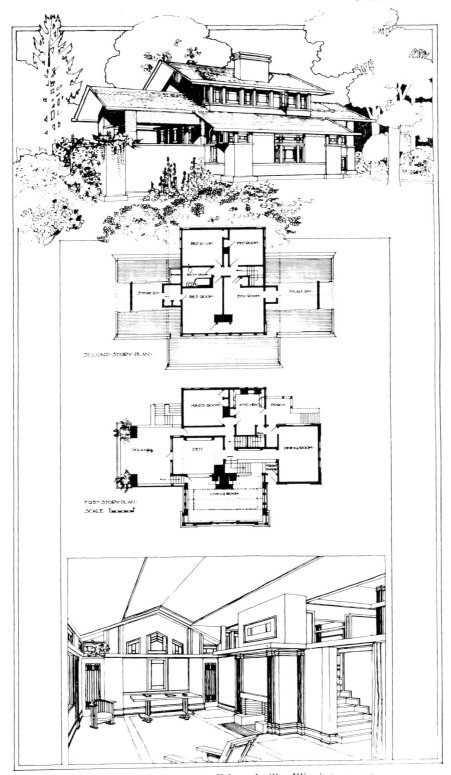

218 *Walter Burghley Griffin. Ralph D. Griffin house, Edwardsville, Illinois (c. 1910)*

219 *Frank Lloyd Wright. Unity Church, interior*

1 Stickley, Gustav *The Craftsman*, Vol. IV, 1903, p. 92

2 Stickley, Gustav Introduction to *More Craftsman Homes*, 1911 in Sanders, Barry (ed.) *The Best of Craftsman Homes*, Peregrine Smith, Santa Barbara and Salt Lake City 1978, p. 7

3 "California's contribution to a national architecture: its significance and beauty as shown in the work of Greene and Greene architects", *The Craftsman*, in Sanders, Barry (ed.) *The Craftsman: an Anthology*, Peregrine Smith, Santa Barbara and Salt Lake City 1978

4 This and much other information about the sources of Greene and Greene architecture is given in Makinson, Randall, L. *Greene and Greene: Architecture as a Fine Art* and *Greene and Greene: Furniture and Related Designs*, Peregrine Smith, Santa Barbara and Salt Lake City 1977 and 1979

5 Cram, Ralph Adams *American Country Houses of Today* 1913, quoted in "Greene and Greene", Makinson, Randall L. in McCoy, Esther *Five Californian Architects*, Reinhold, New York 1960, p. 146

6 Gill, Irving J. "The Home of the Future: the new architecture of the west", *The Craftsman*, May 1916, in Sanders, Barry *The Craftsman, op. cit.*, p. 314

7 Quoted in McCoy, Esther *op. cit.*, p. 69

8 Much information on the foundation and work of the Prairie

School is given by the school's historian Brooks, H. Allen in *The Prairie School* University of Toronto and Buffalo, 1972.

9 *Ibid.*, p. 16. The quotation is from *Architectural Record*, Vol. XV, 1904, pp. 362–3.

10 Wright, F. L. "The Sovereignty of the individual", introduction to *Ausgeführte Bauten Unt Entwürfe*, Wasmuth, Berlin 1910, reprinted in Wright, F. L. *Writings and Buildings*, ed. Kaufmann and Raeburn, Horizon 1960, p. 104

11 Spencer, Robert C. Jr. "The Work of Frank Lloyd Wright", *Architectural Review*, Boston, Vol. I (new series), 1899, p. 68

12 *Ibid.*, p. 72

13 *Ibid.*, p. 62

14 Farr, Finis *Frank Lloyd Wright*, a biography, Cape, London 1962, p. 46

15 Ashbee, C. R. *Memoirs*, typescript in Victoria and Albert Museum library, Vol. I, p. 242

16 *Ibid.*

17 Wright, F. L. "The Art and Craft of the Machine" delivered March 6 1901 at Hull House, printed in *Writings and Buildings, op. cit.*, pp. 65–66

18 Wright, F. L. "Broadacre City; a new community plan", *Architectural Record*, Vol. LXXVII, p. 247

15 Crossing the Channel

Wright's work was published in 1910 and 1911 by Wasmuth of Berlin who had issued Muthesius's *Das englische Haus* a few years earlier. Wright asked Ashbee, his closest European friend, to provide an introduction, and in it the English architect wrote "in a comparison of the work of Frank Lloyd Wright with modern work in England and Germany . . . a certain kinship is significant . . . In Germany the names of Olbrich, Hoffmann, Moser, Bruno Paul, Mohring suggest themselves. In England those of us who are sometimes called the Arts and Crafts men, Lethaby, Voysey, Lutyens, Ricardo, Wilson, Holden, Blow, Townsend, Baillie Scott. We feel that between us and him there is a kinship. We may differ vitally in manner of expression, in our planning, in our touch, in the way we clothe our work, in our feeling for proportion, but although our problems differ essentially, we are altogether at one in our principles. We guard in common the lamp of truth."[1]

Between 1890 and 1910 artistic links between Britain and the German speaking countries were particularly close, and, to some extent, architecture followed parallel courses in the offshore island and in northern and central Europe. These developments were part of a rejection of classicism that swept Europe in the second half of the nineteenth century.* The origins of the reaction have never been properly investigated but they undoubtedly owed something to Ruskinian theory and to the example of Morris and Mackmurdo. Architects as different as the Dutch romantic H. P. Berlage[2] and the great French exponent of Art Nouveau, Hector Guimard,[3] paid tribute to Ruskin, and Morris's designs were well known on the continent by the '90s. Another source of anti-classicism was the writings of the great French Goth, Eugene-Emmanuel Viollet-le-Duc (1814–79). Viollet-le-Duc's analysis made Gothic out to be a much more scientific system of construction than Ruskin had suggested and he proposed various ways of using iron according to Gothic principles. His polemics had great influence throughout the Continent and in America where the young Frank Lloyd Wright was one of his many disciples. In England, there was a vogue for le-Duc's theories in the '70s and '80s.

By 1900, the European anti-classicists could be divided broadly, and with many exceptions on each side, into two camps by a line running roughly, along the Dutch/Belgian border and down through Munich to Vienna. To the south was the territory of Art Nouveau with its sinuous intertwined curves; its profusion of elaborate ornament; its structures curved and twisted to take the shapes of bones and plants. To the north, a much more protestant spirit prevailed. Structures were simple, straightforward and clearly expressed; ornament was restricted and, where it was used, it tended to follow the stiff, heraldic forms of the English Arts and Crafts movement.

In England, Art Nouveau was regarded with some horror. In 1904, the *Magazine of Art* held a colloquium on the subject in which architects as diverse as Jackson, Voysey and Blomfield were united in decrying the southern movement. Voysey, the most eloquent, welcomed "the condition that has made '*Art Nouveau*' possible", but he savaged the manifestation as "distinctly unhealthy and revolting."

"Is it not", he thundered, "merely the work of a lot of imitators with nothing but mad eccentricit guide; good men, no doubt, misled into thinki art is a debauch of sensuous feeling, instead

---

* In America, there was a similar reaction in the Shingle style and the work of Henry Hobson Richardson (1838–1886). Richardson's last work was extremely changeful and bore a powerful personal stamp—great simple planes of rough ashlar penetrated by giant semi-circular arches round the major openings. His work was published spasmodically in Europe and has been said to have influenced architects as different as Townsend and Sonk.

expression of human *thought* and feeling combined."[4]

Jackson described the characteristic feature of Art Nouveau as "the Squirm". It is easy to see how the proper, rather priggish Englishmen were revolted by Art Nouveau's total wilfullness, profusion of decoration and its overt sexuality (naked women figured large in Art Nouveau design, sometimes even forming the structure of chairs), all so alien to ascetic Arts and Crafts folk.

Art Nouveau architects were consciously trying to achieve a new style, derived from nature, in which materials, particularly metal and glass, achieved a writhing plasticity never seen before. The northern architects were much more conscious of their past. Like many Englishmen they turned to late medieval domestic architecture as the chief source of inspiration.

In Scandinavia, echoes of the past were pursued in an attempt to achieve nationally identifiable architectures. All four Scandinavian countries were seeking identity, and all four evolved varieties of what came to be known as national romanticism.

Denmark had a national cultural revival after the loss of Slesvig-Holsten in 1864 and was the first in the

field. Martin Nyrop (1849–1912) designed country houses in local styles throughout Denmark but he also received public commissions,* the largest of which was Copenhagen town hall (built 1892–1905). It was a celebration of brick—the material in which seventeenth-century Copenhagen was constructed—in dramatic contrast to the stuccoed classical public buildings of the previous eighty years. Basically a giant courtyard, the building was saved from symmetry by the great tower with its copper covered spire. The town hall heralded a generation of urban brick buildings, irregular and changeful, by architects such as Ulrick Plesner and Aage Largeland-Mathiesen.

Norway, which got independence from Sweden only in 1906, was as usual quieter than the other Scandinavian countries. Arnsten Arneberg (1882–?) was one of the first to bring the techniques of traditional timber farm building to the suburbs. He spent many years restoring the mighty Akershus

* Unlike the English Arts and Craftsmen, who rarely received public work, the architects of the national romantic movements did get large public works precisely because their work was identified with national aspirations. Their success is an indication that, had the British architects been given a chance, a great civic architecture could been evolved out of Ruskinian principles—a possibility that is denied even today by classicists.

220 *Gesellius, Lindgren and Saarinen. Saarinen's own house, Hviträsk, near Helsinki (1901)*

221 *Gesellius, Lindgren and Saarinen. Finnish National Museum, Helsinki (1905–12)*

castle, hard by Oslo harbour, on principles that would have delighted the British Society for the Protection of Ancient Buildings.

In Finland, struggling to establish separation from Russia, three young architects, Herman Gesellius (1874–1916), Armas Lindgren (1874–1929) and Eliel Saarinen (1873–1959), started to build a group of houses for themselves at Hvitträsk near Helsinki in 1901. The group included a common workshop and studio in the best Arts and Crafts tradition. It consisted of a rough, stone ground floor, partly covered by plaster to give an irregular line (almost Deveyesque in its arbitrary irregularity and the impression it gives of a house built on ancient foundations). On top of this, the first floor was shingled, and the different levels were all tied together by sweeping roofs of pantiles. All materials were taken from local peasant precedents.

When they built in town, for instance in the National Museum, Helsinki (1905–1912), the partners adopted a much tougher style, partly based on romanesque, with a massive base course of squared granite rubble and a tower capped with brick and copper. The minimal decoration was based on traditional Finnish forms and restricted to key areas—over the main door and on gable ends for instance.

Lars Sonk (1870–1956) was even more austere. The squared granite of his Helsinki telephone exchange (1905) was rough, almost brutal; the asymmetrical elevation is banded horizontally by rows of windows, either arched or, on the main floor, with square lintels propped by circular columns, the capitals of which bear almost the whole of the building's simple geometric ornament. There is irony in the romanesque overtones of this building, and of the National Museum, for Finland had no romanesque tradition. National romantic architects were not only fired by Puginian fidelity to tradition, they were quite happy to take and reinterpret themes from the architecture of other nations: even Nyrop's Copenhagen town hall was consciously modelled on Sienna's.

The most splendid of all the northern public buildings was the Stockholm City Hall, built between 1909
and 1923 by Ragnar Östberg (1866–1945). Like
Arneberg, Östberg was a devoted restorer of old
buildings (for instance the hall of state in Uppsala
castle), and in the Stockholm building he mixed
much traditional Swedish detail with themes from
Gothic and Byzantine architecture. It stands reflected
in one of Stockholm's sea canals, a four-square block
of plum coloured brick on rows of Byzantine arches.
It is capped with a curving green copper roof and
pinned down by a huge tapering tower in one corner.
Inside, the glory of many splendid spaces is the Golden Hall, a secular cathedral lined with glowing gold
mosaic which focuses on a great hieratic mosaic
figure, stiff and powerful in the tradition of both
Byzantines and Arts and Craftsmen.

The pioneering architect of the Dutch anti-
classical movement was Hendrik Petrus Berlage
(1856–1934) who, though he practised for a time as a
renaissance architect, then as a formalist Goth,
evolved a much more changeful and savage style in
the '90s.

222 *Ragnar Östberg. Stockholm City Hall (1909–23)*

223 *Östberg. Stockholm City Hall—the Golden Hall*

224 *H. P. Berlage. Amsterdam Stock Exchange (1898–1908), east elevation*

225 *J. M. van der Mey. Amsterdam Shipping office (1913–1916)*

In the Amsterdam stock exchange (built 1898–1908), Berlage married the brick techniques of traditional Dutch architecture with thin metal trusses which carried the glazed roofs on the three main halls. Externally, the building is a large rectangle, anchored, like the Stockholm and Copenhagen town halls, by a big tower in one corner. But the fenestration of Berlage's building is much freer, with the shape and size of windows (generally) dictated by what was going on inside.

Berlage's use of brick in the '90s was a conscious return to roots and rejection of the architecture of stucco or stone. It was an inspiration to national romantics like J. M. van der Mey whose Amsterdam shipping office (1913–16), encrusted with sculpture growing of and out of an austere brick backdrop, all capped with a great grey knobbly metal dragon back, was one of the last and most exuberant examples of savageness. Van der Mey influenced architects of the succeeding generation like Michel de Klerk (1884–1923) and Piet Kramer (1881–1961) whose Amsterdam school of housing, built of brick and tile, full of ebullience and often quirky expression, flourished into the '20s.

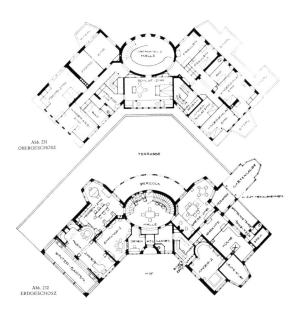

227 *Nikolasee house, ground floor plan*

226 *Hermann Muthesius. House at Nikolasee, Berlin (1907–1908)*

228 *H. M. Baillie Scott. Competition entry for "Ein herrschaflisches Wohnhaus eines Kunstfreundes"* (1900)

In the middle of all these nationalistic architectural movements was Germany, and by the early 1900s, there too, many were calling for an architecture which could clearly be identified as German. Muthesius, for example, ended his introduction to *Das englische Haus* by urging his countrymen to "face our own conditions squarely and as honestly as the English face theirs today, to adhere to our own artistic tradition as faithfully, to embody our customs and habits in the German house as lovingly."[5]

Muthesius's own architecture in the years following his return to Germany was an uneasy blend of English and German. His mansion at Nikolasee, Berlin (1907–1908) appears at first sight to be a Prior butterfly house covered with north German timbering and high tiled roofs. But inside, the layout is quite different from the long, thin Arts and Crafts plan; much more squashed together, and given to German grandiose gestures.

Even while Muthesius was writing, architects like Paul Schultze-Naumburg (1869–1949) and his pupil Heinrich Tessenow were producing much simpler villas and cottages in the north German tradition with white walls, pierced where necessary by simple shuttered windows, sometimes tied together by simple rectilinear half-timbering. These deliberately humble and atavistic buildings were expressions of the northern European romantic search for roots that had started with Old English forty years before. But there were much more direct links between Britain and the German speaking countries at the turn of the century. Baillie Scott and Ashbee were working on the Grand Duke of Hesse's palace in Darmstadt in 1897–1898. Their work and that of Voysey and Mackintosh was illustrated in German and Austrian magazines and, in November 1900, Ashbee and Mackintosh showed work (Mackintosh had a whole room) at the Vienna Secession exhibition.*

In December of the same year, the Darmstadt magazine *Zeitschrift für Innerndekoration* launched a competition for a house for an art lover *"ein herrschaftliches Wohnhaus eines Kunstfreundes"*.[6] No first prize was awarded but Baillie Scott got the largest premium, even though his elevations, which incorporated Scottish baronial drum towers, half-timbering and curious, elegant paraboloid gables were judged to be lacking in the modern spirit. They made a butterfly plan of no great size look like a castle. Mackintosh, though he did not submit enough drawings to qualify, was awarded a special prize. His elevations were a development of Windyhill (p. 105), austere planes of white harling punctuated irregularly by windows all of which had small square panes. The plan was basically rectangular: an elegant version of the long, thin Arts and Crafts layout extending sideways from a double-height hall.

The interiors of the two schemes were radically different. Scott used his dark interior half-timbering, as he had done in the Blackwell hall, enlivened by a simple, diagonal, coloured pattern on the edges of the beams and flowers and painted figures—very much in the Morris tradition. Mackintosh's music room was white and fine-drawn with tapering pilasters and an elaborate, thin, celticly curving, yet symmetrical screen over the piano which formed the focus of the space.

There was a clear affinity between the work of the British and Secession designers. Joseph Hoffmann (1870–1956) came closest to Mackintosh. His first house, the Villa Henneberg near Vienna (1900) echoed the plane walls and irregularly placed small

* The Secession was an association founded in 1897 by artists like Klimt, Olbrich, Moser and Hoffmann in rebellion against the academic management of the *Kunstlerhaus*. It included virtually all the Austrian artists of the *Jugendstil* (the Germanic contemporary of Art Nouveau), and its exhibitions were similar in content to those of the Arts and Crafts Exhibition Society.

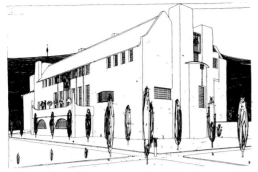

229 *C. R. Mackintosh entry for "Ein herrschaflisches Wohnhaus eines Kunstfreundes" competition (1900)*

paned windows of the Scot.* It even had a (partly)

* British influence in Austria spread further than the Secessionists. One of the sternest critics of Secessionist wilfulness, Adolf Loos (1870–1933), whose pragmatic neo-classicism and hostility to arbitrary ornament earned him the reverence of Modern Movement architects of the next generation, designed cosy interiors complete with inglenooks and (often fake) exposed ceiling beams. Even his House on the Michaelerplatz, a block of flats on top of a store in the middle of Vienna's old city, has a row of Mackintosh-like small paned recessed bay windows between the giant Tuscan columns of the ground floor and the smoothly stripped upper storeys.

230 *Joseph Hoffmann. Haus Henneberg, Hohe Warte, Vienna (1901)*

231 *Hoffmann. Haus Moll II, Hohe Warte, Vienna (1903)*

232 *Hoffmann. Palais Stoclet, Brussels (1905–11). Dining room with Klimt mosaics*

double-height hall, though the plan was compressed into a square round it rather than being strung out in the British fashion. Fernand Khnopff remarked in the *Studio* (which was very much aware of events abroad as well as at home) in 1901 that Hoffmann "is essentially rational and reasonable in all he does. His compositions are never extravagant, never intentionally loud, as are those of his more western *confrères*. He confines himself to . . . proportion and decoration, and thus is enabled to add to the beauty of the original lines of construction without addition and without alteration."[7] One of Hoffmann's clearest debts to Britain is shown in his Haus Moll II (1904), built in Hohe Warte, a northern suburb of Vienna. There, a pyramidally topped two storey block, clad in hung slates is in the process of engulfing an early version of Voysey's Bedford Park tower house, shaved of its bay but complete with smoothly rendered white walls, shallow curved metal roof and a strip of small paned windows pressing up against the eaves.

But Hoffmann's closest personal links were with Mackintosh. Hoffmann and Mackintosh designed rooms for Fritz Wärndorfer's house in 1902. The two architects corresponded, and Hoffmann visited Mackintosh in Glasgow. On the trip, he went to see Ashbee's Guild of Handicraft at Essex House and, full of the experience, he set up the *Wiener Werkstätte* in 1903. His partner was Koloman Moser (1868–1918) and their sponsor was Wärndorfer.*

The Werkstätte's most important commission was the Palais Stoclet, built in Brussels between 1905 and 1911, for a rich art collector who had lived in Vienna. Externally, the building was changeful, building up to a rectilinear stair tower in the middle. It continued Hoffmann and Mackintosh's theme of small paned windows set in plain white walls. But the planes were created in sheets of sawn pale grey Norwegian granite, not simple Scottish harling, and the whole building was tied up by an ornate metal band which ran round every corner of the complex silhouette. The regular vertical windows of the main block give the impression that Palais Stoclet is basically a classical building, carved up and added to rather against its will, instead of one which has grown out of the clash of inner functions which Mackintosh expressed so beautifully in his entry for the *Haus Kunstfreundes*. Inside, the plan has some resemblance to Mackintosh's. The range of Werkstätte skills were used to their full in the most luxurious of materials, marbles and woods from all over Europe. Mackintosh's etiolation and refinement, stripped of his sinuous curves, tapers and witty incidents, form the dominating impression. The furniture and wall surfaces have the overriding rectilinearity of Hoffmann's work except in the dining room, which is enlivened by the complex geometry and brilliant colour of two mosaics by Hoffmann's fellow Secessionist, Gustav Klimt.

The Wiener Werkstätte was one of many communities in Germany and Austria. Some, like Karl Schmidt's Dresden *Werkstätte für Handwerkskunst* (founded 1898), were businesses like the Morris Firm—others were much more idealistic like Ashbee's Guild.

In 1899 Ernst Ludwig, the Grand Duke of Hesse, always indefatigable in his pursuit of the Arts and Crafts, decided to form an artists' colony at Matildenhohe in Darmstadt to act as an inspiration for German design. He called on an Austrian, Joseph Maria Olbrich (1867–1908),* the Secessionist who had designed the group's exhibition gallery in Vienna, to act as chief architect for the colony's houses and for the Ernst Ludwig building, a combination of studios and bachelor quarters in the middle of the complex. W. Fred, reviewing the colony's first exhibition in the *Studio*, remarked that "they have worked together for some purpose. For the first time we are able to take a survey of the extent of art-handicraft. For everything, from the architecture of the exterior to the laid out table and the coverlet of the bed in every house, has been entirely designed by the artist and executed under his supervision."[8] The colony included, besides Olbrich, Peter Behrens (1868–1940), painter, designer and architect (he was the only other artist who designed his own house), and a sculptor, a metal worker, a furniture designer and a painter. Fred emphasized that "Education by means of art-handicraft, not by dilletantism, but by

---

* The *Arbeitsprogramm der Wiener Werkstätte* by Hoffmann and Moser (1905) announced that the organization's message was "a welcoming call for those who invoke the name of Ruskin and Morris . . . We cannot and we do not wish to compete with cheap production; this above all is made at the worker's expense, whilst we consider that our first duty is to give him happiness in his work, and a life worthy of a man." Quoted by Godoli, Ezio in Russell, Frank (ed.) *Art Nouveau Architecture* Academy Editions, London 1979, p. 251.

* Olbrich was another Anglophile—for instance, he managed to spend half his Rome scholarship studying in England. He and Hoffmann were close; both studied under Austria's Norman Shaw, Otto Wagner (1841–1918), and when Olbrich moved to Darmstadt, Hoffmann took over his commissions for houses at Hohe Warte.

233 *Peter Behrens. Own house, Matildenhöhe, Darmstadt (1901)*

234 *Olbrich's house, Matildenhöhe, Darmstadt (1901)*

the daily use of household furniture and utensils, is the special desire of those who in Germany and Austria are fighting for the new art."[9]

Olbrich's houses varied from free reinterpretations of traditional German styles, with big gabled roofs of blue slates and red tiles on top of white walls relieved by stencilling in chequerboard and stylized tree patterns, through an almost Art Nouveau freedom to a severe rectilinear essay in which small paned windows irregularly pierced smooth walls, themselves capped with a pronounced mortar-board roof. His Ernst Ludwig Haus was an essay in strong horizontals with small paned windows symmetrically set about a great, ornate semi-circular door which was flanked by giant free-standing statues—the sort of building that Townsend in his prime might have produced had he ever been give an open site.

The Darmstadt colony was crowned by the *Hochzeitsturm*, designed in 1907 to celebrate Ernst Ludwig's wedding: a tower topped with the shape of a flat hand, with curved copper cascading round the fingers at the top and strapped in the most changeful manner with horizontal bands of windows partially wrapping round the structure. It was Olbrich's most original work and one of his last.

Grand Duke Ernst Ludwig's aim in setting up the Darmstadt colony was to improve the quality of design in Hesse—and thence in all Germany. Another German petty prince, the Grand Duke of Saxony, made a bid for design leadership when he appointed the Belgian Art Nouveau architect and designer Henry van de Velde (1863–1957) as head of the Grand-Ducal school of Arts and Crafts in Weimar in 1902. This grand-ducal competition was not just a matter of late feudal one-up-manship.* Germans regarded good design as vital for the future of the fatherland. Like Britain, Germany was facing tariff walls, but Germany lacked the enormous resources of the British colonies to feed on and sell to. So German products had to sell on quality—but their reputation was not high.

Muthesius commented in 1907 that "in architecture we rank as the most backward country in Europe, because German taste in general is regarded as being at the very bottom of the ladder. In fact our artistic reputation has sunk so low that 'German' and

* Nor was it limited to these two grand dukes; as Wolfgang Pehnt has pointed out, Karlsruhe, Düsseldorf and Berlin merged their academies of art and their schools of craft at about the same time as Weimar. (Pehnt, Wolfgang *Expressionist Architecture*, Thames and Hudson, London 1973 p. 109.)

235 *Adolf Loos. Living room design (1899). Loos, though he attacked the British influenced Secession architects, was himself devoted to Arts and Crafts motifs*

'bad taste' have become practically synonymous."[10]

In the same speech, he pointed out that "helping the modern movement is by no means a commercially unsound proposition. The large number of industrialists who followed the new path as a logical decision have obtained significant financial success. It is enough to mention the Dresdener *Werkstätten für Handwerkskunst*, which in the space of eight years developed from very humble beginnings into a concern with a colossal turnover, capable of employing hundreds of carpenters."[11]

Later in 1907, Muthesius was instrumental in founding the *Deutscher Werkbund*, an organization which brought together architects, artists, designers, industrialists and men from the Werkstätten with the expressed aim of improving German products. In the same year, Peter Behrens of the Darmstadt community was appointed as design consultant to the giant *Allgemeine Elektrizitäts Gesellschaft*. There was no question that machinery should not be used to the full. Morris's teaching that working with machines

made men into slaves was completely ignored in the pursuit of economic success for the German nation, but the arts and crafts were still held in high regard as test bed for product design and as a sort of conscience. Muthesius believed that "the arts and crafts are called on to restore an awareness of honesty, integrity and simplicity in contemporary society."[12]*

As the Werkbund matured, it became increasingly clear that there was little place for craftsmanly elements. The dynamic of the Werkbund was generated by cross-fertilization of artist and industrialist. Walter Gropius (1883–1969), a young architect member, wrote, "The artist has the power to give the lifeless machine made product a soul; it is his creative force that will live on, actively embodied in its outward form. His collaboration is not just a luxury, generously thrown in as an extra, it is an indispensable part of the industrial process and must be regarded as such."[14]

* The attitude was common in the years just after the turn of the century. Even a machine fanatic like Wright believed that the Arts and Crafts shop should be the "experimental station that would represent in miniature the elements of the great pulsating web of the machine."[13]

236 *Joseph Maria Olbrich. Hochzeitsturm, Matildenhöhe (1907–1908)*

Gropius was deeply interested in factory design, believing that "a worker will find that a room well thought out by an artist, which responds to the innate sense of beauty we all possess, relieves the monotony of the daily task and he will be more willing to join in collective undertakings. If the worker is happy, he will take more pleasure in his duties and the productivity of the firm will increase."[15] If the workers were

not to be freed of the tyranny of machine processes, they could at least be kept in order with the new architecture. A new factory building could be good for business too. He was sharply critical of "distorting the true character of the building by allowing it to masquerade in borrowed garments from an earlier period which have absolutely nothing in common with the sterner purposes of a factory. The good name of the firm can only suffer from a building got up in fancy dress."[16] Gropius built several factories before the war, including a model factory at the Werkbund's big exhibition at Cologne in 1914. That was mostly of steel and glass—machine-made elements with craftsmanship reduced to an absolute minimum.*

But when Gropius was made successor to Van der Velde at the Weimar School of Arts and Crafts† and turned it into the Bauhaus, the most renowned art school in the twentieth century, he put great stress on teaching the crafts. The first rule of the school was that "thorough training of all students in the crafts provides the unifying foundation."[17] It was one of the last manifestations of the notion, shared by Ashbee, Wright and Muthesius, that the crafts should be the conscience of industry: the early Bauhaus was a direct descendant of Lethaby's Central School.

Nevertheless, Gropius was in fact wedded to machines, so much so that in 1922 he wrote to his fellow Bauhaus masters praising the work of "young artists . . . beginning to face up to the phenomena of industry and the machine. They try to design what I would call the 'useless' machine."[18]

So the wheel had turned, and William Morris was stood on his head. Instead of the machine being the hated brutalizer of humanity, it was held to be the prime focus of artistic inspiration. The Modern Movement in architecture was being born, and, over the next fifty years, standardization, machine worship

* Apart from contributions by Gropius and his partner Meyer and one or two other architects who built in the machine style, most of the other Werkbund pavilions were vaguely classical. Hoffmann, Behrens and even Muthesius, who had so sorrowfully chronicled Norman Shaw's conversion to classicism, all produced buildings with overtly classical elevations.

Hoffmann's conversion to classicism had begun some years earlier. For instance his Haus Ast (1910), next door to the Haus Moll II, is fluted like a flattened out Doric column pierced by regular rows of windows and topped with a classical cornice covered with curving celtic ornament.

† Eckhart Muthesius, Hermann's son, has told me that Gropius owed his position to Muthesius' recommendation. Eckhart, incidentally, was the godson of Makintosh and Frank Newbery (head of the Glasgow School of Art in the first decade of this century).

and distrust of the craftsman gradually became some of the dominating themes of architecture.

Though the gentler principles like fidelity to place were eschewed, a few Arts and Crafts ideals were taken on board by the Modern Movement. Even changefulness was embraced by some Modern Movement architects, and when the Bauhaus moved to Dessau in 1925, the new building was carefully designed by Gropius to show the difference between living quarters, studios, offices and workshops in a Manx wheel plan with three thin limbs spreading from an ill defined centre.

The Modern Movement took over the Arts and Crafts dislike of period styles (though not its reverence for tradition). Modern Movement architects became fanatical in their hatred of the styles of the past. But in their dominant idea that form should follow function, which had been so clearly spelled out by Pugin, they continued the Arts and Crafts horror of shams—at least theoretically (though many early Modern Movement buildings were built of brick made to look like concrete, just as many Arts and Crafts buildings were given fake half-timbering). And the movement inherited a kind of social idealism; but, while the socialism of Morris had been concerned to liberate everyone, that of the Modern Movement was concerned with standardization and minimal norms, with only the architect free to decide how people should live. The Puginian paradox was finally and brutally resolved, with the designer in complete control and the craftsman reduced to the status of fitter and machine minder.

In the '30s, the authoritarian Modern Movement was banished from Germany* by the even more authoritarian Nazi goverment which, in reaction to machine architecture, reintroduced some of the ideas shared by the Arts and Crafts movement and the National Romantics of the turn of the century.

Art and architecture were, of course, subject to close supervision by the Nazis, perhaps closer than other branches of intellectual endeavour, because of Hitler's own artistic pretentions. He took the arts very seriously: "I am convinced that art, since it forms the most uncorrupted, the most immediate reflection of the people's soul, exercises unconsciously by far the greatest influence on the masses of the people."[19]

237 *Völkisch architecture: Franz Hufnagel, Siedlung Heddernheim (pre 1941)*

Translated into Nazi jargon, the echoes of Morris are clear.

The people—the *volk*—were of great importance to the National Socialists who favoured two styles of architecture which were supposed to be easily understood by everyman. There was a stripped classical style used for great public buildings by architects like Speer—a kind of architecture in which Hitler took particular interest. And, of less interest to the party leaders was *völkisch* architecture, intended for the houses of the masses and based on the vernacular building of rural Germany. Schultze-Naumburg, who had been preaching the virtues of native architecture from early in the century (p. 202), became an enthusiastic Nazi supporter, glorying in the peasant house as "a reservoir of all genuine *völkisch* qualities", whose form was "bound to the blood"[20]. Winfred Wedland, a professor at the Berlin Academy, celebrated the small house as "the seed-core of the *Volk*", in which "everyone who builds . . . must feel the duty to do a small service for art, something to give a house a more beautiful character.

---

* Leading lights of the Modern Movement fled to England, then to America, where they found their machine worship remarkably acceptable in the land of Henry Ford.

This does not always have to be figures for the garden or a painting. A pair of carved beams or a carved door will do."[21] It was a version of Lethaby's brown bread and dewy morning approach to architecture translated to Hansel and Gretel.

Many small *völkisch* houses were built all over Germany, often in small new settlements laid out on Garden City principles, but the most celebrated *völkisch* building was much grander. At Hermann Goering's Karinhall shooting lodge north of Berlin, a courtyard was enclosed by a thatched roof over white walls liberally besprinkled with antlers. The main reception room was a great German hall, focusing on a mighty fireplace complete with inglenook quite in the Arts and Crafts fashion.

Modern Movement critics of the Arts and Crafts have made play with the similarities between the work of Arts and Craftsmen and Nazi architects, implying some sort of guilt by association. Yet evil men may sometimes embrace noble ideals—that does not besmirch the ideals, it improves the men. *Völkisch* architecture can scarcely be added to the horrendous catalogue of crimes perpetrated by the Nazi state. Providing good, simple housing for the people was one of the few decent things that the Nazis did.

The same critics imply that, because the early Modern Movement was execrated by the Nazis, it is in some way virtuous. But it was the Modern Movement that housed ordinary working people in factory-like barrack blocks*: it was that movement which so lovingly embraced the tyranny of the machine, and it wanted to reforge man in quite a new image, free of all the inherited detritus of the past. The final, paradoxical irony of the Arts and Crafts

movement is that, devoted as it was to freedom and individuality, it should have been the reservoir for two such authoritarian streams as *völkisch* architecture and the Modern Movement.

1 Ashbee, C. R. "Frank Lloyd Wright: a study and an appreciation" reprinted in Kaufmann, Edgar *Frank Lloyd Wright, the Early Work*, Horizon, New York 1968, p. 7
2 Singelenberg, Pieter *H. P. Berlage, Idea and Style*, Utrecht 1972, p. 149
3 Guimard, Hector *Architectural Record*, Vol. XII, 1902, p. 127. Guimard was identifying the sources of Art Nouveau for an American audience.
4 Voysey, C. F. A. in "L'art nouveau: a symposium", *Magazine of Art*, Vol. II, 2nd series, 1904, p. 212
5 Muthesius, Hermann *The English House*, trans. Janet Seligman, Crosby Lockwood Staples, London 1979, p. 11
6 Kornwolf, James D. *M. H. Baillie Scott and the Arts and Crafts Movement*, Johns Hopkins, Baltimore and London, 1972 has a detailed discussion of the competition, pp. 216–238.
7 Khnopff, F. *Studio*, Vol. XXII, 1901, p. 264
8 Fred, W. *Studio*, Vol. XXIV, 1902, p. 26
9 *Ibid.*, p. 95
10 Muthesius, Hermann "The meaning of the Arts and Crafts", lecture at Handelshochschule, Berlin 1907. Translated in Benton, T. and C. *Form and Function*, Crosby Lockwood Staples, London, p. 40
11 *Ibid.*, p. 39
12 *Ibid.*, p. 38
13 Wright, F. L. "The art and craft of the machine", in *Frank Lloyd Wright Writings and Buildings*, ed. Kaufmann, E. and B. Raeburn, Horizon 1960, p. 70
14 Gropius, W. "The development of modern industrial architecture" *Jahrbuch des Deutschen Werkbundes* 1913 translated in Benton *op. cit.*, p. 53
15 *Ibid.*, p. 54
16 *Ibid.*, p. 53
17 Gropius, W. "The statutes of the Staatliche Bauhaus in Weimar", translated in Wingler, H. M. *Bauhaus*, M.I.T., Cambridge, Mass and London 1978, p. 44
18 Groupius, W. "The Viability of the Bauhaus Idea", 1922, in Wingler *op. cit.*, p. 51
19 Taylor, Robert R. *The Word in Stone*, University of California, Berkeley & London 1974, p. 31. Taylor, whose book chronicles the architectural theories of the Nazis, is quoting a 1935 utterence.
20 *Ibid.*, p. 224. Taylor is quoting a 1934 book by Schultze-Naumburg
21 *Ibid.*, p. 221. The quotation is from *Kunst und Nation*, 1934.

* I do not wish to suggest that the Nazis who tried to house the *Volk* in decent dwellings, yet kept starving slaves in work camps, were in any way the moral peers of the Modern Movement.

16 Postscript: Looking back

There was more than a half century between the dark night of Nazism and the bright dewy English mornings of the '80s and '90s when Arts and Crafts architecture was born. The whole world had changed. Ideas of freedom had either atrophied or been transmuted into the aids to oppression—by the state or by machinery. Arts and Crafts architectural achievements had either been forgotten or commercialized and bastardized in the suburbs.

Was Arts and Crafts architecture any more than a fashion of the rich: rich architects and designers toying with idealism and rich clients in search of a grand, yet undemonstrative, setting for their lives? Even Morris's own idealism verged at times on the absurd. Ford Madox Brown's grandson, Ford Madox Hueffer, recalled a meeting at Kelmscott House "brought to an end by someone—I presume an Anarchist—putting red pepper in the stove. Poor William Morris, with his enormous mop of white hair, luxuriant white beard and nautical pea-jacket used to preside . . . He disliked the violence that was creeping into his beloved meetings. He had founded them solely with the idea of promoting human kindness and peopling the earth with large bosomed women dressed in Walter Crane gowns and bearing great sheaves of full eared corn. On this occasion his air was most extraordinary as he fled uttering passionate sneezes that jerked his white hairs backwards and forwards like the waves of the sea."[1]

There were no Walter Crane gowns and precious few ears of corn for ordinary building workers. Ruskin and Morris's ideals of free craftsmanship had little effect on workers' lives. Owen, the hero of *The Ragged Trousered Philanthropists*, Robert Tressell's semi-autobiographical novel of life in the building trade, explained the realities of life to his workmate Easton: "when there's no work, you will either starve or get into debt. When—as at present—there is little

work, you will live in a state of semi-starvation. When times are what you call 'good', you will work for twelve or fourteen hours a day and—if you're *very* lucky—occasionally all night. The extra money you then earn will go to pay your debts so that you may be able to get credit again when there's no work . . .

"In consequence of living in this manner, you will die at least twenty years sooner than is natural, or, should you have an unusually strong constitution and live after you cease to be able to work, you will be put in a kind of jail and treated like a criminal for the remainder of your life."[2]

Owen was working for a jobbing decorator who never got contracts from anyone like an Arts and Crafts architect. But the life of building labourers who did work on Arts and Crafts houses does not seem to have been very different. H. G. Wells was horrified by the work he saw on his Voysey-designed Spade House: "It is a house built by hands—and some I saw were bleeding hands—just as in the days of the pyramids."[3]

Of all the Arts and Crafts architects, only Ashbee made serious and consistent attempts to improve the lot of workmen. His effort failed because, to keep the work (so he believed) as interesting and creative as possible, he held machinery to a minimum and put a premium on handwork. Therefore the products and buildings of the Guild of Handicraft were expensive and could only be bought by the rich. And then the rich turned away from modern work to buying antiques or to commercially made imitations. As critic and designer D. S. MacColl wrote in 1903, "It is not the inventor who usually gets the benefit of his idea. It is the shops, which straightway set their own designers or facile students from South Kensington to parody anything in which there seems to be a chance of money."[4]

Ashbee was in a trap: he could sell less and less to

the rich, whose taste was changing, yet he could not fully embrace machine production and compete commercially—that would have been a betrayal of everything he believed in.

The conundrum was just as incapable of solution in architecture as it was in artefact production. Arts and Crafts architects usually charged extra for their special features like individually made ironwork, decorative schemes and their furniture.* This meant that clients were paying a double premium—for having items made by hand which could, without sacrificing convenience, have been more cheaply bought from a mass produced range, and for the architect's special designs (usually charged as a percentage of the cost of production). Or the architect could reduce the client's bill by waiving charges for special designs—but if he did so, he could not make ends meet, as Goodhart-Rendel pointed out (p. 118).

It was the individualness, the specialness, which stemmed from Ruskin's precepts of savageness and changefulness that priced Arts and Crafts architecture out. The wealth of the upper middle class was being gradually eroded and the systematic approach of the classicists became cheaper (for one thing, its standardized details were capable of being produced by machines). The really international style of the '20s and '30s was not the Modern Movement, as some historians have made out, but classicism in different guises, ranging from the people's palaces of Russia and Germany to the quiet neo-colonial and neo-Georgian of Anglo-Saxon suburbs. It was not until after the second world war that the Modern Movement was victorious, when its apparent economies, achieved by elimination of hand labour whenever possible, were desperately needed in the labour-hungry former combatant nations.

Wells foresaw the change after his experiences at Spade House. In 1903, he called for a revolution in building with prefabrication, synthetic materials, electric central heating and self-making beds.[6] His vision was an early example of the building science fiction that dominated much Modern Movement thinking.

Yet as we now see, and as Morris and many of his followers saw perfectly well at the time, substitution of crude machine production for hand work could improve life for workers little, if at all. Certainly it did away with the awfulness of the Rodmarton saw-pit (p.

* For instance, on the Waldbühl house, Baillie Scott charged no less than £560 worth of expenses and fees for special designs on top of the basic fee for the design of the house.[5]

152). But, as building was increasingly made to approximate to machine production, workers fared little better than Tressell's contemporaries. Semi-starvation was obviated by increasingly humane legislation, but workers were still subject to the demands of a notoriously erratic industry. And increasing systemization and mechanization ensured that they lost any opportunity for personal creativity—even Tressell's Owen was allowed to work up and carry out occasional decorative schemes himself, one of the few things that made his life not absolutely bleak.

The only way in which Owen could have had a fundamentally better life and in which Ashbee could have escaped from his trap, the only hope of long term survival of Arts and Crafts building, was the revolution preached by William Morris. Arts and Crafts architecture flourished, briefly, in a time when labour was cheap. Only if labour could have been made free, as it was in *News from Nowhere*, could it have achieved full bloom. But none of Morris's immediate disciples backed his revolutionary socialism to the hilt—even Ashbee held back. And most Arts and Crafts folk must, like Voysey, have shared with their clients a horror of radical social change.

If the Arts and Crafts movement had any coherence at all, it was concerned with the quality of life. The movement had no manifesto. It was far too varied in expression to have a coherent style, for it encompassed Lethaby's Brockhampton church, Prior's Home Place, Mackintosh's art school, Voysey's Sanderson factory and Townsend's Horniman Museum. Yet virtually every Arts and Crafts architect would have agreed with Lethaby when he said that "what I mean by art . . . is not the affair of a few but of everybody."[7]

The Arts and Crafts people knew that quality of life depends on all five senses, and that it is to do with the experience of making and using artefacts. To improve quality, work and leisure, instead of being separated into different compartments as they were by the Industrial Revolution, should be more related to each other. Thinking and making should be brought closer together.

Everyone's ideal of the quality of life must be different. From that understanding sprang the great Arts and Crafts emphasis on individualness. The triumph, first of classical architecture, then of the Modern Movement with its emphasis on standardization and norms, ensured that individualness became less and less important, even ridiculous in an age of mass produced objects. The same emphasis on standardization and universality meant that the Arts and Crafts respect for locality and its humility towards old buildings became regarded as sentimental whimsicality.

Now some of the basic premises of the Modern Movement are being questioned. The vandalism and decay associated with many post-war housing estates throughout the western world are one indication of the falseness of the Movement's belief that satisfaction of people's material needs would in some way automatically ennoble humanity. The realization that supplies of materials are not infinite seriously calls into question the Movement's implicit belief that the whole world would be rebuilt in its image. The end of cheap energy must cast doubt on some of the Movement's theories of building production—for instance, centralized manufacture of bulky and heavy building components must become increasingly uneconomic as transport costs rise.

While resources dwindle, machine production is entering a new phase. At last the subjugation of man to machine, which formed the Arts and Crafts movement's objection to machinery, may be nearly over. There is hope that people need no longer be at all involved in producing chains or planks or refrigerators or television sets. William Morris would surely have welcomed the microchip.* But while the new technology offers freedom from drudgery, it threatens to force millions into the dole queues. At the moment, western societies have simply no answer to the threat of vast unemployment—except the hope that output will increase so greatly that somehow there will be enough machines for everyone to supervise. The prospect seems increasingly unlikely in an age of diminishing resources.

Against such a future, the Arts and Crafts belief in quality and individualness again seems relevant. The Arts and Crafts integration of work and leisure could be a basis for a humane future. In a small way the new life is already growing with the increased middle class interest in craftwork, cooking and gardening. The do-it-yourself explosion (though largely consisting of the assembly of crass commercial decorative products) is another and much more widespread example of a new attitude to work and leisure.

The roles of architect and designer in this kind of future would be much more advisory than directive. The need for very large new buildings will probably be much reduced in an age of advanced telecommunications (which are quite inexpensive in energy terms). So will the need to organize large teams. Sometimes by their own artistic example, more often by smoothing the path, architects and designers would help others to realize their own potential for creativity. To conserve resources, materials would be drawn from more local sources and old buildings be gently adapted, extended and cherished.

1984 is the centenary of the Art Workers' Guild. And it is the year in which Orwell set his nightmare novel. We must, it seems, move towards one or other of these visions. Can anyone doubt which will be better in the end?

---

* In 1883, he wrote: "I want modern science, which I believe to be capable of overcoming all material difficulties, to turn from such preposterous follies as the invention of anthracine colours and monster canon to the invention of machines for performing such labour as is revolting and destructive of self-respect to the men who now have to do it by hand."[8]

1 Ford, Ford Madox "The Spirit of an Age: the Nineties" originally published in *Return to Yesterday*, 1932. Republished in the Bodley Head *Ford Madox Ford*, London 1971, p. 147

2 Tressell Robert *The Ragged Trousered Philanthropists*, Lawrence & Wishart, London 1955, p. 139. Tressell died in 1911 of the deprivations he described so graphically.

3 Quoted in Mackenzie, Norman and Jean, *The Time Traveller*, Weidenfeld & Nicholson, London 1973, p. 149

4 MacColl, D. S. "The Arts and Crafts exhibition" *Architectural Review*, Vol. XIII, 1903, p. 189

5 See the back end papers of Medici-Mall, Katherina *Das Landhaus Waldbühl*, Gesellschaft für Schweizerische Kunstgeschichte, Bern 1979

6 Mackenzie, *op. cit.*, p. 149

7 Lethaby, W. R. "Town Tidying", paper delivered to the Arts and Crafts Society, 1916, reprinted in *Form and Civilization*, *op. cit.*, p. 15

8 Morris, William "Art, Wealth and Riches", lecture 1883 to the Manchester Royal Institution, *Works, op. cit.*, Vol. XXIII, p. 160

Select Bibliography

Anscombe, Isabelle and Charlotte Gere *Arts and Crafts in Britain and America*, Academy Editions, London 1978
Conventional but very well illustrated survey of the craftwork. Very little on buildings.

Arts and Crafts Exhibition Society *Arts and Crafts Essays*, Rivington Percival, London 1893 and New York, C. Scribner's Sons
Lectures delivered to the Arts and Crafts Exhibition Society by its leading members.

Ashbee, C. R. (ed) *The Transactions of the Guild and School of Handicraft*, London 1890
Published and printed by the Guild, the *Transactions* are the first published report on the Guild's activities.

—*A Few Chapters on Workshop Reconstruction and Citizenship*, Guild and School of Handicraft, London 1894
An early polemic on the virtues of handwork.

—*A Book of Cottages and Little Houses*. Batsford, London 1906
An elegant exposition of the architect's country work. Presumably published to attract clients.

—*Craftsmanship in Competitive Industry*, Essex House Press, London and Campden, Gloucestershire 1908
A step in Ashbee's theory of the relationship of the crafts and industry.

—*Should we stop teaching art* Batsford, London 1911
Ashbee's most sophisticated attack on Edwardian capitalism and his most clear development of Morris's theories.

—*Where the Great City Stands: a study in the new civics*, Essex House Press, London 1917
Relatively late Arts and Crafts thoughts on town planning.

—*The Trivialities of Tom*, typescript in the Victoria and Albert Museum (nd)
A semi-autobiographical novella.

—*Memoirs*, typescript in the Victoria and Albert Museum, London (6 vols) (nd)
The *Memoirs* are a version of Ashbee's diaries at King's College, Cambridge, edited by the author in old age. Ashbee is a most informative Virgil to the Inferno of turn of the century architecture from California to Darmstadt.

Baker, Herbert *Architecture and Personalities*, Country Life, London 1944
Autobiographical sketches.

Belcher, John and Mervyn Macartney *Later Renaissance Architecture in England* (2 vols), Batsford, London 1897–1901
A key to the Wrenaissance.

Belcher, John *Essentials in Architecture: an analysis of the principles and qualities to be looked for in buildings*, Batsford, London 1907
Principles of architecture and building, taken principally from classical examples.

Benson, E. F. *Queen Lucia*, Heinemann, London 1970 (reprint of first 1920 edition)
Punishingly ironical fictional description of "arty crafty" ideas and behaviour.

Benton, Tim and Charlotte with Dennis Sharpe (eds) *Form and Function: A Source Book for the History of Architecture and Design, 1890–1939*, Crosby Lockwood Staples, London 1975
Extensive, though quirky, collection of contemporary essays and manifestos, some translated for the first time.

Blomfield, Reginald *A Short History of Renaissance Architecture in England 1500–1800*, George Bell, London 1900
An abridgement of the author's *History of Renaissance Architecture in England, 1500–1800*, London 1897

—*The Mistress Art*, Edward Arnold, London 1908
Lectures on classicism to Royal Academy students.

—*Memoirs of an Architect*, Macmillan, London 1932
Autobiography of a Norman Shaw disciple who started life as an Arts and Craftsman but changed to being one of the chief early twentieth-century proponents of classicism.

—*Richard Norman Shaw*, Batsford, London 1940
The first biography by a (classical) acolyte.

Brandon-Jones, John (and others) *C. F. A. Voysey, Architect and Designer, 1857–1941*, Lund Humphries, London 1978
Catalogue of a major Voysey exhibition first held in Brighton. Well illustrated, it covers the whole of Voysey's work. Contributors include Elizabeth Aslin, Shirley Bury, Joanna Heseltine, Barbara Morris and Duncan Simpson.

Brooks, H. Allen *The Prairie School: Frank Lloyd Wright and his midwest contemporaries*, University of Toronto Press, Toronto, 1972
The fullest description of the School.

—*Prairie School Architecture*, University of Toronto Press, 1975
Edited studies from the contemporary *Western Architect*.

Burne-Jones, Georgina *Memorials of Edward Burne-Jones*, Macmillan, London 1904 (2 vols)
Adoring, detailed, gentle portrait. First volume charmingly describes setting up the Firm and early friendship with Morris.

Butler, A. S. G. *The Architecture of Sir Edwin Lutyens* (3 vols), Country Life, London 1950 and C. Scribner's Sons, New York

The Lutyens memorial volumes, magnificent compilation of Lutyens' main works in drawings, photographs and descriptions.

Campbell, Joan *The German Werkbund. The Politics of Reform in the Applied Arts*, Princeton University Press, Princeton and Guildford 1978
Thorough coverage of the Werkbund from 1907 to 1934.

Cassell, John (publisher) *The Illustrated Exhibitor*, Cassell, London 1951
Popular guide to the Great Exhibition; originally published in parts; copiously illustrated.

Clark, Kenneth *The Gothic Revival: an essay in the history of taste* (3rd edition), John Murray, London 1962

Clark, Robert J. *The Arts and Crafts Movement in America 1876–1916*, Princeton University Press, 1972

Cobden-Sanderson, T. J. *The Arts and Crafts Movement*, Hammersmith Publishing Society, London 1905
Cobden-Sanderson coined the term "Arts and Crafts"; this long essay is an exposition of the movement's early principles.

Cram, Ralph Adams *American Country Houses of Today*, 1913
Cram was Weaver's transatlantic equivalent.

Crane, Walter *Ideals in Art*, G. Bell, London 1905
Credo of an Arts and Crafts designer.

— *An Artist's Reminiscences*, Methuen, London 1907
Memoirs of snobbish socialist. Describes origins of Art Workers' Guild from painters' side.

Creese, Walter L. *The Search for Environment: the Garden City: before and after*, Yale University Press, New Haven and London 1966
Covers the origins and development of the Garden City; focuses on Howard, and Parker and Unwin.

Davidson, Raffles (ed) *The Arts Connected with Building*, Batsford, London 1909
Essays by leading Arts and Craftsmen including Voysey and Baillie Scott

Dixon, Roger and Stefan Muthesius *Victorian Architecture*, Thames and Hudson, London 1978
Outline from Pugin to Mackintosh.

Eastlake, Charles Locke *A History of the Gothic Revival* (ed. with an introduction by J. Mordaunt Crook), Leicester University Press, Leicester and Humanities Press, New York 1970 (second revised edition of original 1872 edition)
Still the most comprehensive history.

Farr, Finis *Frank Lloyd Wright, a biography*, Cape, London 1962
Fawcett, Jane (ed) *Seven Victorian Architects* Thames and Hudson, London 1976 and Pennsylvania State University Press, University Park 1977
The essays on Bodley (by David Verey) and on Lutyens (by Roderick Gradidge) are particularly relevant to the Arts and Crafts movement.

Ferrey, Benjamin *Recollections of Pugin*, Scolar Press, London 1978 (reprint of the first 1861 edition)
The first biography by an architect ecclesiologist.

Ford, Ford Madox *The Bodley Head Ford Madox Ford* (5 vols), Bodley Head, London 1971
Not the collected works, but the next best thing. Reminiscences of the Pre-Raphaelite world surrounding Ford Madox Ford.

Gebhard, David *Charles F. A. Voysey, Architect*, Henessy and Ingalls, Los Angeles 1975
Selection of Voysey's writing and pictures of his designs.

Geretsegger, Hans and Max Peintner *Otto Wagner, 1841–1918: the expanding city, the beginning of modern architecture*, Pall Mall, London 1970 and Academy Editions, London 1979 (translation of original German edition 1964).

Girouard, Mark *The Victorian Country House*, Oxford University Press, 1971; rev. and enl. edition, Yale University Press, New Haven and London 1979
Covers the 1830s to the '90s. Particularly useful on Devey, Shaw and Webb.

— *Sweetness and Light: the 'Queen Anne' Movement 1860–1900*, Oxford: Clarendon Press, 1977
Definitive, scholarly and entertaining.

Goodhart-Rendel, H. S. *English Architecture Since the Regency*, Constable, London 1953
Elegant and ironic analysis ranging from 1820 to 1934 (when the lectures on which the book is based were given). Particularly good on the Picturesque origins of Victorian Gothic designs.

Henderson, Philip *William Morris, His Life, Work and Friends*, Thames and Hudson, London 1967
Particularly good on the life, with many previously unpublished letters.

Hessisches Landesmuseum und Kunsthalle *Darmstadt. Ein Dokument Deutscher Kunst. 1901–1976*, exhibition catalogue (5 vols), Darmstadt 1976–7
Description in detail of the Darmstadt school, and of Jugendstil in general.

Heuffer, Ford Madox, *see* Ford, Ford Madox

Hitchcock, Henry Russell *Architecture: Nineteenth and Twentieth Centuries*, Pelican, London 1958; Penguin Books, Harmondsworth 1968
Still the most comprehensive single volume on the two centuries.

Howard, Ebenezer *Garden Cities of Tomorrow* (2nd edition), Swan Sonnenschein, London 1902
Theoretical basis of the Garden City movement. The first edition (pub 1898) was called *Tomorrow: a Peaceful Path to Reform*.

Howarth, Thomas *Charles Rennie Mackintosh and the Modern Movement*, Routledge and Kegan Paul, London 1952 and 1977
Particularly good on life and contemporaries.

Hoare, Geoffrey and Geoffrey Pyne *Prior's Barn and Gimson's Coxen*, privately published, Budleigh Salterton 1978
The best descriptions of these two Devon buildings.

Hussey, Christopher *The Life of Sir Edwin Lutyens*, Country Life, London 1950
The only biography by an author who knew Lutyens. A spate of modern biographies is being published.

Jackson, T. G. *Recollections* (ed Basil H. Jackson), Oxford University Press 1950
Memoirs of a very successful late Victorian architect.

Jekyll, Gertrude *Home and Garden*, Longmans, London 1900
The Jekyll philosophy of building, living and gardening.

— *Wood and Garden*, Longmans Green, London 1904
Evocative month-by-month description of the new, free garden (Munstead Wood).

— and Lawrence Weaver *Gardens for Small Country Houses*, Country Life, London 1912
Wide ranging description of free and formal gardens from the first

decade of the century. Includes plans, photographs, details of work by Jekyll, Mawson, Lutyens etc.

Kaufmann, Edgar *Frank Lloyd Wright, the Early Work*, Horizon, New York 1968
Extensive survey includes most of Ashbee's original introduction to Wright's 1910 Berlin description of his own work.

Kornwolf, James D. *M. H. Baillie Scott and the Arts and Crafts Movement: pioneers of modern design*, Johns Hopkins Press, Baltimore and London 1972
The only, and exhaustive, biography.

Lane, Barbara Miller *Architecture and Politics in Germany 1918–1945*, Harvard University Press, Cambridge (Mass) 1968

Lethaby, W. R. *Architecture, Mysticism and Myth*, The Architectural Press, London 1974 (new edition of the first 1892 edition)
The cosmology of a young brilliant self-educated Arts and Crafts architect.

— *Architecture*, Williams and Moorgate, London 1911
The history of architecture written by an Arts and Craftsman for laymen.

— (ed) *Ernest Gimson, his Life and Work*, Stratford, London and Oxford 1924
An obituary panegyric to Gimson by friends.

— *Philip Webb and His Work*, Oxford University Press 1935
Still the only biography. Lethaby shows himself to be Webb's devoted disciple.

— *Form in Civilization*, Oxford University Press 1957
Collection of some of his most important essays.

Macartney, Mervyn (ed) *Recent English Domestic Architecture*, special issues of *Architectural Review*, bound specially, London 1908–11
Chronicles the growth of neo-Georgian.

McCoy, Esther *Five California Architects*, Reinhold, New York 1960
Essays on Maybeck, Gill, Greene and Greene and Schindler.

Mackmurdo, A. H. *A History of the Arts and Crafts Movement*, typescript in the William Morris Museum, Walthamstow
A rather chaotic collection of notes made by an old man.

Macleod, Robert *Charles Rennie Mackintosh*, Hamlyn, Feltham 1968
Well illustrated guide to the work.

— *Style and Society: architectural ideology in Britain 1835–1914*, RIBA Publications, London 1971
Lively guide to the theory.

Makail, J. W. *The Life of William Morris* (2 vols), Longmans Green, London 1899
The first biography, weak on politics, useful on life and art.

Makinson, Randell L. *Greene and Greene: architecture as a fine art*, Peregrine Smith, Santa Barbara and Salt Lake City 1977
The most comprehensive book on the buildings so far.

— *Greene and Greene—Furniture and Related Designs*, Peregrine Smith, Santa Barbara and Salt Lake City 1979
Both Makinson's books are well illustrated and are the best available accounts of the architects' work.

Manson, Grant Carpenter *Frank Lloyd Wright to 1910*, Van Nostrand, New York 1958
Particularly good on the earliest designs.

Massé, H. J. I. J. (ed) *The Art Workers' Guild 1884–1934*, Shakespeare Head Press, Oxford 1935

Essays by the original members of the Guild and their close followers.

Mawson, Thomas H. *The Art and Craft of Garden Making*, Batsford, London 1907
The most elaborate work by a contemporary on Arts and Crafts garden making.

Medici-Mall, Katharina *Das Landhaus Waldbühl*, Gesellschaft für Schweizerische Kunstgeschichte, Bern 1979
Beautiful and painstaking description of Baillie Scott's Swiss house.

Morton, Jocelyn *Three Generations in a Family Textile Firm*, Routledge and Kegan Paul, London 1971
Details of Voysey's relationship with his manufacturers.

Morris, May *Works of William Morris*, see Morris, William

— *William Morris, Artist, Writer, Socialist*, Blackwell, Oxford 1935
Much otherwise unpublished work by Morris, and anecdotes about him collated by his daughter. An introductory essay by G. B. Shaw.

Morris, William *The Collected Works of William Morris*, (ed May Morris) (24 vols) Longmans Green, London 1910–15
Comprehensive coverage of the literary works but lacks some essays and lectures.

— *William Morris* (ed G. D. H. Cole), Nonesuch Press, New York 1974
A useful collection of some of Morris's most revealing writing, some of which is not printed in the *Works*.

Muthesius, Hermann *Das englische Haus* (3 vols), Wasmuth, Berlin 1904–5. The first English edition (based on the German 2nd edition, 1908–11) is *The English House*, Crosby Lockwood Staples (1 vol), London 1979
A good translation by Janet Seligman but foolishly truncated.

— *Die englische Baukunst der Gegenwart: Beispiele neuer englischer Profanbauten*, Cosmos, Leipsig and Berlin 1900
Large format illustrated essay. Norman Shaw is already the hero.

Muthesius, Stefan *The High Victorian Movement in Architecture, 1850–1870*, Routledge and Kegan Paul, London and Boston 1972
Analysis of relationships of the theories of Pugin, Ruskin, Street, Butterfield etc.

Naylor, Gillian *The Arts and Crafts Movement: a study of its sources, ideals and influences on design theory*, Studio Vista, London 1971
A pioneering modern work which covers the crafts well but scarcely mentions architecture.

Newton, W. G. *The Work of Ernest Newton, R.A.*, The Architectural Press, London 1925
Life and work by Newton's son.

Parker, Barry, *see also* Unwin, Raymond

— and Raymond Unwin *The Art of Building a Home*, Longmans Green, London 1901
Essays on architecture, art and planning by the two partners.

— *Cottages near a Town*, pamphlet nd (probably 1903)
Expounds an early type-plan evolved by the partnership.

Pehnt, Wolfgang *Expressionist Architecture*, Thames and Hudson, London 1973
The first thorough attempt to recognize expressionist architecture. Focusses on Germany and Holland.

Pevsner, Nikolaus *Pioneers of Modern Design, from William Morris to Walter Gropius*, Penguin Books, Harmondsworth 1960
A revised and largely rewritten edition of *Pioneers of the Modern Movement* (Faber and Faber, London 1936) and originally the first

re-evaluation of the turn of the century. Forces Arts and Crafts into being pioneer of the Modern Movement.

— *The Buildings of England* series, Penguin Books, Harmondsworth 1951 onwards (46 vols)
Sir Nikolaus, as one of the first explorers of the Arts and Crafts movement, has, in his own volumes in this series, a keen eye for its buildings, particularly in his later guides.

Phillips, R. Randal *Small Family Houses*, Country Life, London 1924
Post war Arts and Crafts building. Many examples of neo-Georgian and neo-vernacular.

Powell, Alfred *Country Building and Handicraft in Ancient Cottages and Farmhouses*. Society for Protection of Ancient Buildings, London 1948
The gospel of repair according to Society for Protection of Ancient Buildings.

Prior, E. S. *A History of Gothic Art in England*, George Bell and Sons, London 1900
Gothic as seen by the generation of Shaw's pupils. Illustrated by Horsley.

Pugin, A. W. N. *Contrasts*, London 1836, reprinted in facsimile by Leicester University Press, 1969
Pugin's first and most savage attack on classicism and protestantism.

— *The True Principles of Pointed or Christian Architecture*, London 1841 reprinted in facsimile by St. Barnabas, Oxford 1969 and Academy Editions, London 1973
Detailed prescription of how to design and build in Gothic.

— *An Apology for the Revival of Christian Architecture in England*, London 1843, reprinted in facsimile by St. Barnabas, Oxford 1969
Continues the attack started in *Contrasts*; accepts "modern inventions".

Quennell, Marjorie and C. H. B. Quennell *A History of Everyday Things in England* (3 vols), Batsford, London 1919, 1934
An Arts and Crafts history of design.

Reilly, Charles H. *Representative British Architects of the Present Day*, Batsford, London 1931
Covers Baker, Blomfield, Dawber and others who were still alive when the book was written.

Richards, J. M. and Nikolaus Pevsner (eds) *The Anti Rationalists*, The Architectural Press, London 1973
Essays on individual turn-of-the-century anti-classicists written in the '60s and early '70s.

Robinson, William *The English Flower Garden*, John Murray, London 1883
The first advocate of horticultural naturalness (in the Ruskinian sense), Robinson strenuously opposed clipping and pleaching. The book ran into many editions around the turn of the century.

Ruskin, John *The Complete Works of John Ruskin* (ed E. T. Cook and A. Wedderburn) (39 vols), London 1903–12

Russell, Frank *Art Nouveau Architecture*, Academy Editions, London 1979
Survey of turn-of-the-century architecture from Austria-Hungary to USA. Excludes Scandinavia. Essays vary in quality; illustrations are excellent.

Russell, Gordon *Designer's Trade*, Allen and Unwin, London 1968
As a boy, Russell observed the north Cotswold school at work and grew up under its influence.

Saint, Andrew *Richard Norman Shaw*, Yale 1976
The definitive, endlessly entertaining and informative biography.

Schmutzler, Robert *Art Nouveau*, Thames and Hudson, London 1964

Scott, M. H. Baillie (and others) *Garden Suburbs, Town Planning and Modern Architecture*, Fisher Unwin, London 1910
Essays by Arts and Crafts Garden City enthusiasts (including Unwin) in the first flush of apparent victory.

Scott, M. H. Baillie *Houses and Gardens*, G. Newnes, London 1906 (2nd edition with A. Edgar Beresford 1933)
Essays, photographs, perspectives and plans which explained and publicized the firm's work. Buildings are not dated.

Scully, Vincent J. Jr. *The Shingle Style and the Stick Style*, Yale, New Haven and London, revised edition 1971
Guide to the American contemporary of the Queen Anne style.

Sedding, John Dando *Art and Handicraft*, Kegan Paul, Trench Trübner, London 1893
Essays based on lectures expounding the approach of this early, contradictory Arts and Crafts architect who believed that buildings should be allowed to speak for themselves, unadorned, yet who produced one of the most decorative Arts and Crafts churches.

Service, Alastair *Edwardian Architecture: a Handbook to Building Design in Britain 1890–1914*, Thames and Hudson London 1977.
Quick and useful guide to the period. Useful short bibliographies with addresses of buildings.

— *London 1900*, Granada, London 1979
Wide ranging review of London architecture in the first decade of the twentieth century.

— (ed) *Edwardian Architecture and its origins*, The Architectural Press, London 1975
An extensive quarrying of contemporary *Architectural Review* articles on turn-of-the-century architects, with essays by modern scholars.

Shaw, R. N. and T. G. Jackson (eds) *Architecture: a Profession or an Art*, John Murray, London 1892
The artistic architects' counterblast to the increasing professionalism of the RIBA. Essays by leading Arts and Crafts architects.

Simpson, Duncan *C. F. A. Voysey, an architect of individuality*, Lund Humphries, London 1979
Summary of the architectural work.

Singelenberg, Pieter *H. P. Berlage: Idea and Style: the quest for modern architecture*, Haentjens Dekker & Gumbert, Utrecht 1972
The best description of Berlage in English.

Spencer, Brian *The Prairie School Tradition*, Whitney Library of Design, New York 1979
Record of an exhibition. Has some previously unpublished drawings.

Stanton, Phoebe *Pugin*, Thames and Hudson, London 1971
Particularly useful on relationships with manufacturers. The only modern biography with much previously unpublished material.

Street, Arthur Edmund *Memoir of George Edmund Street, R.A. 1824–1881*, John Murray, London 1888; reprinted by Art Book Company, London 1976
Biography by Street's son.

Taylor, Robert R. *The Word in Stone*, University of California, Berkeley and London 1974
Nazi policies on architecture extensively described from original sources.

Thompson, E. P. *William Morris, Romantic to Revolutionary* (2nd edition), Merlin, London 1977
Exhaustive on the politics—the second edition is more sympathetic to Morris's liberterianism than the first.

Thompson, Paul *William Butterfield*, Routledge and Kegan Paul, London 1971
The only biography.

— *The Work of William Morris*, Quartet, London 1977
Systematically analyses each aspect of Morris's creative work.

Trappes-Lomax, Michael *Pugin, a Medieval Victorian*, London 1932
Fiercely Catholic biography.

Tressell, Robert *The Ragged-Trousered Philanthropists*, Lawrence and Wishart, London 1955
Autobiography in fictional form of a building worker who died in 1911.

Unwin, Raymond, *see* also Parker, Barry

Unwin, Raymond *Cottage Plans and Commonsense*, Fabian tract 109, London 1902
Plea for hygiene, sunlight, greenery in working class housing.

— *Town Planning in Practice*, T. Fisher Unwin, London 1909
Monumental manual for planning practitioners.
Illustrations of ideal townscapes.

— *Nothing Gained by Overcrowding or how the Garden City type of development may benefit both owner and occupier*, Garden Cities and Town Planning Association, London 1912
The economic arguments for low densities.

Victoria and Albert Museum *Victorian Church Art*, catalogue, London 1971

Voysey, Charles F. A. *Individuality*, Chapman and Hall, London 1915
More about Voysey's philosophy than his architecture and design.

— *Tradition and Individuality in Art*, unpublished m.s. 1923, British Architectural Library
Attack on the regrowth of classicism by a late Puginian.

Wingler, Hans Maria *Bauhaus: Weimar, Dessau, Berlin, Chicago*, MIT Press, Cambridge (Mass) and London 1969
Vast collection of Bauhaus materials, including matter never previously published or translated. Originally published in German, 1962.

Weaver, Lawrence *Small Country Houses of Today*, Country Life, London, first series nd (1909?), second series 1919
Weaver was a great and well informed protagonist of Arts and Crafts country work.

Woolf, Virginia *Roger Fry, a biography*, Hogarth, London 1940
Fry's Omega workshops were a late example of Arts and Crafts guild association, though Fry disliked Arts and Crafts styling.

Wright, Frank Lloyd *Ausgefurte Bauten und Entwurfe*, Wasmuth, Berlin 1910
Comprehensive description of Wright's early work with a valuable introduction by Ashbee.

— *Writings and Buildings* (eds Kaufmann, E. and B. Raeburn), Horizon, New York 1960
Compilation of Wright's writings from different periods.

Magazines
During the nineteenth and twentieth centuries, Britain has had an unrivalled range of periodicals on architecture, and these are usually the freshest sources of contemporary ideas. The *Builder* (founded 1842) chronicled the Gothic Revival and the battle of the styles. The *British Architect* (founded 1874) was particularly helpful to the young Voysey. The magazines of the '90s—the *Studio* (founded 1893) and the *Architectural Review* (1896) were, in their early years, solidly for the Arts and Crafts movement. *Country Life* (1897) is particularly good on early Lutyens. *Academy Architecture* (1889) shows the changing taste of the turn of the century. Other useful British magazines include the *Architect* (1869), *Building News* (1857), and the *Journal of the Royal Institute of British Architects*.
Useful American magazines include the *Craftsman*, the *American Architect*, the *Architectural Review* (Boston) and *Architectural Record*.

Index